Artificial Intelligence, Management and Trust

The main challenge related to the development of artificial intelligence (AI) is to establish harmonious human-AI relations, necessary for the proper use of its potential. AI will eventually transform many businesses and industries; its pace of development is influenced by the lack of trust on the part of society. AI autonomous decision-making is still in its infancy, but use cases are evolving at an ever-faster pace. Over time, AI will be responsible for making more decisions, and those decisions will be of greater importance.

The monograph aims to comprehensively describe AI technology in three aspects: organizational, psychological, and technological in the context of the increasingly bold use of this technology in management. Recognizing the differences between trust in people and AI agents and identifying the key psychological factors that determine the development of trust in AI is crucial for the development of modern Industry 4.0 organizations. So far, little is known about trust in human-AI relationships and almost nothing about the psychological mechanisms involved. The monograph will contribute to a better understanding of how trust is built between people and AI agents, what makes AI agents trustworthy, and how their morality is assessed. It will therefore be of interest to researchers, academics, practitioners, and advanced students with an interest in trust research, management of technology and innovation, and organizational management.

Mariusz Sołtysik is a university professor at UEK, College of Management and Quality Sciences at the University of Economics in Krakow. He is also vice-chairman of the Małopolska Regional Group of the International Project Management Association.

Magda Gawłowska is a psychologist and researcher from the Institute of Applied Psychology of the Jagiellonian University. She is mainly interested in the neural basis of cognitive and emotional processes, especially the functioning of the system for detecting erroneous reactions.

Bartlomiej Sniezynski is a university professor at AGH University of Krakow; Faculty of Computer Science, Electronics and Telecommunications; Institute of Computer Science.

Artur Gunia is a philosopher, computer scientist, cognitive scientist, and assistant professor at the Department of Cognitive Science at Jagiellonian University. His research interests include cognitive enhancement with the use of augmented and mixed reality technologies and their impact on cognitive processes, transhumanist philosophy, and especially the issues of morphological freedom and cyborgization.

Routledge Studies in Trust Research
Series editors: Joanna Paliszkiewicz and Kuanchin Chen

Available Titles in this Series:

Trust Building and Boundary Spinning in Cross Border Management
Michael Zhang

Trust, Control, and the Economics of Governance
Philipp Herold

Trust in Epistemology
Edited by Katherine Dormandy

Trust, Digital Business and Technology
Issues and Challenges
Edited by Joanna Paliszkiewicz, Jose Luis Guerrero Cusumano and Jerzy Gołuchowski

Trust and Digital Business
Theory and Practice
Edited by Joanna Paliszkiewicz, Kuanchin Chen and Markus Launer

Trust, Power and Public Sector Leadership
A Relational Approach
Steen Vallentin

Artificial Intelligence, Management and Trust
Edited by Mariusz Sołtysik, Magda Gawłowska, Bartlomiej Sniezynski and Artur Gunia

Artificial Intelligence, Management and Trust

Edited by
Mariusz Sołtysik, Magda Gawłowska,
Bartlomiej Sniezynski and Artur Gunia

Routledge
Taylor & Francis Group
NEW YORK AND LONDON

First published 2024
by Routledge
605 Third Avenue, New York, NY 10158

and by Routledge
4 Park Square, Milton Park, Abingdon, Oxon, OX14 4RN

Routledge is an imprint of the Taylor & Francis Group, an informa business

Library of Congress Cataloging-in-Publication Data
Names: Sołtysik, Mariusz, 1964– editor.
Title: Artificial intelligence, management and trust/edited by Mariusz Sołtysik, Magda Gawłowska, Bartlomiej Sniezynski and Artur Gunia.
Description: New York, NY: Routledge, 2024. | Series: Routledge studies in trust research | Includes bibliographical references and index.
Identifiers: LCCN 2023014632 | ISBN 9781032317939 (hardback) | ISBN 9781032318011 (paperback) | ISBN 9781003311409 (ebook)
Subjects: LCSH: Management—Technological innovations. | Artificial intelligence—Psychological aspects. | Human-computer interaction. | Trust. | Organizational behavior.
Classification: LCC HD30.2. A776 2024 | DDC 658.40380285—dc23/eng/20230330
LC record available at https://lccn.loc.gov/2023014632

ISBN: 978-1-032-31793-9 (hbk)
ISBN: 978-1-032-31801-1 (pbk)
ISBN: 978-1-003-31140-9 (ebk)

DOI: 10.4324/9781003311409

Typeset in Times New Roman
by Apex CoVantage, LLC

Contents

Figures

Tables

Contributors

Urszula Bukowska, PhD in economics in the discipline of management sciences, Assistant Professor at the Department of Labour Resource Management, Cracow of Economics. Her research interests refer to employer branding, personal function, diversity management, and social innovations.

Magda Gawłowska, a psychologist and researcher from the Institute of Applied Psychology of the Jagiellonian University; is mainly interested in the neural basis of cognitive and emotional processes, especially the functioning of the system for detecting erroneous reactions.

Artur Gunia is a philosopher, computer scientist, cognitive scientist, and assistant professor at the Department of Cognitive Science at Jagiellonian University. His research interests include cognitive enhancement with the use of augmented and mixed reality technologies and their impact on cognitive processes, transhumanist philosophy, and especially the issues of morphological freedom and cyborgization. Currently, he conducts research on the impact of social robots on human emotions and thus has the pleasure of working with robots such as Pepper, Nao, Misty 2, and Miro-E. He is the author of a doctoral dissertation entitled: "Cognitive enhancement in the transhumanist context. Theory, practice and consequences of the influence of cognitive technologies on humans" and a dozen or so scientific articles on the impact of information technologies on human cognitive abilities.

Qaisar Iqbal (PhD, Universiti Sains Malaysia) is Postdoctoral Fellow at IRC for Finance & Digital Economy, KFUPM Business School, King Fahd University of Petroleum & Minerals, Saudi Arabia. Previously, he served as Assistant Professor of Human Resource Management at the Sichuan University of Science & Engineering, P.R. China. His research interests are sustainable development, innovation management, leadership and emerging economies with a focus on Asia Pacific.

Szymon Jarosz, Bachelor of Accounting and Controlling, graduated from the University of Economics in Cracow. Master's student at the Cracow University of Economics. Participant of "Szkoła Orłów" Tutoring Programme under the scientific and educational guidance of Prof. Mariusz Sołtysik. President of the Students' Scientific Association of Data Analysis 2021. 2020 The Best Student of the Institute of Management at the Cracow University of Economics winner and 2021 Students' Nobel Prize in Economics laureate.

Marek Koczyński, Department of Labor Resource Management, Krakow University of Economics. HRM specialist interested in recruitment and modern tools of competence management and development. Member of the SEED NGO.

Katarzyna Piwowar-Sulej, PhD, DSc, Associate Professor, Wroclaw University of Economics and Business, head of postgraduate studies for business trainers and postgraduate studies "Management 3.0." Research interests: sustainable human resource management, sustainable project management. Experience in managing HR departments, leading HR and HR-IT projects in business, leading and participating in research projects. Author of more than 140 publications (including articles in high-ranked journals such as the *Journal of Cleaner Production*, *Sustainable Development*, and *International Journal of Managing Projects in Business*) and participant in more than 50 conferences (both academic and business ones) as a lecturer or expert. Active reviewer (cooperation, i.a, with Springer, Emerald, Elsevier).

Grażyna Plichta, Assistant Professor, Department of Market Analysis and Marketing Research, College of Management and Quality Sciences, Krakow University of Economics. The area of research interests includes, in particular, issues related to consumer behavior in e-commerce, the essence and role of trust in shaping relationships between market participants, and the process of transaction execution. She was a coordinator and participant in many research projects on supporting the development of entrepreneurship and factors determining consumer behavior in the B2C market.

Jarosław Plichta, Associate Professor at the Krakow University of Economics in the College of Management and Quality Sciences and In-Charge of the Department of Commerce and Market Institutions. The research interest is related to economics and management, for example, new institutional economy, stakeholders management, inter-organizational cooperation, value chain management, and value co-creation. He was the coordinator participant of many research projects considering consumer and organizational behavior.

Ireneusz Rynduch, Department of Labor Resource Management, Krakow University of Economics. HRM specialist interested in the labor market, multiculturalism, virtualization of teamwork, sustainable management and leadership in organizations. Member of the Students Club of Self Development.

Bartlomiej Sniezynski, Professor, Faculty of Computer Science, Electronics and Telecommunications, Institute of Computer Science, AGH University of Krakow. During his studies, he was a scholarship holder of the Ministry of National

Education and at that time he was employed at the Department of Computer Science at AGH. In 2004, he defended his PhD thesis "Application of the logic of credible reasoning in diagnostic systems" (supervisor Prof. Dr. Edward Nawarecki), and went on an internship at Machine Learning Laboratory, George Mason University, USA, where he worked under the supervision of Prof. Ryszard Michalski, who is a pioneer of machine learning and the creator of one of the first algorithms for learning concepts. In 2014, he was awarded a postdoctoral degree based on the dissertation: "Concept learning by agents as a method of generating strategies." He is the author of over 100 scientific publications on machine learning, diagnostic systems, agent systems, and data mining. He is a member of Polish Information Processing Society.

Mariusz Sołtysik, Professor UEK, College of Management and Quality Sciences at the University of Economics in Krakow. Vice-Chairman of the Małopolska Regional Group of the International Project Management Association. Coordinator of implementation works in the Strategic Program of Scientific Research and Development Works. Contractor in projects financed by the National Science Center, the National Science Center, and the National Center for Research and Development, including the Lider program. The contractor in the H2020-EU program 3.2.4.3. Scientific leader of the research area on the complexity of managing organizations in the conditions of the Fourth Industrial Revolution, in the project entitled Social-economic consequences of the Fourth Industrial Revolution, where he deals with the issue of the human-machine relationship.

Robert Szydło, Department of Labor Resource Management, Krakow University of Economics. HRM specialist and Psychologist. Interested in employability, competence development, gamification, and the usage of psychology in Business. Engaged in various scientific, didactic, and voluntary activities. Leader of the science-based NGO: SEED.

Małgorzata Tyrańska, Associate Professor at the Cracow University of Economics, with a post-doctoral degree in economic science in the discipline of management sciences. Research interests include employment restructuring, organizational structure improvement, job evaluation, competency profile assessment, and employee evaluation. Since 2015, she is a member of the experts' team for the evaluation of projects implemented as part of European programs.

Sylwia Wiśniewska, PhD in economics in the discipline of management sciences, Assistant Professor at the Department of Labour Resources Management, Cracow University of Economics. Research interests include employability, sustainable employability, competencies, and quality of life. She collaborates with business practices and non-governmental organizations, including as an expert.

Introduction

Mariusz Sołtysik, Magda Gawłowska, Bartlomiej Sniezynski and Artur Gunia

0.1 Background

The main challenge related to the development of artificial intelligence is establishing harmonious human-artificial intelligence relations necessary for adequately using its potential.

Artificial intelligence will eventually transform many businesses and industries. However, its pace of development is influenced by the need for more trust on the part of society. Without mature risk awareness and adequate framework and controls, AI applications have not developed much evidence for concepts and single solutions. AI autonomous decision-making is still in its infancy, but AI use cases are evolving at an ever-faster pace. Over time, AI will be responsible for making more decisions, which will be of greater importance.

Creating a framework for using AI and managing risk may seem complicated, but the process is similar to creating controls, policies, and processes already in place with people. We already evaluate human behavior against a set of norms, and as soon as people begin to exceed those norms – as when prejudices affect their judgment – we react. Understanding the risk profile of AI technology and its use cases helps determine the appropriate management framework and controls to be imposed on it. *A special area is a particular human-machine relationship, in this case, the human-humanoid robot relationship.*

The critical question is, how are "robots" supposed to look and behave to work with them effectively? Attention should be paid not only to the objective safety of employees but also to their subjective sense of safety. Research by Carl Benedikt Frey and Michael A. Osborne from Oxford University showed that there are clear grounds for this in the field of professional activities. Nearly 70% of workplaces are more or less threatened by automation and computerization (Frey & Osborne, 2013, p. 37), also in the context of work performed by a human being.

Robots and artificial intelligence are topics that are fascinating and inventive. At the same time, it is a source of some concern, not readily accepted from

DOI: 10.4324/9781003311409-1

a psychological point of view. Many robotics experts believe that harmonious collaboration with humans can easily be achieved if machines are, to some extent, human-like and behave similarly. The second argument often raised is human-humanoid communication, which is extremely important because there is no need to learn new ways of interacting. It is enough for humans to talk to robots and interpret their appearance and gestures as if they were humans.

The human side is still unexplored, that is, how the brain and cognitive mechanisms work during interaction with the robot. To what extent are they similar to the mechanisms activated during interaction with another human being, and to what time they are social mechanisms? It is also crucial to determine whether there are individual differences in the approach to interacting with the robot and what tools are triggered then.

From the earliest ideas to the structuring of a discipline, this academic stream grew as technology and robots became ubiquitous around us. It borrows from philosophy, law, logic, morality, anthropology, industrial design, and science fiction. Various military (e.g., drone systems) and industrial (e.g., Google self-propelled cars) projects already have visions of incorporating such paradigms. The development and design of synthetic trust must be guided by "good moral principles" and not be adopted ab initio.

Some people approach the interaction with a robot highly socially, and others treat it like any other machine. So far, however, we have yet to determine where these differences come from. Certainly, partly from experience, that is, those who have more experience in dealing with a robot will treat it as a machine or a kind of artifact. We will try to answer this question in the monograph.

0.2 Statement of aims

Learning the new functionality of the machine, which has a different, non-human shape, is certainly much more difficult. Therefore, from the point of view of social interaction, it is of great importance, for example, taking into account robots that are to help older people in the future or support education. It is assumed that to establish meaningful human-robot relationships, it is necessary to use generally accepted social mechanisms. One of their key elements is empathy, which is often perceived as the foundation of social relationships, essential for their proper course. However, despite strenuous efforts by scientists, the creation of an emotionally intelligent machine could be better. *Undoubtedly, however, exploring the subject of the relationship between a device and a man can be considered one of the most exciting research directions in recent years. The results of the work carried out are often surprising.* Can we be empathetic toward them despite robots' relatively poor "personality"?

In conditions of excess information and the application of organizational and management solutions, the complexity of these relations will be of great importance in direction. The complexity of management, concerning both systems and processes in enterprises and other types of organizations, is undoubtedly one of the basic features of the Fourth Industrial Revolution. This is due to the basic features of this revolution, that is, the growing importance of knowledge, information, automation, the development of the Internet, and the implementation of artificial intelligence. It is worth noting that the aforementioned features are both causes and effects of the complexity of the Fourth Industrial Revolution. Complexity under the conditions of the Fourth Industrial Revolution involves both measurable components of management and subjective and intersubjective (constructivist) factors. You can then talk about cognitive determinants of complexity. Another area that will be significantly influenced by the effects of complexity in the Fourth Industrial Revolution is human-machine relationships.

Organizational hierarchy may not be extended to the near future; in the world after the Fourth Industrial Revolution, we may not be left with a large amount of corporate hierarchy comparable to the present time. Robots are synthetic creatures and are not influenced by the concept of "flow of control and power" typical of a management system, and this is not enough to instill in robots enthusiasm (implicit measures) and compulsion (explicit criteria) to engage in a given task. Therefore, "trust and cooperation" will have to be channeled differently.

The monograph aims to comprehensively describe Artificial Intelligence technology in three aspects: *organizational, psychological, and technological in the context of the increasingly bold use of this technology in management.*

Recognizing the differences between trust in people and AI agents and identifying the key psychological factors that determine the development of confidence in artificial intelligence is crucial for modern Industry 4.0 organizations. So far, little is known about trust in human-AI relationships, and almost nothing about the psychological mechanisms involved. The monograph will contribute to a better understanding of how trust is built between people and AI agents, which makes AI agents trustworthy, and how their morality is assessed.

Reference will be made to Ronald Arkin's work on managing lethal behavior in military robotic systems in the U.S. Army and Alan Winfield's modular project on an Ethical Robot Engine/AI.

0.3 The following research questions were formulated

1. Are human-AI relationships based on the same principles as human-human relationships, and what is the role of trust in this relationship?
2. How will trust in AI technology affect organizational management processes? How will these technologies shape organizational models, structures, and strategies?

3. What competencies of managers will prove to be important in human-social-robot relations?
4. What are the technological challenges in shaping the human-AI relationship?

At present, books related to the aforementioned questions have yet to be published. The book resulting from our project has two equally important goals.

The first goal is to identify and assess trust in three aspects: organizational, technological, and psychological. *The second goal* is to use the research results as an introduction to further in-depth research focused on the future relationship between trust ideas and social robots.

As a result, the monograph provides interpretations that can form the basis for more profound theoretical and practical applications.

0.4 Bearing in mind the aforementioned considerations, the following assumptions are made

1. Within the methodological framework of trust, three terms related to trust in the organizational aspect, the technological aspect, and the psychological aspect were used.
2. The use of statements related to trust in the human-machine relationship requires reassessment using the latest interdisciplinary and multidisciplinary knowledge from research on trust, also referring to management theory and in-depth knowledge of the specificity of advanced projects in software development and other areas.
3. The proposed reassessment should help to develop more effective interdisciplinary and multidisciplinary approaches in managing various types of projects – not only in software development in terms of the complexity of projects, project teams, and the environment.

0.5 Chapter 1. Trust: a new approach to management

The chapter will present the evolution of trust in management, presenting a critical analysis of existing knowledge. It attempts to respond to the current challenges in the area of research on trust in management sciences, such as:

- building trust in an environment characterized by a low level of trust or distrust,
- experiencing trust in everyday functioning,
- multi-level and contextual nature of the concept of trust.

0.6 Chapter 2. Artificial intelligence and robotization: a new approach to trust?

The chapter attempts to answer the current challenges in the field of research on trust in the area of artificial intelligence and robotization. Particular emphasis will be placed on building confidence in the human-social-robot relationship. A key site in this relationship will be the machine learning aspect.

0.7 Chapter 3. Trust: organizational aspect

Trust is an organizational value that is "closely related" to fairness, commitment, satisfaction, and productivity. Considering the challenges modern organizations face (complexity, cooperation of many people and entities, and the growing role of intellectual capital), a high level of trust is a must. The chapter will cover the following aspects: management and creating trust in company management; trust in relations between colleagues, subordinates, and superiors; and trust between business partners and between the company and its customers.

0.8 Chapter 4. Trust: the psychological aspect

Recognizing the differences between trust in people and AI agents and identifying the key psychological factors that determine the development of confidence in artificial intelligence is crucial for the development of modern organizations. So far, little is known about trust in human-AI relationships, and almost nothing about the psychological mechanisms involved. The human side is still unexplored, that is, how the brain and cognitive agents work during interaction with the robot. To what extent are they similar to the mechanisms activated during interaction with another human being, and to what time they are social mechanisms? It is also crucial to determine whether there are individual differences in the approach to interacting with the robot and what tools are triggered then. This chapter will attempt to answer the aforementioned questions.

0.9 Chapter 5. Neural underpinnings of trust

In the past few decades, there has been rapid development in research that focuses on the neural underpinnings of human behavior. Thanks to the advancement of non-invasive neuroimaging methods, such as functional magnetic resonance imaging (fMRI) and electroencephalography (EEG), we can now observe brain activity in real time. Furthermore, by having study participants engage in specific tasks, we can track the brain activity associated with specific processes such as learning, decision-making, and emotion processing, just to name a few. Many fields of science incorporated neuroimaging techniques into their research.

For example, economists in cooperation with psychologists and neuroscientists started to implement neuroimaging techniques to study decision-making, risk-taking, loss aversion, or propensity to trust, leading to the establishment of the field of neuroeconomics.

0.10 Chapter 6. Trust: the technological aspect

This chapter attempts to answer two questions:

1. Work environments are primarily designed and adapted to the human body, so they should be suitable for humanoid robots. Should robots be as human-like as possible, and what are the technological limitations in this regard?
2. The second argument often raised is human-humanoid communication, which is highly intuitive as there is no need to learn new ways of interacting. It is enough for humans to talk to robots and interpret their appearance and gestures as if they were humans. So, to what extent can we teach the robot to "be independent"?

0.11 Chapter 7. The role of trust in human-machine interaction: cognitive science perspective

Creating a framework for using AI and managing risk may seem complicated, but the process is similar to creating controls, policies, and processes already in place with people. We already evaluate human behavior against a set of norms, and as soon as people begin to exceed those norms – as when prejudices affect their judgment – we react. Understanding the risk profile of AI technology and its use cases helps to identify the appropriate management framework and control measures to be imposed on the technology.

0.12 Chapter 8. Robot ethics and artificial morality

This chapter explains the concepts of trust about the ethics of robots.

0.13 Chapter 9. The importance of trust in the process of generating innovation

This chapter aims to indicate the importance of trust in the process of generating innovation. For the purpose of the article, a review of the subject literature was made. The first part of the article contains the theoretical characteristics of generating innovation in process terms. The second part discusses the relationship between types of innovation and trust. Finally, the paper presents competence as the basis of trust. The article analyzes the research problem by applying a descriptive method.

0.14 Chapter 10. Artificial intelligence as a factor in reducing transaction costs in the virtual space

The number of robots around us is increasing as well as the areas of using them. Due to the innovative approach, young people are familiar with robots on various levels. Two theoretical levels are described (occupational and private life) as well as four levels of exploratory study: social, occupational with robots' main role, occupational with robots' supportive role, and marketing. It was revealed that young people have trust in robots, although the gender differs it in most of the cases. Other factors do not have such an impact.

0.15 Chapter 11. Trust in robots: the experience of the young generation

This chapter attempts to analyze the phenomena related to artificial intelligence and its impact on inefficiencies in the operation of market mechanisms from the point of view of transaction costs, extending these considerations to include the aspect of the importance of artificial intelligence in building market relations between entities operating in virtual space.

The publication was co-financed from the subsidy to the Cracow University of Economics – Project nr 067/ZZS/2022/POT.

References

Archer, M. S., & Maccarini, A. M. (2021). *What is essential to being human? Can AI robots not share it?* Routledge.

Bhaumik, A. (2018). *From AI to Robotics. Mobile, social, and sentient robots*. CRC Press.

Cheng, G. (2015). *Humanoid robotics and neuroscience. Science, engineering and society*. CRC Press.

Frey, C. B., & Osborne, M. A. (2013). *The future of employment: How susceptible are jobs to computerisation?* Technological Forecasting and Social Change. doi:10.1016/j.techfore.2016.08.019

Kanda, T., & Ishiguro, H. (2013). *Human-robot interaction in social robotics*. CRC Press.

Liu, Ch., Tang, T., Lin, H.-Ch., & Tomizuka, M. (2020). *Designing robot behavior in human-robot interactions*. CRC Press.

Tan, F. B. (2001). *Global perspective of information technology management*. doi:10.4018/978-1-931777-11-7

Vallverdú, J. (2014). *Handbook of research on synthesizing human emotion in intelligent systems and robotics*. doi:10.4018/978-1-4666-7278-9

1 Trust

A new approach to management

Mariusz Sołtysik and Szymon Jarosz

1.1 Introduction

Artificial intelligence (AI) informed decision-making is believed to lead to faster and better decision outcomes. It is increasingly used in our society, from making decisions in everyday life, such as recommending movies and books, to making more critical decisions, such as medical diagnosis, predicting credit risk, and selecting talent in recruiting. In 2020, the EU proposed a European approach to excellence and trusted in the White Paper on Artificial Intelligence (European Commission, 2020). They stated that artificial intelligence would change lives, improving healthcare, increasing agricultural productivity, and contributing to climate change mitigation. Therefore, their approach is to improve the quality of life while respecting rights. Among such AI-based decision-making tasks, trust and perceptions of fairness are key drivers of human behavior in human-machine interactions (Zhou et al., 2017, 2021b). As such, trustworthy AI has experienced a significant increase in interest from the research community in various application fields, especially high-stakes fields that usually need to be tested and validated by domain experts not only for security but also for legal reasons (Holzinger et al., 2018; Stöger et al., 2021).

1.2 Understanding trust in management

1.2.1 The concept of trust

An analysis of the literature on trust shows that it is multidimensional and interdisciplinary (Paliszkiewicz, 2013). This concept, apart from management, has been studied in psychology, social psychology, sociology, and economics.

Definitions and approaches to understanding trust can be divided into at least four categories, treating trust as (1) a personality trait, (2) an individual expectation or belief, (3) the basis of interpersonal relationships, and (4) the basis of economic and social exchange. According to Wrightsman (1966), trust is a

DOI: 10.4324/9781003311409-2

personality trait that is reflected in general expectations about the intentions of others. These expectations depend on the socialization process and personal experience of the person.

For Frost et al. (1978), trust is the expectation that other individuals' or groups' behavior (verbal and non-verbal) will be altruistic and beneficial to the trusting person.

Dwyer and Oh (1987) see trust as believing that the exchange partner will not fail credibility. Trust is the trustee's willingness to depend on another person's actions, based on the expectation that the trustee will behave appropriately from the trustee's point of view regardless of the trustee's ability to monitor or control. Paliszkiewicz (2013) emphasizes that trust is the expectation that the other party will have good intentions, can be relied on and neither party will take advantage of the other party's weaknesses, will be credible, and behave in a predictable manner and in accordance with generally accepted standards.

According to Coleman (1990), trust is a relationship of mutual calculations between the trusting entity and the trusting entity. Moorman et al. (1993) say that trust is based on a willingness to rely on others. The fourth of the distinguished perspectives on the recognition of trust in the literature in the field of management sciences draws attention to the nature of mutual relations between people, in which the level of trust in relations is calculated by the partners. This approach is of great importance in e-commerce systems.

Fukuyama (1997) describes trust as a mechanism based on the assumption that other community members are characterized by honest and cooperative behavior, which is rooted in shared norms. Gambetta (1988) defines this concept as the probability that the person with whom we cooperate will perform the entrusted tasks properly or that at least their actions will not be harmful enough to make it necessary to terminate cooperation with them.

Sztompka (1999) defines this concept as a bet made on the uncertain future actions of other people, and Bugdol (2010) has the belief that the actions taken will lead to the achievement of the set goals and the benefits for all stakeholders.

1.2.2 Types and characteristics of trust in the enterprise

Trust comes in many forms. The most common of these is trust: conditional, unconditional, general, specific, simple, blind, basic, organizational, and individual. Some researchers classify trust by taking into account its basis, for example, trust based on institutions – institutional, faith based on characteristics, such as personality traits, process-based, calculation-based, knowledge-based, trust feelings (affective), and cognition (cognitive). Other suggestions that came up in literature are relational, systemic, social, authentic, positional, commercial, technological, systemic, strategic, transactional, self-confidence, structural, decision-making, in-group, outside-group, horizontal, vertical, and organizational.

According to Williamson (1993), trust is divided into calculative, personal, and aggregate. Calculation trust is related to the valuation of the exchange and the profitability of entering into a given relationship. Personal faith is related to the trust placed in another person. This trust is based on a conscious relinquishment of control and attribution of good intentions to the other party. Joint confidence, or institutional trust, refers to social and organizational trust context, such elements as social culture, corporate culture, politics, regulation, professionalism, and networks. Institutional trust, based on features and processes, was presented by Zucker (1986).

He believes trust based on institutions is associated with formal social structures. Trait-based confidence is tied to a person. Process-based faith is related to expected or past experiences, such as reputation. Rousseau et al. (1998) described three basic types of trust: calculative, relational, and institutional. Calculation trust is based on a simple calculation of the costs and benefits of a given relationship. Relational trust builds over time through repeated interactions that enable you to create experiences and predict the behavior of others in the future. Institutional trust is related to institutions, cultural and social norms, and the sense of security associated with guarantees, regulations, or the legal system.

Morris and Moberg (1994) distinguish between personal and interpersonal trust. Personal trust refers to the trust people place in themselves. Interpersonal trust is the trust associated with relationships, for example, between employees. McAllister (1995) distinguished between cognitive trust based on competence, reliability and reliability, and affective trust based on openness, faith, and care for the partner. Affective trust is based on feelings when we form bonds with other people, and cognitive trust is when we choose the person we will want to trust in some circumstances.

1.3 Artificial intelligence in management

1.3.1 The concept of artificial intelligence

Artificial intelligence (AI) is a technology that can demonstrate machine intelligence instead of human intelligence. It can perform cognitive functions such as learning and problem-solving that are typically performed by humans (Chatterjee et al., 2021; Russell & Norvig, 2009). The versatility of AI has attracted the attention of the industrial sector to use these capabilities in organizational operations. This is because AI uses a multi-disciplined approach to accurately collect and analyze data and then share that data without human intervention (Chatterjee, Chaudhuri, Shah et al., 2022; Spanaki et al., 2018). There is great optimism that AI applications will be able to revolutionize various organizational functionalities, including innovation, manufacturing, and operations. Such applications of AI technology are expected to face several interrelated challenges that adversely affect organizational and situational characteristics, technological issues, and the specialized workforce of an organization. These include compatibility, organization complexity, and willingness to adopt AI. Situational risks, including technological dynamics and external competitive pressures, can also create problems. Technical challenges can arise if AI solutions are too difficult to implement or incompatible with existing systems.

1.3.2 Enterprise AI

Several studies have shown that industries face challenges in running their business using technologies adopted before Industry 4.0. These limitations have prompted such initiatives to adopt AI. However, other research has shown that organizations using AI face several organizational, situational, technological, and individual challenges. An organization's ability to embrace innovation depends on the degree to which the organization is ready for a given technology. Many researchers have considered readiness a state of behavioral, psychological, and structural readiness that an organization must achieve before embarking on a particular activity (Chatterjee, 2020b).

The adoption of AI by an organization is influenced by the organizational context and mutual compatibility between it and a given technology. The notion of compatibility includes the aspects of technology-task, technology-organization, and technology-people. Organizational compatibility is defined as "the degree to which an innovation is perceived to be consistent with existing values, past experiences, and the needs of potential users" (Chatterjee, 2020a; Chatterjee, Chaudhuri, & Vrontis, 2022).

Employees' ability to learn needs to be improved to assimilate the technological issues related to artificial intelligence in their organizations (Chatterjee, Chaudhuri, Vrontis et al., 2022). When organizations address all the factors that challenge their adoption of AI, it will be favorable for them to adopt AI. The rationale for implementing artificial intelligence by manufacturing and manufacturing enterprises is using artificial intelligence technology to develop sustainability in their companies (Simons & Mason, 2003). However, Gualandris et al. (2014) suggested that it is challenging to adopt new technology without sincere and practical support from the top management of an organization.

For an organization to adopt innovative technology such as AI, it must be able to unfreeze, freeze, and refreeze available resources supported by the right strategies in the context of dynamic business environments in hyper-competitive markets. This means that to adopt any innovative technology, an organization should be prepared to change its approach to innovation constantly. This is consistent with the theory of organizational readiness, which assumes that an organization's readiness is an assessment of the actual state of preparedness to successfully adopt and use any technology about innovation. Based on organizational readiness theory, we can interpret that readiness has an effect if organizational characteristics favor adoption (Chaudhuri et al., 2022).

The organization's characteristics are crucial to the successful implementation of artificial intelligence to improve manufacturing and manufacturing operations. The time spent installing AI technology in the organization cannot be long. The organization should be able to make effective, intelligent decisions more smoothly with the help of AI applications. In short, there can be no organizational complexity. In addition, employees must develop the necessary skills and expertise to adopt technology such as AI and have the competencies required to use the new technology without any restrictions. The competencies of employees make the organization compatible. The organization must be well equipped when adopting AI so that it is ready to facilitate the implementation without any difficulties. As such, an organization needs to easily implement AI to improve its manufacturing and production units (Chaudhuri et al., 2022).

Kaufmann and Carter (2006) argue that dynamism is a crucial variable when considering industrial adoption behavior; the organization must adapt to keep up with the development of artificial intelligence. Artificial intelligence technology is dynamic (Kaufmann & Carter, 2006). An organization must implement artificial intelligence technology to keep up with the rapidly changing situation to stay caught up to the competition. In addition, the organization should develop at the same pace as modern organizations. This competitive pressure is considered a healthy way to build a competitive advantage (Iacovou et al., 1995).

The rapid technology change can cause problems in the information processing channel. In this regard, organizations should remain vigilant to meet the information processing load and compete in the changing technological environment. Tushman (1979) opined that "a mistake in a threatening environment can be catastrophic to a company; we would expect to find highly rational decision-making procedures used in such an environment." Implementing AI technology in an organization is perceived as a very rational approach to decision-making (Iacovou et al., 1995).

1.3.3 Does artificial intelligence in enterprises require trust?

The application of AI in enterprises can generate tremendous value and significantly improve the efficiency and effectiveness of enterprises (Kolbjørnsrud et al., 2017). For example, AI can improve the accuracy of recommendation systems and increase user trust. Artificial intelligence is beneficial for performance management, employee measurement, and evaluation in enterprises. Artificial intelligence can enhance human capabilities through enterprise decision-making. Artificial intelligence in the enterprise reduces potential conflicts by standardizing decision-making procedures, thus reducing the pressure on supervisors and team leaders (Yu & Li, 2022).

However, whether AI can be successfully integrated into enterprises and become a significant decision-maker depends critically on employees' trust in AI (Glikson & Woolley, 2020). First, AI as a decision-maker has the power to make decisions that are highly relevant to and affect employees. Therefore, trust in the context of AI decision-making is essential and affects the willingness of employees to accept and comply with AI decisions; faith has the potential to promote further behavioral outcomes and attitudes related to the validity of AI decisions (Höddinghaus et al., 2020). Furthermore, when AI is the primary decision-maker, a lack of trust negatively impacts human-AI collaboration in many ways. One reason is that a lack of confidence can lead to fragility in the design and application of decision support systems. If the system's fragility leads to harmful recommendations, it is likely to influence people to make bad decisions strongly. Another reason is that high-trust teams generate less uncertainty and resolve problems more efficiently (Zand, 1972). In addition, if employees do not believe in AI, enterprises or organizations may not be able to adopt AI due to trust issues (Yu & Li, 2022).

1.3.4 AI honesty

The data used to train machine learning models is often historical records or event samples. They usually do not accurately describe the events and hide the discrimination with few details that are very difficult to identify. AI models are also imperfect abstractions of reality due to their statistical nature. This leads to the inevitable imprecision and discrimination (bias) associated with AI. As a result, the study of reliability in AI is becoming an indispensable component of responsible socio-technical AI systems in various decision-making tasks (Berk et al., 2021; Feldman et al., 2015). In addition, extensive research focuses on the definitions of justice and the quantification of injustice. In addition, human perception of fairness (perception of fairness) plays a vital role in AI-based decision-making. AI is often used by humans and to make human-related decisions (Starke et al., 2021).

Duan et al. (2019) argue that AI-powered decision-making can help users make better decisions. Furthermore, the authors propose that AI-based decisions should be accepted mainly by humans when used as a support tool. Therefore, it is crucial to consider people's perception of AI in general and to what extent users would be willing to use such systems. Considerable research on perceived integrity has shown its links with trust, for example, in management and organizations (Berk et al., 2021; Komodromos, 2014).

Users' trust in algorithmic decision-making has been examined from various perspectives. Zhou, Bridon et al. (2015) and Zhou, Sun et al. (2015) argued that communicating user trust is beneficial for evaluating the effectiveness of machine learning approaches. Kizilcec (2016) found that adequate transparency of the algorithms through explanations fostered user trust. Other empirical studies have shown the influence of trust score, model accuracy, and users' experience with system performance on user trust (Angerschmid et al., 2022).

Understanding the relationship between integrity and trust is not trivial in the context of social interactions such as marketing and services.

Kasinidou et al. (2021) examined the perception of fairness in algorithmic decision-making and found that people's perception of the system's decisions as "unfair" affects participants' confidence in the system. Research (Shin, 2020) has shown that the perception of fairness positively affects trust in an algorithmic decision-making system such as recommendations. Zhou et al. (2021a) found similar findings that the introduction of fairness is positively related to users' trust in AI-based decision-making.

This previous work motivates us to explore further how multiple factors, such as AI fairness and AI explanation together impact users' confidence in making AI-based decisions (Angerschmid et al., 2022).

1.3.5 Employees' trust in AI

When an organization is about to adopt technology, the individual characteristics of employees matter a lot in terms of their trust factor and ability to learn. It is common for employees to initially feel uncertain about the results of any technology adopted by their organization. In this context, employee confidence is a factor in adoption (Gagliano et al., 2019). Employees' learning skills affect adoption unless they have adequate knowledge of the technology to be deployed. If not, it adversely affects adoption (Chatterjee, Chaudhuri, Vrontis et al., 2022).

Employees' trust in technology depends on their expectations and subsequent satisfaction from using it (Gefen et al., 2003). This concept is explained in Expectation Unconfirmation Theory (EDT) (Chatterjee & Nguyen, 2021), which suggests that trust influences employees to use technology and then to achieve their results. This leads us to believe that an organization must earn employees' trust to facilitate the adoption of any technology (Gagliano et al., 2019).

In addition, employees' learning abilities are seen as critical to organizational success. Employees must expand their knowledge by gathering up-to-date information on various technological topics. This information leads to the belief that increasing employees' learning ability can motivate them to adopt technology (Gagliano et al., 2019).

1.4 Acknowledgment

The publication was co-financed from the subsidy to the Cracow University of Economics – Project nr 067/ZZS/2022/POT.

References

Angerschmid, A., Zhou, J., Theuermann, K., Chen, F., & Holzinger, A. (2022). Fairness and explanation in AI-informed decision making. *Machine Learning and Knowledge Extraction*, *4*(2), 556–579. https://doi.org/10.3390/make4020026

Berk, R., Heidari, H., Jabbari, S., Kearns, M., & Roth, A. (2021). Fairness in criminal justice risk assessments: The state of the art. *Sociological Methods & Research, 50*(1), 3–44. https://doi.org/10.1177/0049124118782533

Bugdol, M. (2010). *Dimensions and problems of managing an organization based on trust*. Jagiellonian University Publishing House.

Chatterjee, S. (2020a). Internet of Things and social platforms: An empirical analysis from Indian consumer behavioral perspective. *Behavior & Information Technology, 39*(2), 133–149. https://doi.org/10.1080/0144929X.2019.1587001

Chatterjee, S. (2020b). Impact of AI regulation on intention to use robots. *International Journal of Intelligent Unmanned Systems, 8*(2), 97–114. https://doi.org/10.1108/IJIUS-09-2019-0051

Chatterjee, S., Chaudhuri, R., Shah, M., & Maheshwari, P. (2022). Big data-driven innovation for sustaining SME supply chain operation in post COVID-19 scenario: Moderating role of SME technology leadership. *Computers & Industrial Engineering, 168*, 108058. https://doi.org/https://doi.org/10.1016/j.cie.2022.108058

Chatterjee, S., Chaudhuri, R., & Vrontis, D. (2022). Big data analytics in strategic sales performance: Mediating role of CRM capability and moderating role of leadership support. *EuroMed Journal of Business, 17*(3), 295–311. https://doi.org/10.1108/EMJB-07-2021-0105

Chatterjee, S., Chaudhuri, R., Vrontis, D., & Basile, G. (2022). Digital transformation and entrepreneurship process in SMEs of India: A moderating role of adoption of AI-CRM capability and strategic planning. *Journal of Strategy and Management, 15*(3), 416–433. https://doi.org/10.1108/JSMA-02-2021-0049

Chatterjee, S., & Nguyen, B. (2021). Value co-creation and social media at the bottom of the pyramid (BOP). *The Bottom Line, 34*(2), 101–123. https://doi.org/10.1108/BL-11-2020-0070

Chatterjee, S., Rana, N. P., Tamilmani, K., & Sharma, A. (2021). The effect of AI-based CRM on organization performance and competitive advantage: An empirical analysis in the B2B context. *Industrial Marketing Management, 97*, 205–219. https://doi.org/https://doi.org/10.1016/j.indmarman.2021.07.013

Chaudhuri, R., Chatterjee, S., Vrontis, D., & Chaudhuri, S. (2022). Innovation in SMEs, AI dynamism, and sustainability: The current situation and way forward. *Sustainability, 14*(19), 12760. https://doi.org/10.3390/su141912760

Coleman, J. P. (1990). *Foundations of social theory*. Harvard University Press.

Duan, Y., Edwards, J. S., & Dwivedi, Y. K. (2019). Artificial intelligence for decision making in the era of big data – evolution, challenges and research agenda. *International Journal of Information Management, 48*, 63–71. https://doi.org/https://doi.org/10.1016/j.ijinfomgt.2019.01.021

Dwyer, F. R., & Oh, S. (1987). Output sector munificence effects on the internal political economy of marketing channels. *Journal of Marketing Research, 24*(4), 347–358. https://doi.org/10.1177/002224378702400402

European Commission. (2020). *White paper on artificial intelligence – a European approach to excellence and trust*. European Commission.

Feldman, M., Friedler, S., Moeller, J., Scheidegger, C., & Venkatasubramanian, S. (2015). Certifying and removing disparate impact. *Proceedings of the KDD2015*, 259–268.

Frost, T., Stimpson, D. V., & Maughan, MRC (1978). Some correlates of trust. *The Journal of Psychology, 99*, 103–108.

Fukuyama, F. (1997). *Trust. Social capital and the road to prosperity*. PWN Scientific Publishing House.

Gagliano, R., Canterino, F., Longoni, A., & Bartezzaghi, E. (2019). The interplay between smart manufacturing technologies and work organization. *International Journal of Operations & Production Management*, *39*(6/7/8), 913–934. https://doi.org/10.1108/IJOPM-01-2019-0093

Gambetta, D. (1988). *Trust: Making and breaking cooperation relations*. Blackwell.

Gefen, D., Karahanna, E., & Straub, D. W. (2003). Trust and TAM in online shopping: An integrated model. *MIS Quarterly*, *27*(1), 51–90. https://doi.org/10.2307/30036519

Glikson, E., & Woolley, A. W. (2020). Human trust in artificial intelligence: Review of empirical research. *Academy of Management Annals*, *14*(2), 627–660. https://doi.org/10.5465/annals.2018.0057

Gualandris, J., Golini, R., & Kalchschmidt, M. (2014). Do supply management and global sourcing matter for firm sustainability performance? *Supply Chain Management: An International Journal*, *19*(3), 258–274. https://doi.org/10.1108/SCM-11-2013-0430

Höddinghaus, M., Sondern, D., & Hertel, G. (2020). The automation of leadership functions: Would people trust decision algorithms? *Computers Human Behavior, 116*, 106635.

Holzinger, K., Mak, K., Kieseberg, P., & Holzinger, A. (2018). Can we trust machine learning results? Artificial intelligence in safety-critical decision support. *ERCIM News, 2018*.

Iacovou, C. L., Benbasat, I., & Dexter, A. S. (1995). Electronic data interchange and small organizations: Adoption and impact of technology. *MIS Quarterly*, *19*(4), 465–485. https://doi.org/10.2307/249629

Kasinidou, M., Kleanthous, S., Barlas, P., & Otterbacher, J. (2021). *I agree with the decision, but they didn't deserve this*. Proceedings of the 2021 ACM Conference on Fairness, Accountability, and Transparency, pp. 690–700. https://doi.org/10.1145/3442188.3445931

Kaufmann, L., & Carter, C. R. (2006). International supply relationships and non-financial performance-A comparison of US and German practices. *Journal of Operations Management*, *24*(5), 653–675. https://doi.org/10.1016/j.jom.2005.07.001

Kizilcec, R. F. (2016). *How much information?* Proceedings of the 2016 CHI Conference on Human Factors in Computing Systems, pp. 2390–2395. https://doi.org/10.1145/2858036.2858402

Kolbjørnsrud, V., Amico, R., & Thomas, R. J. (2017). Partnering with AI: How organizations can win over skeptical managers. *Strategy & Leadership*, *45*(1), 37–43. https://doi.org/10.1108/SL-12-2016-0085

Komodromos, M. (2014). Employees' perceptions of trust, fairness, and the management of change in three private universities in Cyprus. *Journal of Human Resources Management and Labor Studies*, *2*(2), 35–54.

McAllister, D. J. (1995). Affect- and cognition-based trust as foundations for interpersonal cooperation in organizations. *The Academy of Management Journal*, *38*(1), 24–59. https://doi.org/10.2307/256727

Moorman, C., Deshpande, R., & Zaltman, G. (1993). Factors affecting trust in market research relationships. *Journal of Marketing*, *57*(1), 81–101. https://doi.org/10.1177/002224299305700106

Morris, J., & Moberg, D. (1994). Work organization as context of trust and betrayal. In T. Sarbin, R. Carney, & C. Eoyang (Eds.), *Citizen espionage; Studies in trust and betrayal* (pp. 163–187). Praeger.

Paliszkiewicz, J. (2013). *Confidence in management*. PWN Scientific Publishing House.

Rousseau, D. M., Sitkin, S. B., Burt, R. S., & Camerer, C. (1998). Not so different after all: A cross-discipline view of trust. *Academy of Management Review*, *23*(3), 393–404. https://doi.org/10.5465/amr.1998.926617

Russell, S. J., & Norvig, P. (2009). *Artificial intelligence: A modern approach*. Prentice Hall.

Shin, D. (2020). User perceptions of algorithmic decisions in the personalized AI system: Perceptual evaluation of fairness, accountability, transparency, and explainability. *Journal of Broadcasting & Electronic Media*, *64*(4), 541–565. https://doi.org/10.1080/08838151.2020.1843357

Simons, D., & Mason, R. (2003). Lean and green: 'Doing more with less'. *International Commerce Review: ECR Journal*, *3*(1), 84.

Spanaki, K., Gürgüç, Z., Adams, R., & Mulligan, C. (2018). Data supply chain (DSC): Research synthesis and future directions. *International Journal of Production Research*, *56*(13), 4447–4466. https://doi.org/10.1080/00207543.2017.1399222

Starke, C., Baleis, J., Keller, B., & Marcinkowski, F. (2021). Fairness perceptions of algorithmic decision-making: A systematic review of the empirical literature. *ArXiv:2103.12016*.

Stöger, K., Schneeberger, D., Kieseberg, P., & Holzinger, A. (2021). Legal aspects of data cleansing in medical AI. *Computer Law & Security Review*, *42*, 105587. https://doi.org/10.1016/j.clsr.2021.105587

Sztompka, P. (1999). *Trust: A sociological theory*. Cambridge University Press.

Tushman, M. L. (1979). Work characteristics and subunit communication structure: A contingency analysis. *Administrative Science Quarterly*, *24*(1), 82–98. https://doi.org/10.2307/2989877

Williamson, O. E. (1993). Calculativeness, trust, and economic organization. *The Journal of Law and Economics*, *36*(1, Part 2), 453–486. https://doi.org/10.1086/467284

Wrightsman, L. S. (1966). Personality and attitudinal correlates of trusting and trustworthy behaviors in a two-person game. *Journal of Personality and Social Psychology*, *4*(3), 328–332.

Yu, L., & Li, Y. (2022). Artificial intelligence decision-making transparency and employees' trust: The parallel multiple mediating effect of effectiveness and discomfort. *Behavioral Sciences*, *12*(5), 127. https://doi.org/10.3390/bs12050127

Zand, D. E. (1972). Trust and managerial problem solving. *Administrative Science Quarterly*, *17*(2), 229. https://doi.org/10.2307/2393957

Zhou, J., Arshad, S. Z., Luo, S., & Chen, F. (2017). Effects of uncertainty and cognitive load on user trust in predictive decision making. In G. Dalvi, A. Joshi, D. K. Balkrishan, J. Oneil, & W. M. Bernhaupt Regina (Eds.), *Human-computer interaction – interact 2017* (pp. 23–39). Springer International Publishing.

Zhou, J., Bridon, C., Chen, F., Khawaji, A., & Wang, Y. (2015). *Be informed and be involved*. Proceedings of the 33rd Annual ACM Conference Extended Abstracts on Human Factors in Computing Systems, pp. 923–928. https://doi.org/10.1145/2702613.2732769

Zhou, J., Sun, J., Chen, F., Wang, Y., Taib, R., Khawaji, A., & Li, Z. (2015). Measurable decision making with GSR and pupillary analysis for intelligent user interface.

ACM Transactions on Computer-Human Interaction, 21(6), 1–23. https://doi.org/10.1145/2687924

Zhou, J., Verma, S., Mittal, M., & Chen, F. (2021a). *Understanding relations between perception of fairness and trust in algorithmic decision making.* 2021 8th International Conference on Behavioral and Social Computing (BESC), pp. 1–5. https://doi.org/10.1109/BESC53957.2021.9635182

Zhou, J., Verma, S., Mittal, M., & Chen, F. (2021b). *Understanding relations between perception of fairness and trust in algorithmic decision making.* Proceedings of the International Conference on Behavioral and Social Computing (BESC 2021), Doha, Qatar, pp. 1–5.

Zucker, L. G. (1986). Production of trust: Institutional sources of economic structure, 1840–1920. *Research in Organizational Behavior, 8*, 53–111.

2 Artificial intelligence and robotization

A new approach to trust?

Szymon Jarosz and Bartlomiej Sniezynski

2.1 Introduction

Nowadays, the need for digitization and digitization of enterprises and the use of solutions based on artificial intelligence (AI) is essential. The use of intelligent systems in organizations is not only a *strictly* technical issue but is also important in the management of a modern enterprise. AI innovations are expected to promote economic growth by increasing labor productivity (Purdy & Daughtery, 2017). At the same time, some authors fear that AI solutions will cause a significant drop in the demand for human labor. The literature indicates that the growing use of AI in business and the dependence of companies on employee interaction with advanced technologies make it necessary to understand the factors that build employees' trust in AI used in enterprises (Łapińska et al., 2021). In addition, experts recognize that the broad adoption of AI technologies should be accompanied by legislation promoting the ethical use of AI (WIPO, 2019).

In the managerial context, only the right attitude of employees to artificial intelligence and the promotion of the concept of *lifelong learning* among employees can ensure a satisfactory implementation of these systems, and thus will allow to gain a competitive advantage – so crucial in these times of increased competitiveness and constant technological changes. The aim of this work is to conduct a thorough analysis of the phenomenon of the use of artificial intelligence or humanoid robots in terms of issues related to management and to examine the attitude of young people entering the labor market toward artificial intelligence.

2.2 Artificial intelligence – theoretical background

The science of artificial intelligence was initially based on *symbolic systems*, today called "*good old-fashioned artificial intelligence*." Symbolic systems (in other words: symbolic artificial intelligence) is a term that describes a set of all methods in artificial intelligence research that is based on high-quality symbolic (human-readable) representations of problems, logic, and search (Garnelo & Shanahan, 2019). Symbolic artificial intelligence used tools such as logical

DOI: 10.4324/9781003311409-3

programming or semantic networks, as well as developed solutions such as knowledge-based systems (in particular expert systems), symbolic mathematics or automated planning and scheduling systems. Symbolic systems now have many applications, especially in the subfield of artificial intelligence called planning, which deals with problems that require the formulation of a series of steps to achieve the desired goal with optimal use of the resources at their disposal. Examples of the use of planning include providing a route, packing non-standard packages into trucks, and analyzing contracts and regulations (Kaplan, 2016).

The "new" approach to AI is a data-centric approach (Mitchell, 1997). It consists of the fact that computer programs learn by extracting imperceptible patterns from data. The Internet and ubiquitous digitization mean that this data can take a variety of forms: from hospital visit reports to Facebook "likes" or credit card transactions (Kaplan, 2016). A data-driven approach to AI is emerging in the scientific and media space under several different names, such as machine learning, *big data*, or neutron networks.

2.3 AI's impact on society and management

On the one hand, automated systems, which form the basis of Industry 4.0 theory, are considered a kind of threat: some occupational professions may be vulnerable to automation threats and are likely to be replaced, as artificial intelligence and big data give machines more and more human abilities (Rotman, 2013). In addition, although technology can increase the productivity of many workers, it seems to lead to the employment of a workforce in worse and worse conditions and for less money (after all, a robot is cheaper, can work 24 hours a day, does not get sick, and does not take leave) (Lloyd & Payne, 2009), and low-skilled workers are exposed and constantly under pressure (Lafer, 2004). When it comes to the likelihood of machines replacing a worker, research by Frey and Osborn (2013) indicates that about 47% of workplaces fall into the category of high-risk automation, especially those characterized by routine tasks.

As if in contrast to these claims, Caruso (2017) states that technological innovations do not replace less skilled workers, but so far have produced results that are always achieved in the history of capitalism, such as changing the characteristics and requirements of workers, and even increasing employment in newly created industries. It should also be noted that in practice, automation caused using artificial intelligence replaces certain competences to a greater extent, rather than entire workplaces. The goal of manufacturers of intelligent systems and robots is not to replace people but to provide the right skills to do useful things. This is certainly associated with less demand for employees – especially those whose competencies coincide with those that can be replaced (Kaplan, 2016).

Changes in the labor market caused by the development of information technology and robotization are already observed in a wide range. The Institute for Structural Research addressed the impact of new technologies on employment.

According to a study published in the report "*The impact of ICT and robots on employment and earnings of demographic groups in Europe*," the use of robots and the automation of routine activities is a major saving for companies by increasing productivity.

At the same time, this does not contradict increasing employment in other areas. Robotization affects the types of tasks performed and replacing people with robots polarizes jobs – in Europe, there is a general trend of an increase in the number of employed workers in both low-skilled and highly skilled professions (Albinowski & Lewandowski, 2022). In addition, research indicates that the widespread use of technology has different effects on employees depending on their age or gender. Researchers from the Institute for Structural Research indicate that younger workers are more resilient and better able to cope with the challenges posed by new technologies since they are more familiar with them and more willing to acquire new competences compared to older employees. The deployment of information and communication technologies (ICT) has a positive impact on the employment of women aged 20–49 and a negative impact on women over the age of 60 (in particular those working mentally). Taking ICT has "harmed" men aged 30–59 (especially among employees who perform intensive, non-routine manual work) and those aged 20–49 (routine, manual duties). Interestingly, it was also observed that men aged 50 and over were resistant to the negative effects of technology implementation (Albinowski & Lewandowski, 2022).

There is no doubt that AI technologies are changing the world of work and that today's workers will have to learn new skills and constantly adapt as the characteristics of current ones change and new professions emerge (Dondi et al., 2021). Economy 4.0 requires and will require all its participants (both employers and employees) to develop new knowledge and competences related to the use of technology. In addition to *strictly* technical competences, social and cognitive competences, including digital competences, will play an extremely important role. Due to the epochal changes that are taking place with increasing speed, the key to the proper implementation and success of Industry 4.0 is to educate employees, specialists, and managers with interdisciplinary preparation who will be ready for continuous improvement and learning throughout their professional lives (Strojny et al., 2021).

The literature indicates that the success of Industry 4.0 and the implementation of technologies such as AI largely depends primarily on the skills and competences related to their development and implementation. It is also based on the cultivation and application of new business practices that propose a new paradigm of digitization and networking. The increasing use of new digital technologies in economic and social realities makes trust in new technologies an important issue that requires greater reflection by scientists and management practitioners (Yan & Holtmanns, 2008). Such trust can be seen as the user's willingness to be vulnerable to the actions, decisions, or judgments that digital technology (e.g., AI solutions) indicates to them (Shin, 2011). This involves the assumption that digital trust is knowledge or belief that the operation of new technologies will turn out to be in accordance with our wishes or that the information obtained through them is reliable from the user's perspective. Simply put, this means that new technologies used in economic reality can be trusted (Sołtysik et al., 2022).

Today, companies focus on managing relationships that are based on trust formulated according to the human concept of the word, making them more human-centered. This can cause employees of individual organizations to be vulnerable to possible feelings of distrust of technology, especially when they are replaced (fear of being replaced, reluctance to introduce technology) or at least managed with technology (Mubarak & Petraite, 2020). The lack of appropriate competences necessary to work effectively in the digital environment, as well as the lack of qualified staff, management specialists, and appropriate mentality, are key barriers to the development of Industry 4.0 and technologies related to it, such as AI (Traczyk, 2021). It is pointed out that digital trust is essential for the digital transformation of enterprises (Hurley, 2018).

2.4 Methodology

In the study of the attitude of young people toward artificial intelligence and humanoid robots, a research tool was used, which is a questionnaire. In the survey of young people's attitudes toward solutions based on AI technologies, the research sample consisted of 1357 people, which consisted of 862 women (63.5%) and 495 men (36.5%). As for the age structure of the respondents, it is in the range of 17–30 years. The largest group are people aged 20 (25.5%), 21 years (17.76%), 19 years (16.06%), and 22 years (10.98%). For the purposes of this publication, 3 questions (out of 12) from the author's questionnaire were used.

The first question respondents had to face was to respond to the statement, which read as follows: *"Artificial intelligence is a broad concept that houses many different technologies, among others machine learning. How would you define your understanding of how these technologies work?"* The subjects had to determine their understanding on a 5-point scale from 1 – I have never heard, to 5 – I know this concept very well. The structure of the answers given to question 1 is shown in Figure 2.1.

The largest number of respondents – as many as 548 (40.38%) respondents define their understanding of AI technology at an average level. Good or very good knowledge of these technologies is declared by 39.36% of respondents. Only 42 respondents (3.10%) had never heard of artificial intelligence. The distribution of answers to this question in its structure slightly resembles the normal distribution, which proves that among the people studied, knowledge about AI technology is at an average level.

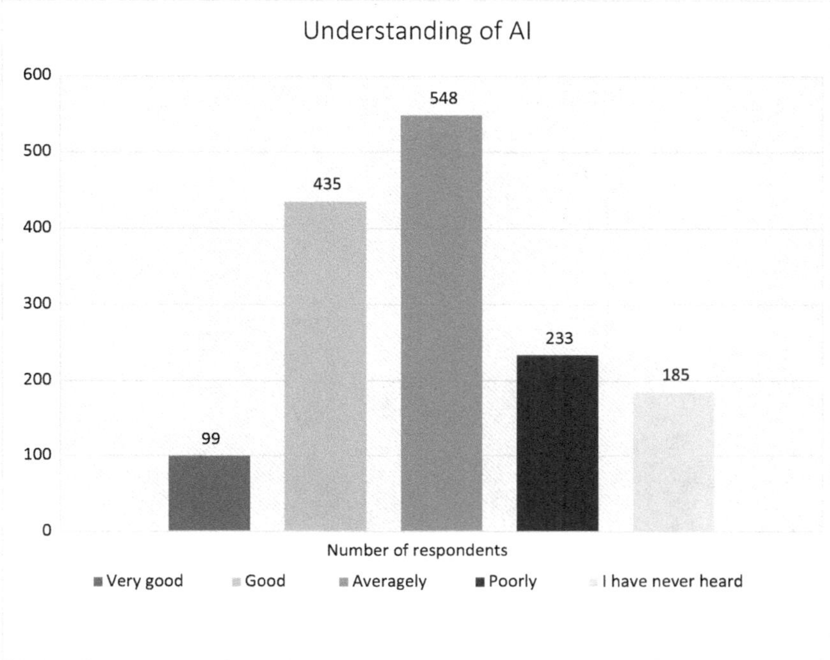

Figure 2.1 Distribution of respondents' responses to a question about understanding how AI works.

Source: Own study.

The fourth question of the questionnaire (Figure 2.2) faced by the *respondents was the definition "from which sources do you most often get information about Artificial Intelligence?"* The following sources were proposed to choose from (it was possible to choose more than one source):

- Scientific conferences
- Specialized websites
- General information portals
- Books/printed press
- From TV
- From the radio
- From movies

The most common sources of knowledge about artificial intelligence used by respondents are general information portals (73.91%), movies (46.06%), and

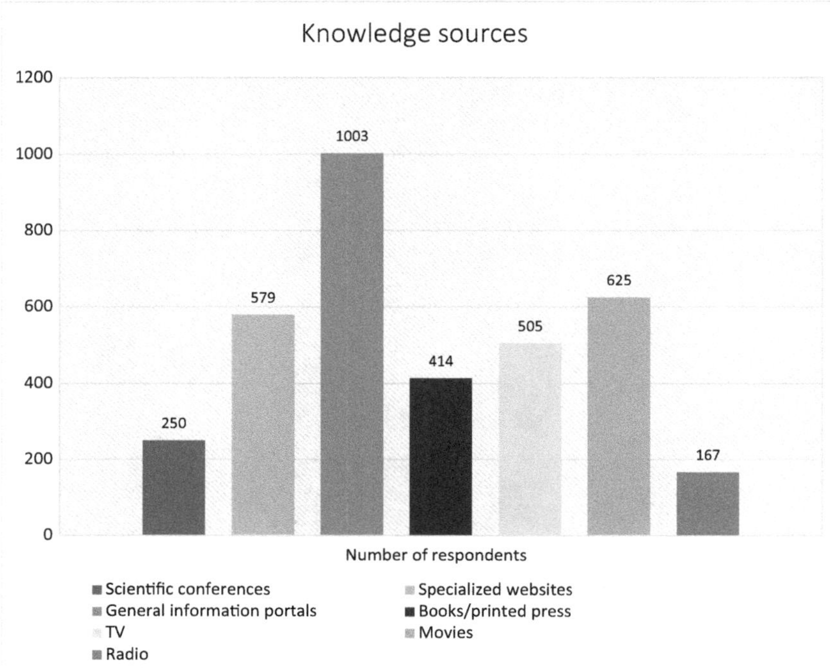

Figure 2.2 Distribution of respondents' responses to a question about the source of knowledge about AI technology.

Source: Own study.

specialized websites (42.67%). The least frequently indicated are scientific conferences (18.42%) and radio (12.31%). The answers given to this question may indicate that most respondents do not use specialized sources of information when it comes to solutions supported by artificial intelligence. This distribution may indicate that respondents' perception of AI may be largely related to the "pop culture" notion.

The last question of the survey questionnaire (results in Table 2.1) set the respondents the goal of responding to the sentences given in the worksheet. The purpose of this question was to study in general attitudes toward AI technology and humanoid robots.

Analyzing the aforementioned data, there are symptoms indicating a lack of trust in AI technology. This is indicated by:

- As many as 72.8% of respondents completely agree with the statement that the relationship between a human and a robot will never be the same as between humans.

Table 2.1 Distribution of respondents' responses to the question about respondents' attitudes toward AI

To what extent do you agree with the following statements? (n=1357)	*Entirely*	*Partly*	*Not at all*	*I do not know*
I would decide to change my own traditional car to an autonomous car using Artificial Intelligence technology.	23.3%	45.4%	24.4%	6.9%
By using AI, people will prefer the use of technology to human contact.	19.1%	49.0%	24.8%	7.1%
Humanoid robots can be equal partners in relations with humans.	7.9%	25.8%	53.6%	12.7%
I believe that digital unemployment will be a big political and social problem.	30.7%	39.1%	15.6%	14.6%
AI will make our privacy vulnerable to constant surveillance.	53.7%	34.6%	6.9%	4.7%
I'm afraid AI will take my place of work.	17.4%	28.5%	45.4%	8.7%
I believe that due to the increasing use of AI, devices will work in a way that is incomprehensible and vague to users.	20.8%	32.3%	37.4%	9.6%
Devices can gain consciousness.	14.6%	26.8%	43.1%	15.5%
I would entrust AI-based programs with activities in the field of legal, financial, or medical services.	10.7%	43.6%	35.3%	10.5%
Artificial intelligence helps people at work and is an equal partner.	19.2%	56.7%	17.9%	6.3%
Human-robot relationships will play an increasingly important role in society.	24.0%	46.0%	19.4%	10.6%
The relationship between man and robot will never be the same as between humans.	72.8%	14.7%	7.0%	5.5%

Source: Own study.

- 30.7% totally and 39.1% of respondents partially agree that digital unemployment will be a big political and social problem.
- 17.9% of respondents disagree at all with the statement that artificial intelligence helps people at work and is an equal partner, 56.7% agree partially, 19.2% completely agree with this opinion.
- 53.7% believe that artificial intelligence will make our privacy vulnerable to constant surveillance; 68.1% fully or partially agree that thanks to the use of artificial intelligence, people will prefer technology to interpersonal contacts.
- 53.6% of respondents disagree that humanoid robots can be equal partners to humans.

This means a significant threat to the management of the organization when it comes to implementing modern solutions in the organization, such as robotization and artificial intelligence. Convincing employees that these technologies are designed to support their work is crucial when it comes to adopting technology and, consequently, streamlining processes in an organization. The fear that the employee may be replaced by robots or the fear of cooperation with artificial intelligence can lead to resistance (or even subconscious sabotage) of employees when implementing such solutions.

2.5 Results

The key issue when it comes to empirical research was the creation and subsequent verification of the developed research model. *The research model* was based on the definition of awareness and knowledge of AI technologies and humanoid robots that have been operationalized (on giving empirical meaning to abstract concepts) in *question 1: "Artificial intelligence is a broad concept that houses many different technologies, among others machine learning. How would you define your understanding of how these technologies work?"* The moderating variable (impact on the intensity and direction of the relationship) in the model is the sources of learning, expressed *in question 4: "From what sources do you most often derive information about Artificial Intelligence?"*

In the model, these variables are classified as independent variables that have an impact on dependent variables. The dependent variables that are the result in the study are the attitude toward these technologies (distrust or trust). This phenomenon was operationalized *in question 7: "To what extent do you agree with the following statements?"* In connection with posing research questions, the next step was to formulate hypotheses, that is, the belief that there is some relationship between variables describing the attributes of the studied phenomenon.

The first research model contains the following two hypotheses:

- Hypothesis 1: Awareness and knowledge of AI technology influences attitudes toward AI and robot technology.
- Hypothesis 2: The source of knowledge from which subjects derive their knowledge about AI moderates the relationship between consciousness and attitudes toward AI.

In the first step of the data analysis, after their preparation, descriptive statistics were determined for the indicators, which for the sake of convenience have been described in the models using abbreviations; Table 2.2 presents the abbreviations for particular research areas. To determine the shape of the distributions obtained, the following statistics were calculated: range (min-max), measures of central tendency (mean) and dispersion (standard deviation), measures of asymmetry and concentration (skewness, kurtosis), and tests of distribution normality.

Table 2.2 Descriptive statistics of study indicators (N = 1357)

Abreviation	*Variable*	*R*	*M*	*SD*	*Mdn*	*Sk*	*Kurt*	*D*
KNO	Knowledge	0–4	2.23	.92	2.00	–.16	–.27	.21**
SGNF	validity/relevance of specialized AI	1–5	3.52	.63	3.55	–.47	.41	.06**
	Perception of AI technology							
THLP	AI technology is assistive	0–1	.88	.21	1.00	–1.92	3.66	.43**
TAUT	AI technology is autonomous	0–1	.35	.37	.50	.54	–1.04	.30**
TDEV	AI technology is pro-development	0–1	.65	.31	.67	–.47	–.69	.22**
	Source of knowledge							
KSPC	Specialist sources	0–1	.31	.30	.33	.62	–.52	.24**
KNSPC	Non-specialist sources	0–1	.42	.26	.50	.33	–.47	.22**
	Role of AI/attitude toward AI							
FRS	Fears	0–3	1.33	.67	1.33	.29	–.51	.08**
CHNCS	Opportunities	0–3	1.04	.55	1.00	.64	.26	.11**

* p <.05, ** p <.01

Source: Author's own table.

To check whether the distributions thus obtained differ from the theoretical normal distribution, Kolmogorov–Smirnov tests were calculated, suggested in the case of trials involving relatively large numbers (Bedyńska, 2012). The statistical values thus obtained showed that all variables were characterized by significant deviations from the normal distribution. The THLP index showed features of a clear left-skewed asymmetry (a predominance of high scores). The kurtosis statistics for TAUT indicated clear platykurticity, that is, a significant dispersion of results relative to the mean, while THLP was characterized by a clear concentration around the mean (leptokurticity of distributions).

To confirm compliance of the theoretical model with the empirical data, an analysis was performed based on the structural modeling (SEM) method. The first model analyzed the impact of the awareness and knowledge of AI technology (a self-descriptive indicator of knowledge) on attitudes toward I (fears and opportunities) with the mediating influence of sources of knowledge (specialist and non-specialist) about AI.

To estimate the quality of the model the following were used: classic fit indices, that is, $\chi2$/df and RMSEA with confidence intervals (less than 0.05 is considered satisfactory, but an acceptable threshold is often taken as 0.10), the Jöreskog and Sörbom GFI goodness-of-fit index and the adjusted Jöreskog goodness-of-fit index, the Sörbom AGFI (which can be deemed satisfactory from a level of

0.800), and as the complementary CFI relative fit index and the Tucker–Lewis TLI coefficient based on F0 (Bedyńska, 2012), which are less sensitive to sample size. The TLI and CFI indices have fit acceptance thresholds that do not correspond to AGFI and GFI, but which can also be used to determine whether a fit model results from too many parameters (Bedyńska, 2012).

To increase the readability of the tested models, abbreviations of the names of the variables were used in the path diagrams. The charts present the values of standardized coefficients, and the specific coefficient values for the individual models are presented in the tables.

The research model (Figure 2.3) matched the data relatively well: [$\chi2/df = 8.34$; RMSEA = 0.074 (0.034–0.123); GFI = 0.998; AGFI = 0.963; TLI=0.832; CFI = 0.983]. The RMSEA indices are acceptable and indicate a moderate fit, but at the same time, quite good values were also obtained for the other fit indices used. On the other hand, the influence of the explanatory variables on the response variables is small; predictors in the model explain 2.9% of the variance of the variable responsible for perceived opportunities in AI and 3.3% of the variance in the variable understood as fears about AI.

In the case of the individual path coefficients (Table 2.3), a positive relationship can be observed between the level of self-descriptive knowledge and the sources of knowledge: the greater the knowledge declared by the respondents, the more they used specialist knowledge and to a lesser extent non-specialist knowledge; the self-descriptive level of knowledge is more strongly associated with specialist sources than with non-specialist sources. The self-declared level of knowledge of the respondents also effectively reduced the perception of AI as threatening, but did not positively affect perceptions of it as an opportunity for development (expressing also general trust in the AI) (the path factor is negligible).

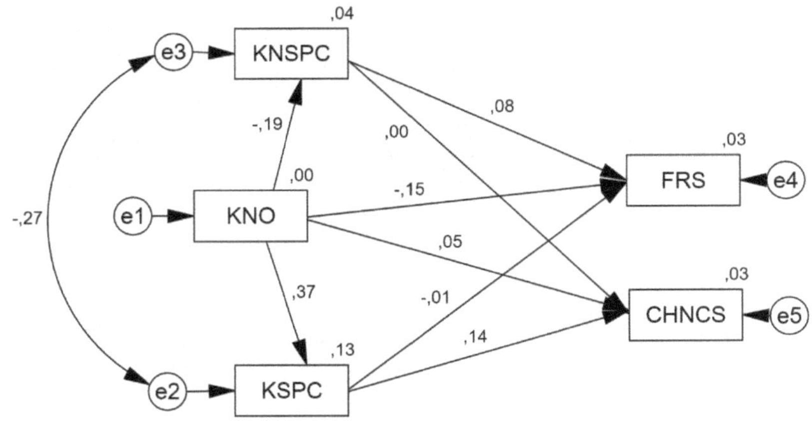

Figure 2.3 Structural model verifying the first theoretical model: standardized coefficients.
Source: Author's own diagram.

Table 2.3 Path coefficients for model 1 – detailed summary

Ścieżka	*B*	*beta*	*P*
KSPC<—KNO	0,117	0,365	<0,001
KNSPC<—KNO	−0,054	−0,195	<0,001
FRS<—KNO	−0,106	−0,146	<0,001
CHNCS<—KSPC	0,264	0,143	<0,001
CHNCS<—KNO	0,032	0,053	0,064
FRS<—KSPC	−0,013	−0,006	0,849
CHNCS<—KNSPC	−0,005	−0,002	0,940
FRS<—KNSPC	0,210	0,080	0,005
CHNCS<<—KNO	0,031	0,052	<0,001
FRS<<—KNO	−0,013	−0,018	0,106
e2<-->e3	−0,019	−0,274	< 0,001

Source: Author's own table.

Note: Statistical significance of indirect effects was calculated using Bootstrap modeling for a 95% confidence interval and 5000 observations; <—direct impact; <<—indirect impact; <--> covariance.

Specialist knowledge slightly increased perceptions of AI as an opportunity for development, but did not affect perceptions of the level of threat associated with AI; non-specialist knowledge only very slightly increased the perception of AI as a threat but did not affect perceptions of it as an opportunity. Taking into account the indirect impact – knowledge interacted with the level of knowledge specialization, thereby slightly increasing perceptions of AI as an opportunity, but the path factor is very small and it may be an artifact. No indirect impact of self-descriptive knowledge was observed in interaction with the acquisition of knowledge from non-scientific sources.

2.6 Conclusions

The analysis indicates that a relationship has been shown between the level of knowledge about AI declared by respondents and the perception of this technology as an opportunity/threat. In addition, expertise (i.e., drawn from sources such as specialist literature or scientific conferences) increased the perception of AI as an opportunity for development but did not affect the perception of the level of threats due to AI. Noteworthy is also the positive relationship between the level of self-descriptive knowledge and sources of knowledge: the more knowledge the subjects declared, the more they used specialist knowledge and the less they used non-specialist knowledge. In view of this situation, it should be assumed that the hypotheses put forward in the research model:

- Hypothesis 1: Awareness and knowledge of AI technology influences attitudes toward AI and robot technology.

- Hypothesis 2: The source of knowledge from which subjects derive their knowledge about AI moderates the relationship between consciousness and attitudes toward AI.

can be verified *positively*, so referring to the research problem posed, it can be assumed that knowledge of AI technologies and humanoid robots affects the perception of their role in society and attitude (trust/distrust) toward them, and the source of knowledge about these technologies is a moderating variable in this relationship.

The results of the survey show that the degree of digital trust among our respondents is at a low level, and the degree of trust in new technologies increases with the increase in knowledge about them. Having a robot or artificial intelligence as a partner in the work environment requires knowledge and a positive attitude toward the other side of the human-robot relationship. An important implication for the future, both for the business sector and the education system, is the fact that the appropriate competences needed by the digital labor market will not only allow employees to function seamlessly in the digital reality but will also enable them to break down barriers, gain digital trust in new technologies and consequently, efficiently implement new technologies. This, in turn, increases the possibility of using on a wider scale the possibilities offered by modern Industry 4.0 solutions.

To sum up, it should be assumed that the knowledge of artificial intelligence technologies and humanoid robots significantly affects their perception. This has significant practical implications. The results of the research show that the senior management of the organization must take care of the appropriate level of training of employees, which will allow them to perceive modern technologies not as a threat, but as support and an opportunity for development and innovation. The lack of appropriate competences, but also the attitude of employees – "digital trust" built on the basis of reliable knowledge of employees, may become one of the key barriers to the implementation of these systems (but also in general all technologies related to Industry 4.0) or stand behind the lack of productivity development after the implementation of such systems, due to the internal resistance of employees, lack of conviction or fear of "being replaced" by a robot or AI.

The study has its limitations. The research group was limited to young people from Polish. To better investigate the phenomenon of digital trust, further research on the issue should focus on extending the aforementioned research to people from other age groups or other countries. This will determine the impact of age differences as well as cultural differences when it comes to the human-machine relationship. In addition, these results show how important it is to update curricula so that young people entering the robotic and automated labor market do not feel threatened by modern technologies.

The use of intelligent systems in organizations is not only a *strictly* technical issue but is also important in the management of a modern enterprise – especially in terms of the key human potential of the organization.

Artificial intelligence means that some competences or activities in the workplace will be automated. However, according to the predictions of scientists, AI will not completely replace a human being, but only (or as much) change the characteristics of his workplace. It will make a person have to focus on more creative activities, based on a completely different set of competences.

References

Albinowski, M., & Lewandowski, P. (2022). *Wpływ technologii ICT i robotów na zatrudnienie oraz zarobki grup demograficznych w Europie*. IBS Working Paper, WP 04/2022, ISSN: 2451–4373

Bedyńska, S., & Książek, M. (2012). *Praktyczny przewodnik wykorzystania modeli regresji oraz równań strukturalnych*. Akademickie Sedno, wydanie 1.

Caruso, L. (2017). Digital innovation and the fourth industrial revolution: Epochal social changes? *AI Society*, *33*(3), 379–392. https://doi.org/10.1007/s00146-017-0736-1

Dondi, M., Klier, J., Panier, F., & Jörg Schubert, J. (2021). *Defining the skills citizens will need in the future world of work*. McKinsey Global Institute. Retrieved July 26, 2022, from www.mckinsey.com/industries/public-and-social-sector/our-insights/defining-the-skills-citizens-will-need-in-the-future-world-of-work

Frey, C. B., & Osborne, M. A. (2013, September). *The future of employment: How susceptible are jobs to computerization?* (pp. 1–72). Technological Forecasting and Social Change.

Garnelo, M., & Shanahan, M. (2019). Reconciling deep learning with symbolic artificial intelligence: Representing objects and relations. *Current Opinion in Behavioral Sciences*, *29*, 17–23. https://doi.org/10.1016/j.cobeha.2018.12.010

Hurley, J. (2018). *Digital trust – the foundation of digital transformation*. Information Services Group. Inc., ISG Confidential. Retrieved July 18, 2022, from www.unisys.com/Style%20Library/Unisys/usi2018/reports/DigitalTrust_TheFoundationofDigitalTransformation.pdf

Jarosz, S., Sołtysik, M., & Zakrzewska, M. (2020). The fourth industrial revolution in the light of social and competence changes. *European Research Studies Journal*, *XXIII*(1), 530–548. https://doi.org/10.1051/10.35808/ersj/1776

Jarosz, S., & Zakrzewska, M. (2020). Świadomość studentów w zakresie konsekwencji Czwartej Rewolucji Przemysłowej w sektorze. In *Interesariusze w gospodarce cyfrowej – modele zachowań współczesnego rynku*. Naukowe Wydawnictwo IVG, Szczecin, ISBN PL (IVG) 978-83-62062-85-0

Kaplan, J. (2016). *Artificial intelligence. What everyone needs to know*. Oxford University Press, ISBN: 978-0-19060-239-0

Lafer, G. (2004). *Conceptual confusions: Emotion work as skilled work*. In I. F. C. Warhurst (Ed.), *The skills that matter: Clinical perspectives on work and organisations* (pp. 109–127). Palgrave Macmillan.

Łapińska, J., Escher, I., Górka, J., Sudolska, A., & Brzustewicz, P. (2021). Employees' trust in artificial intelligence in companies: The case of energy and chemical industries in Poland. *Energies*, *14*, 1942. https://doi.org/10.3390/en14071942

Lloyd, C., & Payne, J. (2009). Full of sound and fury, signifying nothing': Interrogating new skill concepts in service work – the view from Two UK call centres. *Work, Employment and Society*, *23*(4), 617–634.

Mitchell, T. (1997). *Machine learning*. McGraw Hill. ISBN 0-07-042807-7

Mubarak, M. F., & Petraite, M. (2020). Industry 4.0 technologies, digital trust and technological orientation: What matters in open innovation? *Technological Forecasting and Social Change*, *161*, 120332. https://doi.org/10.1016/j.techfore.2020.12

Purdy, M., & Daughtery, P. (2017). *Why artificial intelligence is the future of growth*. Accentury. Retrieved September 15, 2022, from https://dl.icdst.org/pdfs/files2/2aea5d87070f0116f8aaa9f545530e47.pdf

Rotman, D. (2013, June 12). How technology is destroying jobs. *MIT Technology Review*. Retrieved July 26, 2022, from www.technologyreview.com/featuredstory/515926/how-technology-is-destroying-jobs

Shin, D. (2011). Understanding e-book users: Uses and gratification expectancy model. *New Media & Society*, *13*(2), 260–278. https://doi.org/10.1177/1461444810372163.

Sołtysik, M., Zakrzewska, M., & Jarosz, S. (2022). *The fourth industrial revolution – new technology adoption and trust*. In J. Paliszkiewicz, J. L. Guerrero Cusumano, & J. Gołuchowski (Eds.), *Trust, digital business and technology: Issues and challenges* (1st ed.). Routledge. https://doi.org/10.4324/9781003266495

Strojny, P., Nowak, P., Hetmańczyk, M., Malaka, J., & Skrzek, K. (2021). *Standardy kształcenia kompetencji przyszłości*. Platforma Przemysłu Przyszłości.

Traczyk, W. (2021). *7 barier wdrożenia czwartej rewolucji przemysłowej*. Magazyn Przemysłowy. Retrieved August 7, 2022, from www.magazynprzemyslowy.pl/artykuly/przemysl-4-0-7-barier-wdrozenia-czwartej-rewolucji-przemyslowej?fbclid=IwAR06zs0BSivg-TCRg-_mn2cwUtn8y3HJPyYRd9y_Z2YcqsKyXBXNKOgEE00

World Intellectual Property Organization. (2019). *WIPO technology trends 2019 – artificial intelligence*. https://doi.org/10.34667/tind.29084

Yan, Z., & Holtmanns, S. (2008). Trust modeling and management: From social trust to digital trust. In R. Subramanian (Ed.), *Computer security, privacy and politics: Current issues, challenges and solutions* (pp. 290–323). IGI Global. https://doi.org/10.4018/978-1-59904-804-8.ch013

3 Trust

Organizational aspect

Katarzyna Piwowar-Sulej and Qaisar Iqbal

3.1 Managing and creating trust in business management

Trust is one of the most used concepts and at the same time one of the least understood. The researchers do not agree on the nature and definition of the concept of trust (Huang & Wilkinson, 2013). Van Zeeland-van der Holst and Henseler (2018) pointed that one of the first definitions of trust in management science was adopted from psychology. In psychology, trust is associated with intrapersonal states toward the other person (expectations, intentions, faith, emotions, or attitudes). However, one can distinguish deterrence-based trust which is based on the assumption that other will keep their word, knowledge-based trust which is grounded in our familiarity with other to predict their behavior, and identification-based trust which is based on the internalization of the preferences of the other (Lewicki et al., 2006). More trust will lead to more risk-taking, proactive behaviors toward this person (Mayer & Gavin, 2005). Trust changes over time. It develops, builds, declines, and even resurfaces in long-standing relationships (Harrison, 2020). Moreover, it is situational, voluntary, conscious, relevant, not linear, dynamic, and action-oriented (Paliszkiewicz, 2011). The way how trust develops is also national culture specific (Doney et al., 1998). National political systems (e.g., neotraditional communistic) also affect interpersonal trust (Fulmer & Gelfand, 2012).

Trust is one of the organizational values that is "closely related" to fairness, commitment, satisfaction, and productivity. In business, trust is also associated with the expectations of ethical behavior of the other person, group, or company within a joint venture or economic exchange (Hosmer, 1995). Taking into account the challenges faced by modern organizations (cooperation of many people and entities, the growing role of intellectual capital), a high level of trust is a must. The greater the ambiguity, uncertainty, and complexity of a situation, the more trust becomes crucial. However, trust is subjective in its nature and is hard to map trust into computational models (Ruan & Durresi, 2016). Therefore, organizations must put much effort to efficiently manage trust in different organizational settings.

DOI: 10.4324/9781003311409-4

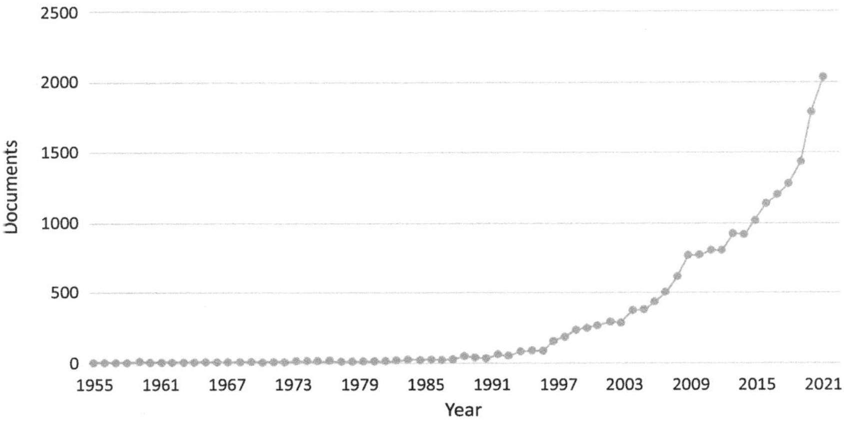

Figure 3.1 Number of publications which addressed the issue of trust in the management domain indexed in Scopus.

Source: Scopus database (July 22, 2022).

On July 22, 2022, Scopus showed the result of 218,507 documents when using the following simple searching strategy: TITLE-ABS-KEY ("trust"). After providing some limitations (EXCLUDE (PUBYEAR, 2023) OR EXCLUDE (PUBYEAR, 2022)) AND (LIMIT-TO (PUBSTAGE, "final")) AND (LIMIT-TO (DOCTYPE, "ar")) AND (LIMIT-TO (SUBJAREA, "BUSI")) AND (LIMIT-TO (LANGUAGE, "English") the result was 21,245 documents. Figure 3.1 demonstrates the growing interest in the issue of trust in the field of business and management.

The growing interest in the issue of trust is caused by such processes and phenomena as: globalization, advances in information technology and increasing number of virtual organizations, outsourcing, an interest in "soft" aspects of management (justice, solidarity) also in the context of misconduct of organizations toward their employees and increase of cynicism among employees, increasing importance of intangible factors, development of social institutions (Rudzewicz, 2017). The aforementioned factors are worldwide phenomena. Therefore, on the list of countries which mainly explored the issues of trust, different continents are represented (see Figure 3.2).

Since there is a possibility of exporting a base which data of only 2,000 documents, the authors ordered the articles taking into account the decreasing number of citations received. At this point, it is worth indicating that the most influential paper, which received 4,503 citations.

In the database of 2,000 articles, 5,442 keywords were used, considering both author keywords and index keywords. Five hundred and forty-one keywords met

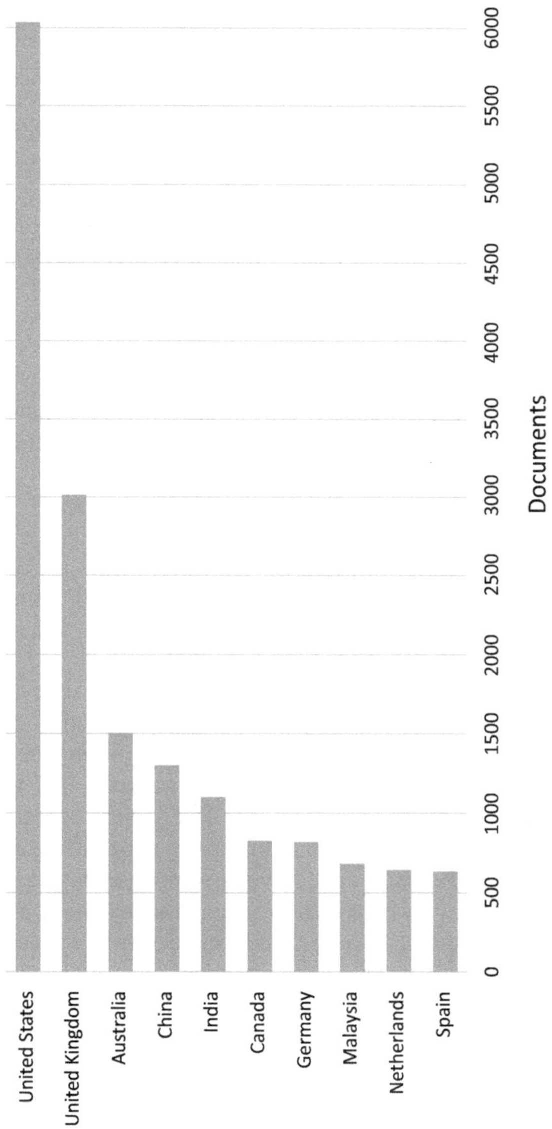

Figure 3.2 Number of publications indexed in Scopus which addressed the issue of trust in management with a focus on most productive countries.

Source: Scopus database (July 22, 2022).

the threshold of 5 as a minimum number of occurrences. First, based on the analysis of keywords, the key theories used in the studies on trust have been identified. They are: social exchange theory (16 occurrences), agency theory and game theory (each has 7 occurrences), theory of reasoned actions (6 occurrences), and theory of planned behavior and signaling theory (each has 5 occurrences). This supports Fulmer and Gelfand's (2012) findings that research on trust has drawn heavily on social exchange theory.

After cleaning this list of keywords (eliminating duplicates, unification of terminology), the authors created – with the use of VosViewer (van Eck & Waltman, 2014) – the map which showed 309 interrelated keywords (see Figure 3.3).

As Figure 3.3 shows, the most explored topics in the context of trust are e-commerce, Internet, supply chain management, and social capital. To go deeper into these topics, 33 keywords were selected which met the threshold of 25 occurrences (Figure 3.4). They constituted three clusters:

1. The red cluster (with supply chain management in its "heart"), which included keywords such as: strategic alliances, collaboration, project management, terms related to knowledge and information management, innovation, performance leadership, and social capital.
2. The blue cluster (with e-commerce in its center). It consists of keywords such as Internet, consumer behavior, corporate social responsibility, decision-making, risk perception and management.
3. The green cluster (with customer satisfaction as main issue), which covers also relational marketing, customer satisfaction, commitment, and loyalty.

Organizations develop and function through exchanges between entities which is emphasized in the social exchange theory (Cropanzano et al., 2017). These exchanges take place as part of the interactions between organizations and between members of these organizations. As the aforementioned analysis of cluster shows, a large part of literature on trust in management domain focuses mainly on organizational efforts toward building trust with business partners in order to achieve relational effects. In this way, companies make better use of the opportunities created by turbulent environments and achieve a competitive advantage. However, in the first cluster practices related to employees and/or leaders are also indicated (e.g., knowledge sharing). The other most popular research area – reflected in blue and green clusters – covers relationships between organizations and customers (from customer point of view or marketing perspective).

The academic literature distinguishes many detailed groups of companies' stakeholders. For example, Friedman and Miles (2006) listed: employees, customers, suppliers, competitors, governments, investors (shareholders), government, regulators, policymakers, political groups, communities, trade associations, media, the public in general, business partners, future generations,

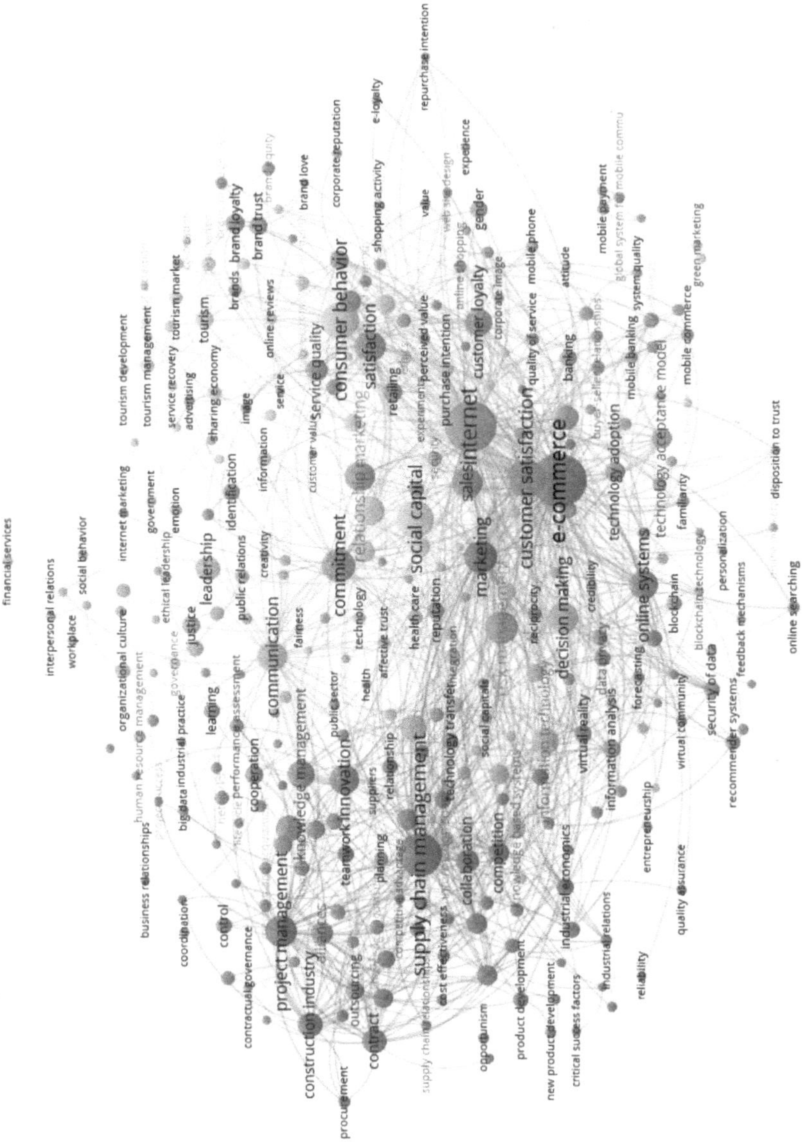

Figure 3.3 The keywords' network map (result as for threshold of 5 occurrences).

Source: Own work (picture generated with the use of VosViewer (van Eck & Waltman, 2014)).

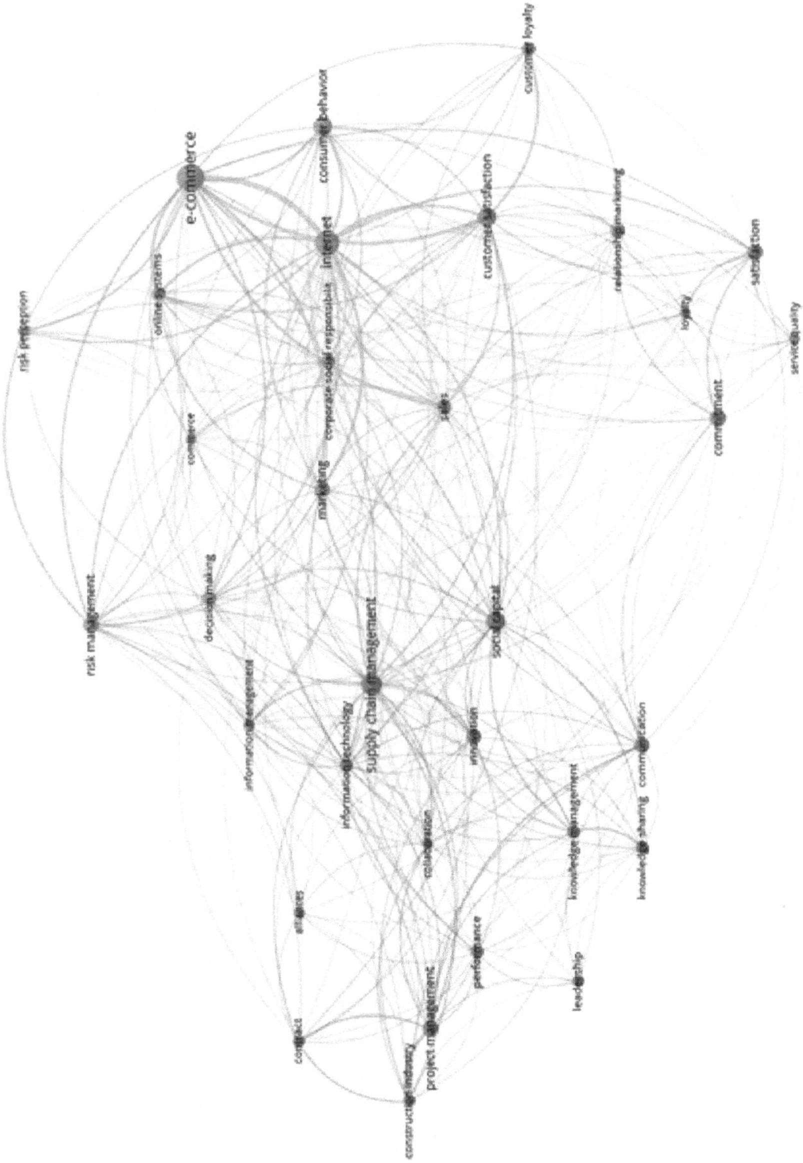

Figure 3.4 The keywords' network map (result as for threshold of 20 occurrences).

Source: Own work (picture generated with the use of VosViewer (van Eck & Waltman, 2014)).

past generations (founders of organizations), academics, competitors, NGOs or activists (individuals and stakeholder representatives, e.g., trade unions), and financiers other than stockholders (e.g., creditors). Leaders may also be treated as a separate group of stakeholders (Nilsson & Fagerström, 2006). However, as resulted from the cluster analysis, trust is mainly examined in the context of companies external stakeholders such as business partners and customers and relationships between employers and employees and leaders who are internal stakeholders. Therefore, the next two sections will be devoted to a brief description of the role of trust in relations within the company and between organization and its external stakeholders indicated earlier based on the narrative review of existing literature. This type of literature review reports the author's findings in a condensed format that can provoke further developments. It presents many pieces of information together in a readable format which is helpful in showing a broad perspective on a topic (Green et al., 2006).

3.2 Trust in intraorganizational relations

Trust within an organization should be examined in terms of four following areas of relations: (1) between employees, (2) employees toward the leader, and (3) leader toward employees. In this intraorganizational context, trust is a backbone of social capital which creates value by facilitating successful collective action (Leana & Van Buren, 1999). However, one may also indicate one more important area of relation: (4) employees trust in organization.

Team members who trust each other learn to feel comfortable with each other; they are open to each other, they are not afraid to reveal their own weaknesses, and talk about failures and even fears (Lencioni, 2016). Therefore, such positive outcomes of trust have been observed as knowledge sharing (Chiu et al., 2006; Collins & Smith, 2006), team learning (Bogenrieder & Nooteboom, 2004), effective cooperation in teamwork (Jones & George, 1998), creativity (Javed et al., 2018), and innovation (Shazi et al., 2015). Trust builds more slowly when there is a lack of face-to-face interactions in a real time. Trust develops through communication (Ruppel & Harrington, 2000) which differs between traditional and virtual organizational settings. Therefore, the importance of trust has been for many years examined in the context of virtual teamwork (Alsharo et al., 2017; Ardichvili et al., 2003; Chiu et al., 2006; Jarvenpaa et al., 1998; Jarvenpaa & Leidner, 1999).

Managers are initiators of trust. There are many guidelines for them on how to build and maintain trust. For example, Convey (2008) provided leaders with the list of behaviors which enhance trust under the conditions they are balanced. It covers, i.a., listening first, talking straight, clarifying expectations and practicing accountability, creating transparency, showing respect and loyalty, delivering results, confronting reality, getting better, and keeping commitments. Moreover, five categories of behavior influence employees' perceptions of managerial trustworthiness. They are: behavioral consistency, behavioral integrity, sharing and delegation of control, an open communication, and demonstration of concern (E. M. Whitener et al., 1998). Literature examined also how "big five" personality aspects of managers influence employees trust (Martins, 2002). Burke et al. (2007) proposed that expert coaching provided by a leader is an indicator of benevolence and thus increases trust in leadership. Literature also emphasizes the importance of fulfilling psychological contract which exists between a leader and employee (Coyle-Shapiro, 2002).

There are also types of leadership which increases trust both toward leaders and among employees. Among them, ethical leadership (Brown et al., 2005), transformational leadership (Bass & Steidlmeier, 1999; Podsakoff, 1996), authentic leadership (Gardner et al., 2005), charismatic leadership (Conger et al., 2000), empowering leadership (Wibowo & Hayati, 2019), relational leadership (Brower et al., 2000), and servant leadership (Chinomona et al., 2013) have been found as drivers of trust. Leaders with strong ethical values "generally honor their word and commitments made and communicate the same to their employees, which further reinforces their employees' trust in them" (Javed et al., 2018) (p. 399). Transformational leadership's behaviors cover promoting shared vision and team cooperation, transcending a leader's own self-interests for the sake of organizational interests, influencing employees' values and aspirations as well as activating their higher-order needs through intellectual stimulation (Bass & Steidlmeier, 1999). Authentic leaders are honest, inspire, and motivate subordinates through positive moral views, express supportive behaviors, and shape transparent relationships (Crawford et al., 2020). To be a charismatic leader means to be perceived by employees as a person with a great desire to change, shared and idealized vision and sensitive in terms of environmental opportunities, constraints, and followers' needs (Conger et al., 2000). Relational leaders put efforts in building positive relationships with subordinates (Brower et al., 2000). Finally, servant leaders serve people. They build community, value and development employees, share power (similarly to empowering leaders) and status for the common good of all company stakeholders (Joseph & Winston, 2005). When employees trust in leader they do not experience a fear of failure which increases their work engagement (Kleynhans et al., 2022), job satisfaction (Burke et al., 2007), and creativity (Javed et al., 2018). In turn, if employees spend time and energy worrying about what the management or organization may do to adversely impact them, the less cognitive resources they have for productive efforts (Mayer & Gavin, 2005). Moral management is the best way of management (Ruppel & Harrington, 2000).

At this point, it is worth mentioning that scant attention is paid in the literature to a leader's trust in employees. However, leaders undergo conditions such as ethical work climate which increases their trust in employees (Ruppel & Harrington, 2000). Moreover, one of the key constructs of relational leadership includes the employees' perception on how much leader trust in them (Brower et al., 2000).

Trust in coworkers (Tan & Lim, 2009) and trust in leader (Aryee et al., 2002; Joseph & Winston, 2005) may correlate with organizational trust because networks with coworkers constitute organizational social capital and leaders are agents of organizations (Li et al., 2012). Trust in leaders and organization is positively related to organizational commitment, organizational citizenship behavior, and employee loyalty (Fulmer & Gelfand, 2012). However, the antecedents of trust in the organization differ to some extent from those of trust in coworkers and the leader. In particular, different human resource policies and practices which create good working conditions (Kiefer, 2005), involve people in decision -making (Searle et al., 2011), provide justice in organization (Aryee et al., 2002; Cohen-Charash & Spector, 2001), job security (W. Wang et al., 2018), ethical cultural norms (Li et al., 2012) and perceived support (Fulmer & Gelfand, 2012) positively affect employees' perception of trust. In turn, a high level of formalization decreases employees' trust in organization (Li et al., 2012). Moreover, organizational cultural values and a reward system that promote teamwork enhance trust in teams (between employees) (Fulmer & Gelfand, 2012). Corporate social responsibility has been found as predictor of employee trust (Hansen et al., 2011). However, out of four CSR components (CSR toward social and nonsocial stakeholders; employees-, customers-, government-directed CSR), employees-directed CSR has the strongest impact on employees' trust (Farooq et al., 2014).

Many of the positive outcomes of trust presented earlier are not universal. There are studies which did find evidence for a positive main effect of trust on employee performance, team performance, and organizational citizenship behavior (Fulmer & Gelfand, 2012; E. Whitener, 2001). For example, according to Molina-Morales and Martínez-Fernández (2009), after a certain point of development, the social capital effectiveness decreases. There is an inverted U-shaped relationship of social interactions and trust with firm value creation. For a long-lasting team, team membership is embedded in social capital and is vital than trust which is not. As compared to team membership, trust, which comprises benevolence trust, integrity trust, and capability trust, appears as a poor predictor of knowledge-sharing practices in a team (Bakker et al., 2006). Therefore, future context-specific research on multidimensional trust is needed. One of the current contexts in research on trust is the COVID-19 pandemic. As research shows the pandemic made managers and employees equal which, in turn, increased the level of trust in leaders. Managers and employees found themselves in the same situation, trying to cope with the risk of being infected and with remote working (Vozza, 2022). Moreover, managers have put great effort into constant communication with employees which also contributed to trust (Men et al., 2022).

There is also a timely topic on the use of IT systems to measure the level of trust, for example, between people (Hale et al., 2018) and collaborating organizations (Ait Aali et al., 2018). The other emerging research area – discussed in other chapters in this monograph – is trust in human-machine teaming (Kohn et al., 2021).

3.3 Trust between organization and its external stakeholders

Transparency is viewed as a highly vital element to improve trust among stakeholders (Schnackenberg & Tomlinson, 2016). Considering the institutional and transactional uncertainty as core features, competition is neither price nor measurable quality dependent but follows networked reputation and experience-based trust (Glückler & Armbrüster, 2003). McKnight et al. (2002) have introduced trust as a multidimensional construct with four dimensions namely institution-based trust, trusting intentions, trusting beliefs, and disposition to trust. Inter-organizational and multi-functional networking are increasingly portrayed as new and potentially more effective forms of organization, especially where innovation is important. The success of a network is highly reliant on the pre-existing commonalities between its members (Huggins, 2000). Integrating mechanisms such as trust between the parties is essential if such networks are to be effective in coordinating the work of a diverse range of partners (Newell & Swan, 2000). Communication and cooperation between stakeholders are substantially important for the project success (Diallo & Thuillier, 2005).

Inter-firm interaction fosters trust-based ties in the shape of social capital which influences knowledge sharing (Mu et al., 2008). Weak ties enable firms to develop initial relationship. Strong ties are a source of getting high-quality knowledge. Reputable trust-brokers play the role of intermediator in effective networks. Having a good reputation enables the government to play as a trust-broker except areas where it lacks competency to intermediate effectively (Casson & Giusta, 2007).

As far as relationships between stakeholders in supply chain management are concerned, in relation to complex interorganizational networking, high density and frequency of interactions between partners, perceived competence of partners, expected future benefits of cooperation play a vital role in the development of trust among partners (Klijn et al., 2010). Trust has also been found to indirectly affect the supply chain project success through project-level factors such as between-firm communication and within-firm commitment (Brinkhoff et al., 2015). However, it has been proved that the supply chain project success requires the presence of trust among its partners but is not fully dependent on this (Dubey et al., 2018). Knowledge sharing – as the outcome of trust – is vital to improve supply-chain performance. According to Youn et al. (2013), the mutual trust level among supply chain partners promotes strategic information sharing. Yet, there is no evidence about the significant impact of mutual trust among partners on their operational information sharing (Youn et al., 2013). Both technical exchange and technology sharing, two types of knowledge sharing, among supply chain partners are significantly affected by trust and power but with greater magnitude at the former end (Cai et al., 2013). The justification behind the quick knowledge sharing is operational, market-specific, and technological experience which promotes trust among partners. As in the case of trust in a team of employees, social interaction-trust on value creation relationship is explained with the help of an inverted U-shaped relationship (Molina-Morales & Martínez-Fernández, 2009).

One of the main groups of company external stakeholders is customers. The issue of trust in the context of customers' decision when buying goods or services has received much attention in the literature. Online businesses and organizational activities in Internet are specific research areas related to customer's trust. For example, perceived relationship investment and perceived shopping risk have been found indirectly affecting relationship intention through trust (Wang & Head, 2007). The perceived price, convenience, and recreational benefit along with trust of the initiator (perceived reputation, structural assurance, and website trustworthiness) have been found to significantly positively influence consumers' attitudes toward online group buying (Liu et al., 2013). Moreover, physical distant retail store or lack of a physical store gives rise to distrust among its customers. Contrary to this, the website images of an office building or the owner's name and appearance positively affect customer's trust (Darke et al., 2016).

Subject literature also focuses on specific online and mobile businesses. One of them is online/mobile brokerage services. Lin et al. (2011) claim that trust in the first type of business significantly and positively affects perceived ease of use, usefulness, structural assurance, and initial trust in the second type of brokerage services. Moreover, perceived usefulness and structural assurance in mobile brokerage services also promote initial trust in these services. Yet, the perceived ease of use of mobile brokerage services is not significantly positively related to initial trust in the services (Lin et al., 2011).

Lee and Jeong (2014) provided evidence that online-offline brand image congruity significantly affects customers' trust toward the hotel's brand. To develop online trust, offline trust, word-of-mouth, and expected sanctioning power are strong determinants (Kuan & Bock, 2007). Moreover, word-of-mouth is more powerful than offline trust on the basis of an individual's personal experience with the physical stores. Socio-economic background and cooperative behavior influence trust toward strangers and beliefs about the fairness and helpfulness of others (Gächter et al., 2004). In online social networks, the strength of both ties and trust is mandated to promote social and emotional support and information sharing among individuals (Grabner-Kräuter, 2009).

Trust is a crucial factor in e-commerce. Cyr (2013) has found that users in high institutional trust, high social capital, and low uncertainty avoidance countries always perceive positively about information content, information design, visual design, and navigation design of a website. However, consumers are less likely to trust unknown Web sites. Considering the associative network model of memory and information integration theory, it has been proven that branding alliances and website quality are vital to developing initial trust (Lowry et al., 2008). On social network sites, participation motivation promotes brand loyalty and trust through customer participation. Moreover, both brand loyalty and brand trust significantly affect brand co-creation in brand communities in social media (Kamboj et al., 2018). Moreover, individuals are using Web 2.- applications to generate content and interact with other people on the Internet (Hajli, 2015). Employing social commerce constructs enhances an individual's trust and intention to purchase.

At this point, it is worth mentioning that during the 2008–2009 financial crisis, companies with high social capital had stock returns that were 4–7 percentage points higher than firms with low social capital. This finding shows that the trust between an organization and its stakeholders pays off when the overall level of trust in different markets is decreased (Lins et al., 2017). There are also research addressing the issue of trust in the context of the COVID-19 pandemic. For example, it has been found that risk perception was developed by trust in medical professional and government (Dryhurst et al., 2020). Moreover, the trust in leadership of any nation was crucial to take collective action toward such a crisis, that is, COVID-19, which was based on the government's willingness to hire subject matter experts, mobilize the population, and employ coping mechanism (Wilson, 2020). The widespread misinformation sharing appeared a serious threat to the COVID-19 response. Such rapid sharing of misinformation was actually led by information overload (Iqbal et al., 2020) and an individual's trust in online information (Krause et al., 2020). Ultimately, cyberchondria merged because of these factors along with the pandemic severity and vulnerability (Krause et al., 2020; Laato et al., 2020). In relation to the pandemic, both electronic and print media also generated positive, negative, and neutral sentiments. Approximately 52% of news headlines promoted negative sentiments and scored high on the emotional scale. These headlines mostly focused on the spreading of trust, anger, sadness, and fear as core motions (Aslam et al., 2020).

Turning back to the issue of online sales during the pandemic, food delivery apps emerged as an online-to-offline mobile technology, proving beneficial in rescuing catering enterprises and satisfying customers' mental exceptions in this pandemic. Here, trust also contributed significantly to influencing directly and indirectly users' continuance intention toward these apps during the pandemic (Zhao & Bacao, 2020).

As presented previously, there are many detailed research areas related to trust between intraorganizational actors as well as between organizations and their external stakeholders. The academic knowledge on trust evolves with changes that take place in companies and their environment.

References

Ait Aali, N., Baina, A., & Echabbi, L. (2018). Trust management in collaborative systems for critical infrastructure protection. *Security and Communication Networks, 2018*, 1–15. https://doi.org/10.1155/2018/7938727

Alsharo, M., Gregg, D., & Ramirez, R. (2017). Virtual team effectiveness: The role of knowledge sharing and trust. *Information & Management, 54*(4), 479–490. https://doi.org/10.1016/j.im.2016.10.005

Ardichvili, A., Page, V., & Wentling, T. (2003). Motivation and barriers to participation in virtual knowledge-sharing communities of practice. *Journal of Knowledge Management, 7*(1), 64–77. https://doi.org/10.1108/13673270310463626

Aryee, S., Budhwar, P. S., & Chen, Z. X. (2002). Trust as a mediator of the relationship between organizational justice and work outcomes: Test of a social exchange model. *Journal of Organizational Behavior, 23*(3), 267–285. https://doi.org/10.1002/job.138

Aslam, F., Awan, T. M., Syed, J. H., Kashif, A., & Parveen, M. (2020). Sentiments and emotions evoked by news headlines of coronavirus disease (COVID-19) outbreak. *Humanities and Social Sciences Communications, 7*(1), 1–9.

Bakker, M., Leenders, R. T. A. J., Gabbay, S. M., Kratzer, J., & Van Engelen, J. M. L. (2006). Is trust really social capital? Knowledge sharing in product development projects. *The Learning Organization, 13*(6), 594–605.

Bass, B. M., & Steidlmeier, P. (1999). Ethics, character, and authentic transformational leadership behavior. *The Leadership Quarterly, 10*(2), 181–217. https://doi.org/10.1016/S1048-9843(99)00016-8

Berggren, N., & Bjørnskov, C. (2011). Is the importance of religion in daily life related to social trust? Cross-country and cross-state comparisons. *Journal of Economic Behavior & Organization, 80*(3), 459–480.

Bogenrieder, I., & Nooteboom, B. (2004). Learning groups: What types are there? A theoretical analysis and an empirical study in a consultancy firm. *Organization Studies, 25*(2), 287–313. https://doi.org/10.1177/0170840604040045

Brinkhoff, A., Özer, Ö., & Sargut, G. (2015). All you need is trust? An examination of inter-organizational supply chain projects. *Production and Operations Management, 24*(2), 181–200.

Brower, H. H., Schoorman, F. D., & Tan, H. H. (2000). A model of relational leadership. *The Leadership Quarterly, 11*(2), 227–250. https://doi.org/10.1016/S1048-9843(00)00040-0

Brown, M. E., Treviño, L. K., & Harrison, D. A. (2005). Ethical leadership: A social learning perspective for construct development and testing. *Organizational Behavior and Human Decision Processes, 97*(2), 117–134. https://doi.org/10.1016/j.obhdp.2005.03.002

Burke, C. S., Sims, D. E., Lazzara, E. H., & Salas, E. (2007). Trust in leadership: A multilevel review and integration. *The Leadership Quarterly, 18*(6), 606–632. https://doi.org/10.1016/j.leaqua.2007.09.006

Cai, S., Goh, M., De Souza, R., & Li, G. (2013). Knowledge sharing in collaborative supply chains: Twin effects of trust and power. *International Journal of Production Research, 51*(7), 2060–2076.

Casson, M., & Giusta, M. Della. (2007). Entrepreneurship and social capital: Analysing the impact of social networks on entrepreneurial activity from a rational action perspective. *International Small Business Journal*, *25*(3), 220–244.

Chinomona, R., Mashiloane, M., & Pooe, D. (2013). The influence of servant leadership on employee trust in a leader and commitment to the organization. *Mediterranean Journal of Social Sciences*. https://doi.org/10.5901/mjss.2013.v4n14p405

Chiu, C.-M., Hsu, M.-H., & Wang, E. T. G. (2006). Understanding knowledge sharing in virtual communities: An integration of social capital and social cognitive theories. *Decision Support Systems*, *42*(3), 1872–1888. https://doi.org/10.1016/j.dss.2006.04.001

Cohen-Charash, Y., & Spector, P. E. (2001). The role of justice in organizations: A meta-analysis. *Organizational Behavior and Human Decision Processes*, *86*(2), 278–321. https://doi.org/10.1006/obhd.2001.2958

Collins, C. J., & Smith, K. G. (2006). Knowledge exchange and combination: The role of human resource practices in the performance of high-technology firms. *Academy of Management Journal*, *49*(3), 544–560. https://doi.org/10.5465/amj.2006.21794671

Conger, J. A., Kanungo, R. N., & Menon, S. T. (2000). Charismatic leadership and follower effects. *Journal of Organizational Behavior*, *21*(7), 747–767.

Convey, S. (2008). *Speed of trust: The one thing that changes everything*. Harper Collins Publishers.

Coyle-Shapiro, J. A.-M. (2002). A psychological contract perspective on organizational citizenship behavior. *Journal of Organizational Behavior*, *23*(8), 927–946. https://doi.org/10.1002/job.173

Crawford, J. A., Dawkins, S., Martin, A., & Lewis, G. (2020). Putting the leader back into authentic leadership: Reconceptualising and rethinking leaders. *Australian Journal of Management*, *45*(1), 114–133. https://doi.org/10.1177/0312896219836460

Cropanzano, R., Anthony, E. L., Daniels, S. R., & Hall, A. V. (2017). Social exchange theory: A critical review with theoretical remedies. *Academy of Management Annals*, *11*(1), 479–516. https://doi.org/10.5465/annals.2015.0099

Cyr, D. (2013). Website design, trust and culture: An eight country investigation. *Electronic Commerce Research and Applications*, *12*(6), 373–385.

Darke, P. R., Brady, M. K., Benedicktus, R. L., & Wilson, A. E. (2016). Feeling close from afar: The role of psychological distance in offsetting distrust in unfamiliar online retailers. *Journal of Retailing*, *92*(3), 287–299.

Dearmon, J., & Grier, K. (2009). Trust and development. *Journal of Economic Behavior & Organization*, *71*(2), 210–220.

Diallo, A., & Thuillier, D. (2005). The success of international development projects, trust and communication: An African perspective. *International Journal of Project Management*, *23*(3), 237–252.

Doney, P. M., Cannon, J. P., & Mullen, M. R. (1998). Understanding the influence of national culture on the development of trust. *Academy of Management Review*, *23*(3), 601–620. https://doi.org/10.5465/amr.1998.926629

Dryhurst, S., Schneider, C. R., Kerr, J., Freeman, A. L. J., Recchia, G., Van Der Bles, A. M., Spiegelhalter, D., & Van Der Linden, S. (2020). Risk perceptions of COVID-19 around the world. *Journal of Risk Research*, *23*(7–8), 994–1006.

Dubey, R., Luo, Z., Gunasekaran, A., Akter, S., Hazen, B. T., & Douglas, M. A. (2018). Big data and predictive analytics in humanitarian supply chains: Enabling visibility and coordination in the presence of swift trust. *The International Journal of Logistics Management*, *29*(2), 485–512.

Farooq, O., Payaud, M., Merunka, D., & Valette-Florence, P. (2014). The impact of corporate social responsibility on organizational commitment: Exploring multiple mediation mechanisms. *Journal of Business Ethics*, *125*(4), 563–580. https://doi.org/10.1007/s10551-013-1928-3

Friedman, A. L., & Miles, S. (2006). *Stakeholders: Theory and practic*. Oxford University Press.

Fulmer, C. A., & Gelfand, M. J. (2012). At what level (and in whom) we trust. *Journal of Management*, *38*(4), 1167–1230. https://doi.org/10.1177/0149206312439327

Gächter, S., Herrmann, B., & Thöni, C. (2004). Trust, voluntary cooperation, and socio-economic background: Survey and experimental evidence. *Journal of Economic Behavior & Organization*, *55*(4), 505–531.

Gardner, W. L., Avolio, B. J., Luthans, F., May, D. R., & Walumbwa, F. (2005). "Can you see the real me?" A self-based model of authentic leader and follower development. *The Leadership Quarterly*, *16*(3), 343–372.

Gefen, D., Karahanna, E., & Straub, D. (2003). Trust and TAM in online shopping: An integrated model. *MIS Quarterly*, *27*(1), 51. https://doi.org/10.2307/30036519

Glückler, J., & Armbrüster, T. (2003). Bridging uncertainty in management consulting: The mechanisms of trust and networked reputation. *Organization Studies*, *24*(2), 269–297.

Grabner-Kräuter, S. (2009). Web 2.0 social networks: The role of trust. *Journal of Business Ethics*, *90*(4), 505–522.

Green, B. N., Johnson, C. D., & Adams, A. (2006). Writing narrative literature reviews for peer-reviewed journals: Secrets of the trade. *Journal of Chiropractic Medicine*, *5*(3), 101–117. https://doi.org/10.1016/S0899-3467(07)60142-6

Hajli, N. (2015). Social commerce constructs and consumer's intention to buy. *International Journal of Information Management*, *35*(2), 183–191.

Hale, J., Payne, M. E., Taylor, K. M., Paoletti, D., & De C Hamilton, A. F. (2018). The virtual maze: A behavioural tool for measuring trust. *Quarterly Journal of Experimental Psychology*, *71*(4), 989–1008. https://doi.org/10.1080/17470218.2017.1307865

Hansen, S. D., Dunford, B. B., Boss, A. D., Boss, R. W., & Angermeier, I. (2011). Corporate social responsibility and the benefits of employee trust: A cross-disciplinary perspective. *Journal of Business Ethics*, *102*(1), 29–45. https://doi.org/10.1007/s10551-011-0903-0

Harrison, K. (2020). *Why trust is vital to your organization*. https://cuttingedgepr.com/trust-vital-to-your-organization/

Hosmer, L. T. (1995). Trust: The connecting link between organizational theory and philosophical ethics. *The Academy of Management Review*, *20*(2), 379. https://doi.org/10.2307/258851

Huang, Y., & Wilkinson, I. F. (2013). The dynamics and evolution of trust in business relationships. *Industrial Marketing Management*, *42*(3), 455–465. https://doi.org/10.1016/j.indmarman.2013.02.016

Huggins, R. (2000). The success and failure of policy-implanted inter-firm network initiatives: Motivations, processes and structure. *Entrepreneurship & Regional Development*, *12*(2), 111–135.

Iqbal, Q., Ahmad, N. H., & Nawaz, R. (2020). Perceived information pollution: Conceptualization, measurement, and nomological validity. *Online Information Review*. https://doi.org/10.1108/OIR-10-2018-0322

Jarvenpaa, S. L., Knoll, K., & Leidner, D. E. (1998). Is anybody out there? Antecedents of trust in global virtual teams. *Journal of Management Information Systems*, *14*(4), 29–64. https://doi.org/10.1080/07421222.1998.11518185

Jarvenpaa, S. L., & Leidner, D. E. (1999). Communication and trust in global virtual teams. *Organization Science*, *10*(6), 791–815. https://doi.org/10.1287/orsc.10.6.791

Javed, B., Rawwas, M. Y. A., Khandai, S., Shahid, K., & Tayyeb, H. H. (2018). Ethical leadership, trust in leader and creativity: The mediated mechanism and an interacting effect. *Journal of Management & Organization*, *24*(3), 388–405. https://doi.org/10.1017/jmo.2017.56

Jones, G. R., & George, J. M. (1998). The experience and evolution of trust: Implications for cooperation and teamwork. *Academy of Management Review*, *23*(3), 531–546. https://doi.org/10.5465/amr.1998.926625

Joseph, E. E., & Winston, B. E. (2005). A correlation of servant leadership, leader trust, and organizational trust. *Leadership & Organization Development Journal*, *26*(1), 6–22. https://doi.org/10.1108/01437730510575552

Kamboj, S., Sarmah, B., Gupta, S., & Dwivedi, Y. (2018). Examining branding co-creation in brand communities on social media: Applying the paradigm of stimulus-organism-response. *International Journal of Information Management*, *39*, 169–185.

Kiefer, T. (2005). Feeling bad: Antecedents and consequences of negative emotions in ongoing change. *Journal of Organizational Behavior*, *26*(8), 875–897. https://doi.org/10.1002/job.339

Kleynhans, D. J., Heyns, M. M., Stander, M. W., & de Beer, L. T. (2022). Authentic leadership, trust (in the leader), and flourishing: Does precariousness matter? *Frontiers in Psychology*, *13*. https://doi.org/10.3389/fpsyg.2022.798759

Klijn, E.-H., Edelenbos, J., & Steijn, B. (2010). Trust in governance networks: Its impacts on outcomes. *Administration & Society*, *42*(2), 193–221.

Kohn, S. C., de Visser, E. J., Wiese, E., Lee, Y.-C., & Shaw, T. H. (2021). Measurement of trust in automation: A narrative review and reference guide. *Frontiers in Psychology*, *12*. https://doi.org/10.3389/fpsyg.2021.604977

Krause, N. M., Freiling, I., Beets, B., & Brossard, D. (2020). Fact-checking as risk communication: The multi-layered risk of misinformation in times of COVID-19. *Journal of Risk Research*, *23*(7–8), 1052–1059.

Kuan, H.-H., & Bock, G.-W. (2007). Trust transference in brick and click retailers: An investigation of the before-online-visit phase. *Information & Management*, *44*(2), 175–187.

Laato, S., Islam, A. K. M. N., Islam, M. N., & Whelan, E. (2020). What drives unverified information sharing and cyberchondria during the COVID-19 pandemic? *European Journal of Information Systems*, *29*(3), 288–305.

Leana, C. R., & Van Buren, H. J. (1999). Organizational social capital and employment practices. *Academy of Management Review*, *24*(3), 538–555. https://doi.org/10.5465/amr.1999.2202136

Lee, S. A., & Jeong, M. (2014). Enhancing online brand experiences: An application of congruity theory. *International Journal of Hospitality Management*, *40*, 49–58.

Lencioni, P. (2016). *Overcoming the five dysfunctions of teamwork. A practical guide for leaders, managers, and moderators*. MT Biznes.

Lewicki, R. J., Tomlinson, E. C., & Gillespie, N. (2006). Models of interpersonal trust development: Theoretical approaches, empirical evidence, and future directions. *Journal of Management*, *32*(6), 991–1022. https://doi.org/10.1177/0149206306294405

Li, P. P., Bai, Y., & Xi, Y. (2012). The contextual antecedents of organizational trust: A multidimensional cross-level analysis. *Management and Organization Review*, *8*(2), 371–396. https://doi.org/10.1111/j.1740-8784.2011.00219.x

Lin, J., Lu, Y., Wang, B., & Wei, K. K. (2011). The role of inter-channel trust transfer in establishing mobile commerce trust. *Electronic Commerce Research and Applications*, *10*(6), 615–625.

Lins, K. V., Servaes, H., & Tamayo, A. (2017). Social capital, trust, and firm performance: The value of corporate social responsibility during the financial crisis. *The Journal of Finance*, *72*(4), 1785–1824. https://doi.org/10.1111/jofi.12505

Liu, M. T., Brock, J. L., Shi, G. C., Chu, R., & Tseng, T-H. (2013). Perceived benefits, perceived risk, and trust: Influences on consumers' group buying behaviour. *Asia Pacific Journal of Marketing and Logistics*, *25*, 225–248.

Lowry, P. B., Vance, A., Moody, G., Beckman, B., & Read, A. (2008). Explaining and predicting the impact of branding alliances and web site quality on initial consumer trust of e-commerce web sites. *Journal of Management Information Systems*, *24*(4), 199–224.

Martins, N. (2002). A model for managing trust. *International Journal of Manpower*, *23*(8), 754–769. https://doi.org/10.1108/01437720210453984

Mayer, R. C., & Gavin, M. B. (2005). Trust in management and performance: Who minds the shop while the employees watch the boss? *The Academy of Management Journal*, *48*(5), 874–888. www.jstor.org/stable/20159703

McKnight, D. H., Choudhury, V., & Kacmar, C. (2002). Developing and validating trust measures for e-commerce: An integrative typology. *Information Systems Research*, *13*(3), 334–359.

Men, L. R., Qin, Y. S., & Jin, J. (2022). Fostering employee trust via effective supervisory communication during the COVID-19 pandemic: Through the lens of motivating language theory. *International Journal of Business Communication*, *59*(2), 193–218. https://doi.org/10.1177/23294884211020491

Molina-Morales, F. X., & Martínez-Fernández, M. T. (2009). Too much love in the neighborhood can hurt: How an excess of intensity and trust in relationships may produce negative effects on firms. *Strategic Management Journal*, *30*(9), 1013–1023.

Mu, J., Peng, G., & Love, E. (2008). Interfirm networks, social capital, and knowledge flow. *Journal of Knowledge Management*. https://scholar.google.com/citations?user=-gPt1JsAAAAJ&hl=th

Newell, S., & Swan, J. (2000). Trust and inter-organizational networking. *Human Relations*, *53*(10), 1287–1328.

Nilsson, P., & Fagerström, B. (2006). Managing stakeholder requirements in a product modelling system. *Computers in Industry*, *57*(2), 167–177. https://doi.org/10.1016/j.compind.2005.06.003

Paliszkiewicz, J. O. (2011). Trust management: Literature review. *Management*, *6*(4), 315–331.
Podsakoff, P. (1996). Transformational leader behaviors and substitutes for leadership as determinants of employee satisfaction, commitment, trust, and organizational citize. *Journal of Management*, *22*(2), 259–298. https://doi.org/10.1016/S0149-2063(96)90049-5
Ruan, Y., & Durresi, A. (2016). A survey of trust management systems for online social communities–trust modeling, trust inference and attacks. *Knowledge-Based Systems*, *106*, 150–163.
Rudzewicz, A. (2017). Zaufanie w przedsiębiorstwie – znaczenie i pomiar. *Zarządzanie i Finanse*, *15*(2), 291–304.
Ruppel, C. P., & Harrington, S. J. (2000). The relationship of communication, ethical work climate, and trust to commitment and innovation. *Journal of Business Ethics*, *25*(4), 313–328. https://doi.org/10.1023/A:1006290432594
Schnackenberg, A. K., & Tomlinson, E. C. (2016). Organizational transparency: A new perspective on managing trust in organization-stakeholder relationships. *Journal of Management*, *42*(7), 1784–1810.
Searle, R., Den Hartog, D. N., Weibel, A., Gillespie, N., Six, F., Hatzakis, T., & Skinner, D. (2011). Trust in the employer: The role of high-involvement work practices and procedural justice in European organizations. *The International Journal of Human Resource Management*, *22*(5), 1069–1092. https://doi.org/10.1080/09585192.2011.556782
Shazi, R., Gillespie, N., & Steen, J. (2015). Trust as a predictor of innovation network ties in project teams. *International Journal of Project Management*, *33*(1), 81–91. https://doi.org/10.1016/j.ijproman.2014.06.001
Tan, H. H., & Lim, A. K. H. (2009). Trust in coworkers and trust in organizations. *The Journal of Psychology*, *143*(1), 45–66. https://doi.org/10.3200/JRLP.143.1.45-66
van Eck, N. J., & Waltman, L. (2014). Visualizing bibliometric networks. In *Measuring scholarly impact* (pp. 285–320). Springer International Publishing. https://doi.org/10.1007/978-3-319-10377-8_13
van Zeeland-van der Holst, E. M., & Henseler, J. (2018). Thinking outside the box: A neuroscientific perspective on trust in B2B relationships. *IMP Journal*, *12*(1), 75–110. https://doi.org/10.1108/IMP-03-2017-0011
Vozza, S. (2022). *Has the pandemic improved trust in the workplace?* www.shrm.org/resourcesandtools/hr-topics/people-managers/pages/pandemic-breeds-trust-.aspx
Wang, F., & Head, M. (2007). How can the web help build customer relationships? An empirical study on e-tailing. *Information & Management*, *44*(2), 115–129.
Wang, W., Mather, K., & Seifert, R. (2018). Job insecurity, employee anxiety, and commitment: The moderating role of collective trust in management. *Journal of Trust Research*, *8*(2), 220–237. https://doi.org/10.1080/21515581.2018.1463229
Whitener, E. M. (2001). Do "high commitment" human resource practices affect employee commitment? A cross-level analysis using hierarchical linear modeling. *Journal of Management*, *27*(5), 515–535. https://doi.org/10.1016/S0149-2063(01)00106-4
Whitener, E. M., Brodt, S. E., Korsgaard, M. A., & Werner, J. M. (1998). Managers as initiators of trust: An exchange relationship framework for understanding managerial trustworthy behavior. *Academy of Management Review*, *23*(3), 513–530. https://doi.org/10.5465/amr.1998.926624

Wibowo, A., & Hayati, N. R. (2019). Empowering leadership and trust on team learning behavior. *Journal of Management Development*, *38*(3), 238–248. https://doi.org/10.1108/JMD-11-2018-0335
Wilson, S. (2020). Pandemic leadership: Lessons from New Zealand's approach to COVID-19. *Leadership*, *16*(3), 279–293.
Youn, S., Yang, M. G. M., Hong, P., & Park, K. (2013). Strategic supply chain partnership, environmental supply chain management practices, and performance outcomes: An empirical study of Korean firms. *Journal of Cleaner Production*, *56*, 121–130.
Zhao, Y., & Bacao, F. (2020). What factors determining customer continuingly using food delivery apps during 2019 novel coronavirus pandemic period? *International Journal of Hospitality Management*, *91*, 102683.

4 Trust

The psychological aspect

Magda Gawłowska

4.1 Defining trust

Trust is a psychological state characterized by a willingness to be vulnerable based on the positive expectations of the intentions or behavior of another entity (Rousseau et al., 1998).

Trust plays a crucial role in fostering cooperation and building relationships in diverse social, economic, and political settings and it is based on the belief in the reliability and honesty of another person, shaped by factors such as personality, communication, cultural background, and past experiences (Freitag & Bauer, 2016). Interpersonal trust is complex and dynamic, it requires an expectation of the other person to act in a favorable manner, despite having the opportunity to betray. In a majority of cases, trust involves taking a risk by relying on another person's actions in uncertain circumstances. Thus, from an evolutionary perspective, trusting behaviors can be difficult to explain (Engelmann & Herrmann, 2016).

Rotenberg et al. (2005) proposed a model of interpersonal trust, according to which there are three key elements that constitute interpersonal trust: reliability, emotional, and honesty. Reliability refers to the expectation that others will fulfill given promises; emotional refers to the belief that others will not cause emotional harm; whereas honesty refers to anticipation that others will be truthful. These elements are further divided into cognitive/affective and behavioral domains. The cognitive/affective domain holds an individual's beliefs and emotional experiences regarding the three bases of trust, whereas the behavioral domain refers to individuals' behavioral tendency to rely on others to act in a trustworthy manner. The bases of trust and the domains are further divided into dimensions based on the target of trust, including the specificity of trusted individuals and their level of familiarity.

4.2 Development of trust

The extent of a person's trust is influenced by various internal and external factors. However, from a psychological standpoint, early childhood experiences

DOI: 10.4324/9781003311409-5

play a significant role in shaping the foundation for the level of trust a person has in others later in life.

According to Erik Erikson's (Erikson, 1964) psychosocial theory of development, an individual goes through eight developmental stages in the course of life. Each stage of development involves a conflict that can be resolved in either a healthy or unhealthy manner. The way the conflict is resolved at one stage influences an individual's ability to successfully address conflicts in later stages. Trust is a crucial aspect of early childhood development. Erikson believed that during the first stage of development, known as the "trust vs. mistrust" stage, which lasts for the first 18 months of life, infants develop a sense of trust or mistrust toward the world and others based on their early experiences with caregivers. If infants are provided with a supportive and responsive environment, they will develop a sense of trust in the world and in others. This sense of trust allows them to feel secure and confident in their surroundings, which lays the foundation for future healthy relationships and a positive sense of self. On the other hand, if infants are subjected to neglect, inconsistency, or abuse, they may develop a sense of mistrust toward the world and others. This mistrust can lead to feelings of insecurity and fear, which can negatively impact future relationships and a sense of self. Erikson believed that trust is essential for psychological well-being. When people experience trust, they feel safe and secure and are more likely to take risks and explore the world around them. In contrast, when trust is lacking, individuals may become cautious, withdraw from others, and develop feelings of anxiety and insecurity. In later stages of life, trust continues to play an important role in a person's relationships with others. For example, in adolescence, young people must establish trust in their peers and their own abilities in order to develop a sense of identity. In adulthood, trust is crucial for forming intimate relationships and for trusting institutions and society at large.

Second of the theories, which points at crucial role of trust in the earliest stages of life is attachment theory, first introduced by psychologist John Bowlby (Bowlby, 1969, 1973, 1977), and it has since been further developed and expanded upon by numerous researchers in the field of psychology. Some of the key figures in the field of attachment theory include Mary Ainsworth (Ainsworth et al., 2015) or Cindy Hazan and Phillip Shaver (Hazan & Shaver, 1994), who applied attachment theory to adult romantic relationships. Attachment theory explains the nature of the emotional and physical bonds between infants and their caregivers and the influence these bonds have on the child's future relationships and emotional regulation. Trust is an essential aspect of attachment theory, as it refers to the child's belief that their needs will be met by their caregiver and that they are safe and protected in their presence. Based on their relationship with the caregiver, an infant can develop one of the three attachment styles: secure, insecure-ambivalent, and insecure-avoidant. To assess the attachment style, Ainsworth developed a laboratory procedure called "Strange Situation" (Ainsworth & Bell, 1970), designed to observe and measure attachment security in infants. The procedure involves placing an infant in a series of gradually more stressful situations, for example, the caregiver leaving the room and a stranger entering the room, while observing their behavior and the interactions with their caregiver. The infant's behavior, such as crying, seeking proximity to the caregiver, and exploring the environment, is recorded and analyzed. Infants with a secure attachment display distress when separated from their caregiver, seek comfort and proximity upon reunion, and are able to freely explore their environment while their caregiver is present. Insecure-ambivalent attachment is characterized by the infant showing distress upon separation and an inconsistent response to reunion, while insecure-avoidant attachment is characterized by the infant showing little distress upon separation and avoiding the caregiver upon reunion. A secure attachment relationship is characterized by trust and reliability, and it lays the foundation for the child's ability to trust others and regulate their emotions in later life.

It should be noted that early childhood experiences shape the baseline for basic trust, and as an individual's life progresses, multiple, either internal or external factors can influence the amount of trust they are likely to exhibit.

4.3 Factors influencing trust

In general, research on factors influencing the level of trust and trust formation revolves around two main theoretical perspectives (Freitag & Bauer, 2016). The first perspective states that trust is a consequence of past experiences in social interactions. If an individual has had positive experiences and views the social environment as trustworthy in the past, they are more likely to trust in the future, and vice versa. The second perspective views trust as a relatively stable disposition that is not significantly impacted by situational events. It argues that the level of trust is determined by, for example, gender, personality traits, or heritability. Despite the differing definitions of the origins of trust in these two theoretical approaches, both offer insightful perspectives from research on the factors that may influence the level of trust and perceived trustworthiness.

Multiple researchers analyzed and provided evidence for the relationship between personality traits and trust. For instance, Hiraishi et al. (2008) conducted a twin study on a group of 540 twin pairs (both, identical and fraternal) and they found that general trust was positively correlated with extraversion and agreeableness. Moreover, the relations they observed were heritable. In another twin study, Oskarsson et al. (2012) investigated the relationship between psychological traits and social trust in a sample of 2000 twin pairs and found that extraversion, personal control, and intelligence were correlated with social trust, with no gender-related differences observed. Additionally, as in research conducted by Hiraishi et al., they observed the influence of heritability. Uslaner (2002) points to the positive relation between optimism, sense of control, and general trust. In contrast, Couch and Jones (1997) conducted a study on a group of students involved in a romantic relationship and found a negative correlation between trust and jealousy, shyness, and suspiciousness. Finally, there is an interesting relationship between trust and locus of control. For example, Gopinath et al. (2000) found that external locus of control was related to both, unwillingness to comply with the therapy demands and reduced trust in the medical system.

Gender is another interesting factor to consider when studying differences in trust and perceived trustworthiness. Maddux and Brewer (2005) examined the relationship between gender and trust by implementing the Dictator Game paradigm, in which participants interacted with players from different social connections – players from their social group, players they had relationship with them, or players from the outside of social circle. The results showed that men were more likely to trust individuals based on their shared group affiliations, while women tended to trust those with whom they had direct or indirect personal connections. In a separate study, Buchan et al. (2008) utilized Investment Game to explore gender differences in the level of trust and trustworthiness. They found that men tended to display more trust, but the trust can be interpreted as instrumental – in the Investment Game the only way to maximize outcome is by sending money to the responder and trust the money would be returned. Women, on the other hand, were found to be more trustworthy, as they were more likely to return money to the sender. Another interesting study by Haselhuhn et al. (2015) explored the gender differences in trust after trust violation. Results indicate that women tend to be less prone to losing trust and more inclined to regain trust in someone who has betrayed them compared to men. Higher level of trust observed in women may be a result of them placing a higher importance on preserving relationships, which influences the connection between gender and trust behavior.

Haselhuhn et al. (2015) demonstrated that previous experiences, such as a breach of trust, can affect the level of trust. The same can be said for the socioeconomic status in childhood. Individuals who come from low socio-economic status backgrounds often face more dangers, leading them to be highly attuned to their surroundings and generally more distrustful of others in adulthood (Stamos et al., 2019). Moreover, the experience of income inequality, mediated by lower life satisfaction, may lead to a lower overall level of trust toward others (Graafland & Lous, 2019).

It is worth noting that the trust we are willing to allocate in others is often influenced by situational variables, which may fluctuate over time, such as experienced emotions or cognitive processes happening outside of awareness (Lount & Pettit, 2012). In a series of studies, Dunn and Schweitzer (2005) found that happy participants were more trusting than sad participants, and sad participants were more trusting compared to angry ones. Additionally, emotions with appraisal of other-person control (i.e., anger or gratitude) influence the level of trust significantly more than those with appraisal of personal control (i.e., pride or guilt).

The list of factors that influence trust presented earlier is by no means complete. The purpose of previous section was not to come up with a finite list, but rather to demonstrate to the reader that there are multiple variables that can affect how we place our trust and that these variables can interact in various ways and different configurations.

4.4 Trust and AI

Previous paragraphs of this chapter focused on trust in an interpersonal setting. However, we are currently witnessing a rapid development of intelligent systems designed to perform tasks once requiring human intelligence, with minimal or no human supervision. As these systems – collectively called artificial intelligence (AI) – leave laboratories and enter new areas of our lives, the question appears whether individuals are able to trust AI. What factors are critical in shaping this trust? Is trust in AI different from trust in social interactions?

People allocate a higher level of trust in agents similar to them. When AI comes with a "packaging," for example, we are presented with an AI-based robot, we tend to trust more the ones which are more similar to humans, that is, with a high level of anthropomorphism or the system which acts like human, for example, expresses emotions (de Visser et al., 2016; Sanders et al., 2011; Waytz et al., 2014).

When we look at the characteristics of human agent, Chien et al. (2016) found that personality differences had a significant impact on trust in automation. Participants with higher scores in agreeableness or conscientiousness tended to trust automation more. Further, humans with high self-confidence are less likely to trust in robotic systems, as opposed to humans with low self-confidence, who are more likely to trust a robot more than they should (Freedy et al., 2007). However, personality traits were good predictors of declared trust in AI, but not trust behaviors (Alarcon et al., 2018).

Logg et al. (2019) looked at how people perceive the advice whether they believed it was coming from an algorithm or a person. In general, people undervalued advice, but when they believed it was from an algorithm, they were more likely to trust it than if it came from a human, especially if they were not experts. This effect disappeared when experts were asked to choose between advice from the algorithm and their own judgment.

What distinguishes the human-human and human-AI trust is once trust in humans is violated, it is quite easily restored, contrary to trust in AI – once broken, it is unlikely to be reestablished (de Visser et al., 2012). Therefore, it seems crucial to identify areas of possible transgressions, the violation of which may result in loss of trust.

Hoff and Bashir (2015) developed a model of trust in automation that identifies three main sources of variation in trust upon AI: dispositional (the human operator), situational (the environment), and learned (the system itself). Additionally, the dispositional layer is influenced by culture, age, gender, and personality traits of human. Thus, this model of trust in automation bears a striking resemblance to models of trust in social interactions. However, Lockey et al. (2021) point at five AI-specific areas that are crucial for AI to be trusted: transparency and explainability, accuracy and reliability, automation, anthropomorphism, and mass data extraction. Transparency and explainability point to the need to present the user with information regarding the rules the system operates by. If the utilized algorithm is explainable, people are more likely to trust it (Gretton, 2018), especially if they are naïve users (Andras et al., 2018). Further, to be trusted AI should be accurate and reliable. Studies show that when the accuracy of AI decreases the same can be observed for the level of user's trust (Moran et al., 2013). Automation, understood as complete autonomy of system, is probably one of the most sensitive and fear-inducing areas of cooperation and trust between human and AI. People are reluctant, especially with regard to medical care, to trust decisions made by AI without human support present (Longoni et al., 2019). Another topic discussed earlier is anthropomorphism. As stated before, people are more likely to trust AI that is equipped in human-like features, either physical or behavioral (de Visser et al., 2016; Sanders et al., 2011; Waytz et al., 2014). Finally, issues concerning mass data extraction, especially fear of bridge of privacy, can heavily influence trust. Up until now, there is a very limited number of studies that address this concern; however, Kaur and Rampersad (2018) showed that users were more likely to trust autonomous cars if they had less privacy concerns.

In conclusion, the objective of this chapter is to provide a psychological perspective on both interpersonal trust and trust directed toward Artificial Intelligence. While the studies of interpersonal trust have been conducted for decades, trust toward AI is a relatively new topic. Nevertheless, as the field of AI is rapidly advancing, examining the factors that impact human-AI interactions is crucial as new forms of AI will increasingly be incorporated into various facets of human life.

References

Ainsworth, M. D. S., & Bell, S. M. (1970). Attachment, exploration, and separation: Illustrated by the behavior of one-year-olds in a strange situation. *Child Development*, *41*(1). https://doi.org/10.1111/j.1467-8624.1970.tb00975.x

Ainsworth, M. D. S., Blehar, M. C., Waters, E., & Wall, S. N. (2015). Patterns of attachment. In *Patterns of attachment: A psychological study of the strange situation*. Psychology Press. https://doi.org/10.4324/9780203758045

Alarcon, G. M., Lyons, J. B., Christensen, J. C., Bowers, M. A., Klosterman, S. L., & Capiola, A. (2018). The role of propensity to trust and the five factor model across the trust process. *Journal of Research in Personality*, *75*, 69–82. https://doi.org/10.1016/J.JRP.2018.05.006

Andras, P., Esterle, L., Guckert, M., Han, T. A., Lewis, P. R., Milanovic, K., Payne, T., Perret, C., Pitt, J., Powers, S. T., Urquhart, N., & Wells, S. (2018). Trusting intelligent machines: Deepening trust within socio-technical systems. *IEEE Technology and Society Magazine*, *37*(4), 76–83. https://doi.org/10.1109/MTS.2018.2876107

Bowlby, J. (1969). Attachment and loss, vol. 1: Attachment. Attachment and loss. *Attachment*, *33*, 371–399.

Bowlby, J. (1973). Attachment and loss: Vol.2. Seperation: Anxiety and anger. *The International Psycho-Analytical Library*, *95*(1973).

Bowlby, J. (1977). The making and breaking of affectional bonds. *British Journal of Psychiatry*, *130*(5). https://doi.org/10.1192/bjp.130.5.421

Buchan, N. R., Croson, R. T. A., & Solnick, S. (2008). Trust and gender: An examination of behavior and beliefs in the Investment Game. *Journal of Economic Behavior and Organization*, *68*(3–4), 466–476. https://doi.org/10.1016/j.jebo.2007.10.006

Chien, S. Y., Lewis, M., Sycara, K., Liu, J. S., & Kumru, A. (2016). Relation between trust attitudes toward automation, Hofstede's cultural dimensions, and big five personality traits. *Proceedings of the Human Factors and Ergonomics Society*, 840–844. https://doi.org/10.1177/1541931213601192

Couch, L. L., & Jones, W. H. (1997). Measuring levels of trust. *Journal of Research in Personality*, *336*(31), 319–336.

de Visser, E. J., Krueger, F., McKnight, P., Scheid, S., Smith, M., Chalk, S., & Parasuraman, R. (2012). The world is not enough: Trust in cognitive agents. *Proceedings of the Human Factors and Ergonomics Society*, 263–267. https://doi.org/10.1177/1071181312561062

de Visser, E. J., Monfort, S. S., McKendrick, R., Smith, M. A. B., McKnight, P. E., Krueger, F., & Parasuraman, R. (2016). Almost human: Anthropomorphism increases trust resilience in cognitive agents. *Journal of Experimental Psychology: Applied*, *22*(3), 331–349. https://doi.org/10.1037/xap0000092

Dunn, J. R., & Schweitzer, M. E. (2005). Feeling and believing: The influence of emotion on trust. *Journal of Personality and Social Psychology*, *88*(5), 736–748. https://doi.org/10.1037/0022-3514.88.5.736

Engelmann, J. M., & Herrmann, E. (2016). Chimpanzees trust their friends. *Current Biology*, *26*(2), 252–256. https://doi.org/10.1016/j.cub.2015.11.037

Erikson, E. H. (1964). *Childhood and society* (2nd ed.). W. W. Norton. https://psycnet.apa.org/record/1965-10989-000

Freedy, A., DeVisser, E., Weltman, G., & Coeyman, N. (2007, June). *Measurement of trust in human-robot collaboration*. Proceedings of the 2007 International Symposium on Collaborative Technologies and Systems, CTS, pp. 106–114. https://doi.org/10.1109/CTS.2007.4621745

Freitag, M., & Bauer, P. C. (2016). Personality traits and the propensity to trust friends and strangers. *Social Science Journal*, *53*(4), 467–476. https://doi.org/10.1016/j.soscij.2015.12.002

Gopinath, B., Radhakrishnan, K., Sankara Sarma, P., Jayachandran, D., & Alexander, A. (2000). A questionnaire survey about doctor–patient communication, compliance and locus of control among South Indian people with epilepsy. *Epilepsy Research*, *39*(1), 73–82. https://doi.org/10.1016/S0920-1211(99)00112-6

Graafland, J., & Lous, B. (2019). Income inequality, life satisfaction inequality and trust: A cross country panel analysis. *Journal of Happiness Studies*, *20*(6), 1717–1737. https://doi.org/10.1007/s10902-018-0021-0

Gretton, C. (2018). Trust and transparency in machine learning-based clinical decision support. In *Human and machine learning* (pp. 279–292). https://doi.org/10.1007/978-3-319-90403-0_14

Haselhuhn, M. P., Kennedy, J. A., Kray, L. J., Van Zant, A. B., & Schweitzer, M. E. (2015). Gender differences in trust dynamics: Women trust more than men following a trust violation. *Journal of Experimental Social Psychology*, *56*, 104–109. https://doi.org/10.1016/j.jesp.2014.09.007

Hazan, C., & Shaver, P. R. (1994). Attachment as an organizational framework for research on close relationships. *Psychological Inquiry*, *5*(1), 1–22. https://doi.org/10.1207/s15327965pli0501_1

Hiraishi, K., Yamagata, S., Shikishima, C., & Ando, J. (2008). Maintenance of genetic variation in personality through control of mental mechanisms: A test of trust, extraversion, and agreeableness. *Evolution and Human Behavior*, *29*(2), 79–85. https://doi.org/10.1016/j.evolhumbehav.2007.07.004

Hoff, K. A., & Bashir, M. (2015). Trust in automation: Integrating empirical evidence on factors that influence trust. *Human Factors*, *57*(3), 407–434. https://doi.org/10.1177/0018720814547570

Kaur, K., & Rampersad, G. (2018, November). Trust in driverless cars: Investigating key factors influencing the adoption of driverless cars. *Journal of Engineering and Technology Management – JET-M*, *48*(2017), 87–96. https://doi.org/10.1016/j.jengtecman.2018.04.006

Lockey, S., Gillespie, N., Holm, D., & Someh, I. A. (2021). *A review of trust in artificial intelligence: Challenges, vulnerabilities and future directions*. Proceedings of the Annual Hawaii International Conference on System Sciences, 2020-Janua, pp. 5463–5472. https://doi.org/10.24251/hicss.2021.664

Logg, J. M., Minson, J. A., & Moore, D. A. (2019, December). Algorithm appreciation: People prefer algorithmic to human judgment. *Organizational Behavior and Human Decision Processes*, *151*(2018), 90–103. https://doi.org/10.1016/j.obhdp.2018.12.005

Longoni, C., Bonezzi, A., & Morewedge, C. K. (2019). Resistance to medical artificial intelligence. *Journal of Consumer Research*, *46*(4), 629–650. https://doi.org/10.1093/jcr/ucz013

Lount, R. B., & Pettit, N. C. (2012). The social context of trust: The role of status. *Organizational Behavior and Human Decision Processes*, *117*(1), 15–23. https://doi.org/10.1016/j.obhdp.2011.07.005

Maddux, W. W., & Brewer, M. B. (2005). Gender differences in the relational and collective bases for trust. *Group Processes and Intergroup Relations*, *8*(2 SPEC. ISS.), 159–171. https://doi.org/10.1177/1368430205051065

Moran, S., Pantidi, N., Bachour, K., Fischer, J. E., Flintham, M., Rodden, T., Evans, S., & Johnson, S. (2013, March). Team reactions to voiced agent instructions in a pervasive game. International Conference on Intelligent User Interfaces, Proceedings IUI, pp. 371–382. https://doi.org/10.1145/2449396.2449445

Oskarsson, S., Dawes, C., Johannesson, M., & Magnusson, P. K. E. (2012). The genetic origins of the relationship between psychological traits and social trust. *Twin Research and Human Genetics*, *15*(1), 21–33. https://doi.org/10.1375/twin.15.1.21

Rotenberg, K. J., Fox, C., Green, S., Ruderman, L., Slater, K., Stevens, K., & Carlo, G. (2005). Construction and validation of a children's interpersonal trust belief scale. *British Journal of Developmental Psychology*, *23*(2), 271–293. https://doi.org/10.1348/026151005X26192

Rousseau, D. M., Sitkin, S. B., Burt, R. S., Camerer, C., Rousseau, D. M., & Burt, R. S. (1998). Not so different after all: A cross- discipline view of trust. *The Academy of Management Review*, *23*(3), 393–404.

Sanders, T., Oleson, K. E., Billings, D. R., Chen, J. Y. C., & Hancock, P. A. (2011). A model of human-robot trust. *Proceedings of the Human Factors and Ergonomics Society*, 1432–1436. http://dx.doi.org/10.1177/1071181311551298

Stamos, A., Altsitsiadis, E., & Dewitte, S. (2019, June). Investigating the effect childhood socioeconomic background on interpersonal trust: Lower childhood socioeconomic status predicts lower levels of trust. *Personality and Individual Differences*, *145*(2018), 19–25. https://doi.org/10.1016/j.paid.2019.03.011

Uslaner, E. M. (2002, October). The moral foundations of trust. *SSRN Electronic Journal*. https://doi.org/10.2139/ssrn.824504

Waytz, A., Heafner, J., & Epley, N. (2014). The mind in the machine: Anthropomorphism increases trust in an autonomous vehicle. *Journal of Experimental Social Psychology*, *52*, 113–117. https://doi.org/10.1016/J.JESP.2014.01.005

5 Neural underpinnings of trust

Magda Gawłowska

5.1 Trust in neuroeconomic research

Before examining the results of studies upon trust, it is necessary to outline several general assumptions to improve our understanding of the type of research conducted in the field of neuroeconomics. Firstly, the aim of the conducted research is to link trust behavior with underlying brain activity. Secondly, it is crucial to properly define the concept of trust behavior and define its key components. Thirdly, it is necessary to design the experimental setting that allows to effectively elicit trust behaviors, observe its components, and finally tie them with their neural underpinnings.

Krueger and Meyer-Lindenberg (2019) proposed a very compelling model of the components of trust behavior called the Neuropsychoeconomic Model of Trust (NMT). According to the NMT (Figure 5.1), trust behavior arises from the interaction of motivational, affective, and cognitive systems, each with its own neural representation, reflected in the activity of specific brain networks (Figure 5.2).

Motivational system is engaged in anticipating the outcome of interaction between the trustor and trustee, that is, whether the trusting behavior will be rewarded. Through repeated interaction with trustees, the trustor learns to predict how likely it is that trust will elicit reciprocity. On the neural level, this prediction is encoded by the reward prediction error, which reflects the difference between the expected and obtained reward. The reward prediction error serves as a learning signal to update the trustor's expectations for upcoming interactions (Schultz, 2017). The neural basis for the motivational system lays in the activity of structures that together form a reward network. Further, the affective system encodes aversion associated with the possibility of trust being violated. The greater the perceived risk, the less likely trustor will engage in trust behavior. On the neural level, affective system is represented by the activity of structures forming the salience network, including the amygdala, structure engaged in fear processing and salience attribution (Cunningham & Brosch, 2012), the anterior insula, engaged in encoding subjective feelings (Namkung

DOI: 10.4324/9781003311409-6

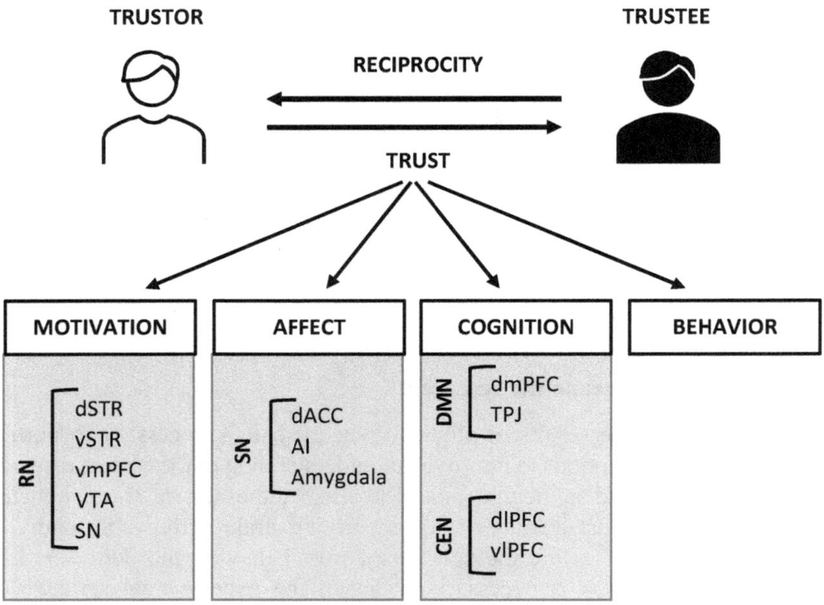

Figure 5.1 Components of trust with its neural underpinnings. RN – reward network; SN – salience network; DMN – default-mode network; CEN – central-executive network; AI – anterior insula; dACC – dorsal anterior cingulate cortex; dlPFC – dorsolateral prefrontal cortex; dmPFC – dorsomedial prefrontal cortex; dSTR – dorsal striatum; SN – substantia nigra; TPJ – temporoparietal junction; vlPFC – ventrolateral prefrontal cortex; vmPFC – ventromedial prefrontal cortex; vSTR – ventral striatum; VTA – ventral tegmentum area.

Source: Own elaboration based on Krueger and Meyer-Lindenberg, 2019.

et al., 2017), and the dorsal anterior cingulate cortex, associated with conflict monitoring and evaluation of behavior (Shenhav et al., 2016). Finally, the cognitive system is rooted in the activity of the central-executive network and the default-mode network. Structures forming the central-executive network are engaged in cognitive control and flexible adaptation of behavior to changing situational demands (Miller, 2001), while the default-mode network is associated with the mentalization process, that is, inferring about other people's intentions and emotions (Li et al., 2014). Trust behaviors result from evaluating available data, filtered through the lens of the aforementioned systems.

When exploring neural correlates of trust, researchers largely focus on designing paradigms that mimic the situations of cooperation based on trust. One of the most frequently implemented experimental tasks is the Trust Game, which implements both, trusting and reciprocal behaviors. In another popular experimental paradigm, participants are presented with faces and based on the

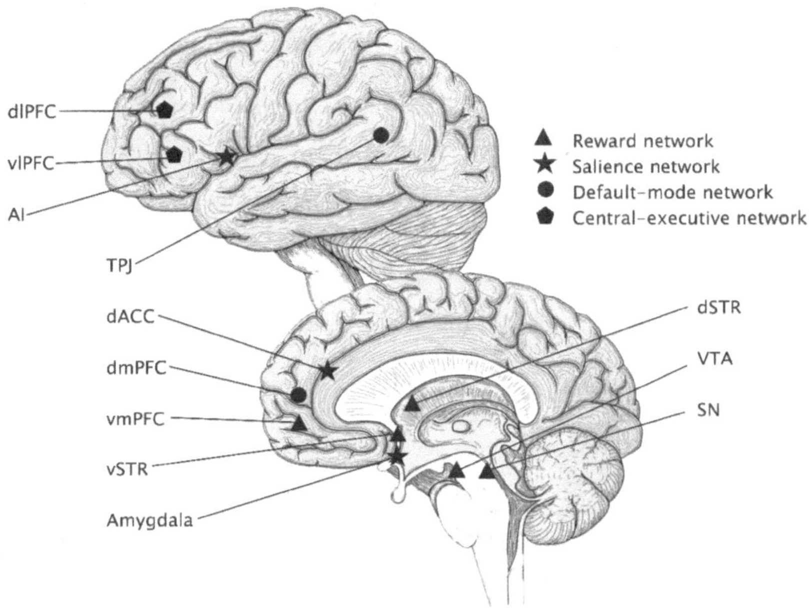

Figure 5.2 Neural networks engaged in trust behavior. AI – anterior insula; dACC – dorsal anterior cingulate cortex; dlPFC – dorsolateral prefrontal cortex; dmPFC – dorsomedial prefrontal cortex; dSTR – dorsal striatum; SN – substantia nigra; TPJ – temporoparietal junction; vlPFC – ventrolateral prefrontal cortex; vmPFC – ventromedial prefrontal cortex; vSTR – ventral striatum; VTA – ventral tegmentum area.

Source: Own elaboration based on Krueger and Meyer-Lindenberg, 2019.

provided information (or lack of it) they are expected to assess the trustworthiness of prospective trustee. Of course the list of experimental paradigms used in research upon trust is much longer; however, the paradigms mentioned earlier have gained the greatest popularity.

5.2 Neural underpinnings of interpersonal trust

Looking for the cause of individual differences in tendency to trust, scientists largely focused on functional data. However, there are some studies pointing at the anatomical differences brain structure between people more and less likely to exhibit trust behaviors. For example, in the study by Haas et al. (2015) participants underwent MRI anatomical scan. Additionally, they were asked to rate on a 7-point scale the trustworthiness of faces presented on photos and to complete NEO PI-3 personality inventory to assess their tendency to trust, reflected in the trust facets of agreeableness subscale scores. Analysis of the obtained data revealed that participants with greater tendency to trust were characterized by an increase in the gray matter volume in the vmPFC and insula. On the contrary, greater gray matter volume in the right amygdala was correlated with both greater and smaller tendency to trust.

Moving to the functional data, Castle et al. (2012) looked at the age-related differences in the tendency to trust. Older and younger adults were asked to rate faces that differed in the context of cues predicting trustworthiness. There was no between-group difference in rating faces with a high number of trust cues. On the contrary, older adults perceived untrustworthy faces as more trustworthy compared to younger adults. On the neural level, there have been differences in the activation of anterior insula. Younger adults showed greater activation in this region when presented with untrustworthy, compared to trustworthy faces. Older adults presented muted response of the anterior insula when presented with faces high in untrustworthiness cues. Belfi et al. (2015) compared neurotypical adults and individuals with damage to the insula. As expected, neurotypical adults exhibited an increase in trust in rection to partners increase and vice versa. In the case of the individuals with insula damage, when acting as a trustor they were expressing trust irrespective of the partner's behavior. However, when in the role of trustee, they consistently violated partner's trust. In yet another study, Jiménez et al. (2022) analyzed the influence of social closeness on the perception of trustworthiness. They implemented a modified version of the Trust Game where partner was a computer, a stranger, or a real friend. fMRI data showed that participants exhibited increased functional coupling between the anterior insula and intraparietal sulcus during anticipation of reciprocal behavior in real friends compared to strangers. Similar tendency in functional coupling was observed between the right parietal cortex and both, the fusiform gyrus, and the inferior temporal gyrus. Together, these three studies point to the role of the insula in expressing adequate interpersonal trust.

Another compelling data comes from the study of Fett et al. (2014). The aim of the study was to analyze the trust behaviors in a group of participants ranging in age from adolescence to mid-adulthood. The behavioral results show a positive correlation between the age and both, initial propensity to trust and an increase in trust in cooperation with fair partner. On the neural level, age was correlated with increased activity in the TPJ, posterior cingulate and precuneus. Moreover, there was an age-related increase in ACC activity after interaction with an untrustworthy partner. The study by Fett et al. (2014) is especially interesting in the light of data from Castle et al. (2012) mentioned in the previous paragraph. Together, these studies suggest that there is an age-related, U-shaped dynamic of trust behavior after an interaction with an untrustworthy partner. From adolescence to mid-adulthood, there is a decrease in the tendency to trust after partner's trust violation. However, this tendency shifts, so that older adults are once again more likely to trust their untrustworthy partner.

In their fMRI study, Engelmann et al. (2019) implemented experimental manipulation to induce a negative effect. Subjects were informed that they may receive an electric shock while performing task. Under these circumstances participants were less trusting on the behavioral level, which was accompanied by reduced activity in TPJ and functional connectivity between TPJ and amygdala. Moreover, functional connectivity between posterior superior temporal sulcus and TPJ was associated with trust in no-threat conditions but introducing threat disorganized this association.

Baumgartner et al. (2009) conducted an fMRI study in which they look for the neural markers of breaking given promise in social interaction. Participants were engaged in the modified version of the Trust Game, divided into three stages. The first stage of the task was intended for making a promise to the partner whether the participant is willing to resend money given to him or not. In the second stage, participants were supposed to predict whether the promise would influence partners decision. In the final stage, participants were free to keep the promise or break it. Breaking the promise was associated with increased activation in the dlPFC, ACC, and amygdala, suggesting an emotional reaction to violating given declaration, the trust, due to the suppression of the honest response. What is more, the intended breach of promise was to be predicted based on the activity of anterior insula, ACC, and inferior frontal gyrus, before the promise was actually broken.

Interesting data comes from resting-state studies. The goal of the resting-state paradigm is to uncover the spontaneous fluctuations in neural activity that reflect the functional architecture of the brain (Lee et al., 2013). In this experimental setting, participants are not required to perform any task but are simply asked to stay alert with their eyes open.

Hahn et al. (2014) used EEG to record brain activity before participants engaged in the Trust Game. Later, they compared behavioral results from the game, specifically the Investor's willingness to transfer money to their partner at different stages of the game, with pre-recorded brain activity. They found that resting-stated functional connectivity was a good predictor of propensity to trust at the initial stage of the game, when the partner's reciprocal behavior was unknown to Investor. However, this effect was absent in the later stages of the game. In another study, Bellucci et al. (2019) implemented a similar experimental paradigm; however, instead of EEG, they collected resting-state fMRI activity. The level of trust and reciprocity was predicted by the activity in the default-mode network, known to be engaged in mentalizing. Additionally, reciprocity was predicted by the activity in salience network and central-executive network, responsible for cognitive control. Finally, Lu et al. (2019) found that a tendency to trust was reflected in the resting-state functional connectivity between the amygdala, lateral PFC, TPJ and temporal pole, thus the connections between salience network, default-mode network, and central-executive network.

A review of research on interpersonal trust would not be complete without mentioning the role of oxytocin in trust behaviors. Oxytocin is a neuropeptide hormone produced by the hypothalamus and released to brain as well as peripheries. In the last decades, oxytocin has received increased attention in research due to its role in not only maternal but also social behaviors (Nave et al., 2015). Multiple studies have investigated the influence of oxytocin on the propensity to trust or assessing trustworthiness in others. Baumgartner et al. (2008) conducted an fMRI study in which subjects were administered intranasal oxytocin or placebo. Participants in the placebo group decreased the level of trust in the Trust Game after their partner violated their trust, whereas participants in the oxytocin group were insensitive to this information. Additionally, the oxytocin group demonstrated reduced activity in regions associated with encoding fear and adaptation to feedback information, that is, amygdala and midbrain regions, and dorsal striatum, respectively. In another fMRI study, Frazier et al. (2021) looked at the combined effect of age and oxytocin on trust behaviors. Groups of younger and older adults were administered oxytocin or placebo via intranasal spray before taking part in the Trust Game. As it was shown in previous studies (e.g., Castle et al., 2012), younger participants were less likely to trust their partners after their trust was violated, whereas the behavior of older participants was not affected. There was no observable effect of oxytocin on a behavioral level, but older adults administered with oxytocin exhibited decreased activity in the superior temporal gyrus after the trust violation. This result is supported by previous findings, suggesting that oxytocin-related decrease in the activity of the superior temporal gyrus is associated with negative social feedback (Gozzi et al., 2017).

Together, there is an ever-growing number of studies on the neural correlates of trust in social interactions. In the meantime, another branch of research on the neural underpinnings of trust has started to emerge, namely studies exploring trust between humans and artificial intelligence.

5.3 Neural correlates of trust toward artificial intelligence

There is an extensive number of behavioral studies exploring trust behaviors toward automated agents and factors influencing human tendency to trust autonomous systems. The same cannot be said about the exploration of the neural underpinnings of trust toward robots. Available data is still extremely limited, but there are some studies that allow us to glimpse into this interaction.

In an fMRI study by Goodyear et al. (2017), participants took part in the luggage screening task paradigm. They were asked to determine whether luggage contains knife or not. Every participant received advice regarding the presence of knife (60% accuracy) either from another human (human-adviser group) or from the robot (robot-adviser group). The behavioral data showed that there was a greater decrease in utilizing the information from robot adviser. On the neural level, there was a stronger functional connectivity between the lingual gyrus and ACC, anterior precuneus, and cuneus for human advice, compared to robot advice. Moreover, all the areas except the ACC had higher activation for the human-advisor, compared to robot-advisor group. It is likely that participants receiving advice from humans were less focused on monitoring for errors than participants receiving advice from robot.

de Visser et al. (2018) conducted an experiment where participants observed algorithms of varying reliability and credibility performing a flanker task while their brain activity was recorded through EEG. The data analysis focused on the error-related event-related potentials, specifically the observational ERN and observational Pe. The ERN reflects an automatic error detection signal, while the Pe is believed to indicate error awareness, and both components are generated in dorsal anterior cingulate cortex (Debener et al., 2005). Results obtained through the analysis showed that participants were significantly more aware of errors made by more reliable and credible algorithms, what was reflected in the increased amplitude of the observational Pe. As participants perceived these algorithms as more trustworthy, errors committed by them were perceived as more evident.

In the fNIRS study, Hopko and Mehta (2022) explored the neural underpinning of trust in the human–robot collaboration task. Participants were asked to finish polishing the surface by using the automated arm. The algorithm operating the arm differed with regard to the reliability and assistance level to modulate the level of trust toward robot. The analysis of neural data indicated that when both, the reliability of robots and trust perception decreased, there was a decrease in the number and strength of functional connections and an increase in activation in the medial dlPFC region. This trend was even more pronounced when the robots provided more assistance. After adjusting for the effects of workload on trust and neural activity, it was also noted that decreased reliability in robots led to an increase in activation in the right dorsolateral prefrontal cortex, a region linked to paying attention to negative emotions.

Taken together, the data on neural correlates of trust in human-robot/algorithm/autonomous system interactions is scarce. However, the studies cited earlier show some common patterns of results, such as activation in the ACC and EEG components generated in the ACC. Undoubtedly, given the rapid advancement of artificial autonomous systems, it is crucial to further investigate human-robot interaction in order to better understand how to make it safe and credible for humans.

References

Baumgartner, T., Fischbacher, U., Feierabend, A., Lutz, K., & Fehr, E. (2009). The neural circuitry of a broken promise. *Neuron*, *64*(5), 756–770. https://doi.org/10.1016/j.neuron.2009.11.017

Baumgartner, T., Heinrichs, M., Vonlanthen, A., Fischbacher, U., & Fehr, E. (2008). Oxytocin shapes the neural circuitry of trust and trust adaptation in humans. *Neuron*, *58*(4), 639–650. https://doi.org/10.1016/j.neuron.2008.04.009

Belfi, A. M., Koscik, T. R., & Tranel, D. (2015). Damage to the insula is associated with abnormal interpersonal trust. *Neuropsychologia*, *71*(3), 165–172. https://doi.org/10.1016/j.neuropsychologia.2015.04.003

Bellucci, G., Hahn, T., Deshpande, G., & Krueger, F. (2019). Functional connectivity of specific resting-state networks predicts trust and reciprocity in the trust game. *Cognitive, Affective and Behavioral Neuroscience*, *19*(1), 165–176. https://doi.org/10.3758/s13415-018-00654-3

Castle, E., Eisenberger, N. I., Seeman, T. E., Moons, W. G., Boggero, I. A., Grinblatt, M. S., & Taylor, S. E. (2012). Neural and behavioral bases of age differences in perceptions of trust. *Proceedings of the National Academy of Sciences of the United States of America*, *109*(51), 20848–20852. https://doi.org/10.1073/pnas.1218518109

Cunningham, W. A., & Brosch, T. (2012). Motivational salience: Amygdala tuning from traits, needs, values, and goals. *Current Directions in Psychological Science*, *21*(1), 54–59. https://doi.org/10.1177/0963721411430832

de Visser, E. J., Beatty, P. J., Estepp, J. R., Kohn, S., Abubshait, A., Fedota, J. R., & McDonald, C. G. (2018, August). Learning from the slips of others: Neural correlates of trust in automated agents. *Frontiers in Human Neuroscience*, *12*, 1–15. https://doi.org/10.3389/fnhum.2018.00309

Debener, S., Ullsperger, M., Siegel, M., Fiehler, K., Cramon, V., Yves, D., & Engel, A. K. (2005). Trial-by-trial coupling of concurrent electroencephalogram and functional magnetic resonance imaging identifies the dynamics of performance monitoring. *Journal of Neuroscience*, *25*(50), 11730–11737. http://dx.doi.org/10.1523/JNEUROSCI.3286-05.2005

Engelmann, J. B., Meyer, F., Ruff, C. C., & Fehr, E. (2019). The neural circuitry of affect-induced distortions of trust. *Science Advances*, *5*(3). https://doi.org/10.1126/sciadv.aau3413

Fett, A. K. J., Gromann, P. M., Giampietro, V., Shergill, S. S., & Krabbendam, L. (2014). Default distrust? An fmri investigation of the neural development of trust and cooperation. *Social Cognitive and Affective Neuroscience*, *9*(4), 395–402. https://doi.org/10.1093/scan/nss144

Frazier, I., Lin, T., Liu, P., Skarsten, S., Feifel, D., & Ebner, N. C. (2021). Age and intranasal oxytocin effects on trust-related decisions after breach of trust: Behavioral and brain evidence. *Psychology and Aging*, *36*(1), 10–21. https://doi.org/10.1037/pag0000545

Goodyear, K., Parasuraman, R., Chernyak, S., de Visser, E., Madhavan, P., Deshpande, G., & Krueger, F. (2017). An fMRI and effective connectivity study investigating miss errors during advice utilization from human and machine agents. *Social Neuroscience*, *12*(5), 570–581. https://doi.org/10.1080/17470919.2016.1205131

Gozzi, M., Dashow, E. M., Thurm, A., Swedo, S. E., & Zink, C. F. (2017). Effects of oxytocin and vasopressin on preferential brain responses to negative social feedback. *Neuropsychopharmacology*, *42*(7), 1409–1419. https://doi.org/10.1038/npp.2016.248

Haas, B. W., Ishak, A., Anderson, I. W., & Filkowski, M. M. (2015). The tendency to trust is reflected in human brain structure. *NeuroImage*, *107*, 175–181. https://doi.org/10.1016/j.neuroimage.2014.11.060

Hahn, T., Notebaert, K., Anderl, C., Teckentrup, V., Kabecker, A., & Windmann, S. (2014). How to trust a perfect stranger: Predicting initial trust behavior from resting-state brain-electrical connectivity. *Social Cognitive and Affective Neuroscience*, *10*(6), 809–813. https://doi.org/10.1093/scan/nsu122

Hopko, S. K., & Mehta, R. K. (2022). Trust in shared-space collaborative robots: Shedding light on the human brain. *Human Factors: The Journal of the Human Factors and Ergonomics Society*. https://doi.org/10.1177/00187208221109039

Jiménez, S., Mercadillo, R. E., Angeles-Valdez, D., Sánchez-Sosa, J. J., Muñoz-Delgado, J., & Garza-Villarreal, E. A. (2022). Social closeness modulates brain dynamics during trust anticipation. *Scientific Reports*, *12*(1), 1–12. https://doi.org/10.1038/s41598-022-20827-y

Krueger, F., & Meyer-Lindenberg, A. (2019). Toward a model of interpersonal trust drawn from neuroscience, psychology, and economics. *Trends in Neurosciences*, *42*(2), 92–101. https://doi.org/10.1016/j.tins.2018.10.004

Lee, M. H., Smyser, C. D., & Shimony, J. S. (2013). Resting-state fMRI: A review of methods and clinical applications. *American Journal of Neuroradiology*, *34*(10), 1866–1872. https://doi.org/10.3174/ajnr.A3263

Li, W., Mai, X., & Liu, C. (2014, February 1). The default mode network and social understanding of others: What do brain connectivity studies tell us. *Frontiers in Human Neuroscience*, *8*, 1–15. https://doi.org/10.3389/fnhum.2014.00074

Lu, X., Li, T., Xia, Z., Zhu, R., Wang, L., Luo, Y. J., Feng, C., & Krueger, F. (2019). Connectome-based model predicts individual differences in propensity to trust. *Human Brain Mapping*, *40*(6), 1942–1954. https://doi.org/10.1002/hbm.24503

Miller, E. K. (2001). The prefrontal cortex and cognitive control. *Nature Reviews Neuroscience*, *1*(1), 59–65. papers3://publication/uuid/1194A5EB-F854-4A4F-BC2F-E63CF052E51A

Namkung, H., Kim, S. H., & Sawa, A. (2017). The insula: An underestimated brain area in clinical neuroscience, psychiatry, and neurology. *Trends in Neurosciences*, *40*(4), 200–207. https://doi.org/10.1016/j.tins.2017.02.002

Nave, G., Camerer, C., & McCullough, M. (2015). Does oxytocin increase trust in humans? A critical review of research. *Perspectives on Psychological Science*, *10*(6), 772–789. https://doi.org/10.1177/1745691615600138

Schultz, W. (2017). Reward prediction error. *Current Biology*, *27*(10), R369–R371. https://doi.org/10.1016/j.cub.2017.02.064

Shenhav, A., Cohen, J. D., & Botvinick, M. M. (2016). Dorsal anterior cingulate cortex and the value of control. *Nature Neuroscience*, *19*(10), 1286–1291. https://doi.org/10.1038/nn.4384

Zak, P. J. (2004). Neuroeconomics. *Philosophical Transactions of the Royal Society B: Biological Sciences*, *359*(1451), 1737–1748. https://doi.org/10.1098/rstb.2004.1544

6 Trust

The technological aspect

Bartlomiej Sniezynski

6.1 Technological challenge of the human-robot relationship

There are many technological problems which need to be solved to achieve a harmonious human-robot relationship. A good review of the most important challenges can be found in Riek (2010). Classical robotics issues (like appropriate mechanical design, efficient power supply, and environment recognition) are completed with the following problems related to social environment:

1. Dynamic Spaces – instead of standard environment typical for industrial robots social robot has to operate in areas with humans present, which makes the environment much more complex.
2. Social Learning – social robot should be able to adapt to humans, which means lifelong learning because Humans change their environment and behaviors.
3. Sustainability – relation between the robot and its user should be long-lasting and still interesting. As a result, some creativity in robot behavior, taking into account user's emotions and context will be helpful.
4. Affect and Social Signal Awareness – affect and social signals (expressed by facial expressions, gaze, posture and gestures, proxemics and prosody) should be recognized and generated by the social robot. Visual communication can be considered as a component of natural language usage.
5. Social Norms – a social robot should know social norms and act accordingly. It is difficult because norms are context dependent and require a lot of knowledge.
6. Societal Issues – problems such as privacy, security and acceptability. Companies producing robots need to have their products accepted, which is not only technological problem but also sociological.

In this chapter problems related to reasoning and learning in the context of trust are discussed from the AI perspective. In the literature there are many architectures that may be used to design social robot software (Moulin-Frier et al., 2017; Lazzeri et al., 2018; Bono et al., 2020; Jarosz et al., 2021; Kopp & Hassan,

DOI: 10.4324/9781003311409-7

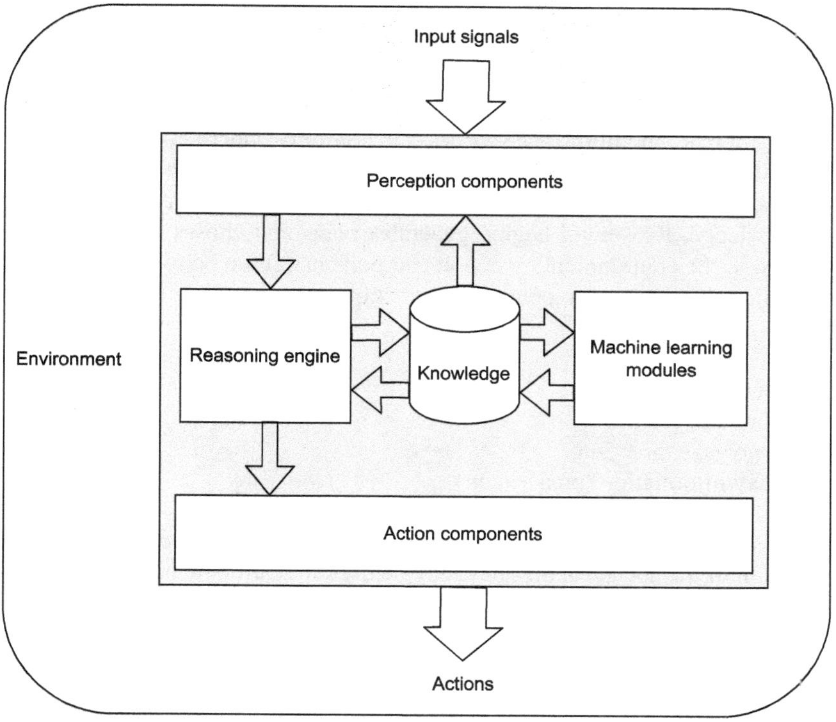

Figure 6.1 Social robot software architecture.

2022). To focus the discussion, let us consider a simplified software architecture for a social robot presented in Figure 6.1 that may be applied to do build a software for the social robot. It is very general but can be used to present most important technological challenges.

On the top there are perception components responsible for processing input signals from the environment. Types of the inputs depend on the type of the robot. For a humanoid robot, we can distinguish components like:

- Object recognition,
- Localization,
- Posture, gestures, and proxemics detection,
- Face recognition,
- Emotions classification,
- Speech, intonation, and prosody recognition,
- Natural language understanding,
- Gaze direction detection.

Processing input signals is a very complex task an may involve complicated computational methods like deep neural networks, for example, for image or signal processing and object or facial expression recognition (Ruiz-del-Solar et al., 2018) or data fusion, for example, for localization based on various sensors, like camera, LiDAR, and ultrasonic sensors data (Barreto-Cubero et al., 2021).

Results of processing are sent to the Reasoning engine, which processes it and stores its representation in a form of facts in the Knowledge base. Based on the knowledge, Reasoning engine generates plans and choses actions that are executed in the environment by action components (at the bottom). In case of a humanoid robot, they are responsible for actions like:

- Movement,
- Speech generation,
- Posture and gestures,
- Change gaze direction,
- Display information (on a screen).

The last component is a set of Machine learning modules that are responsible for adaptation of the social robot. They may be used to learn new or improve existing capabilities. For example, the robot can learn:

- navigate in a new areas,
- recognize new people,
- new words or games,
- operate new devices,
- habits, preferences, and interests of the owner,
- correlate behavior of the owner with her or his emotions.

Although some of these problems are AI-Complete or NP-Complete, recent advantages in AI, especially with use of transformer architecture of neural networks (e.g., good performance of ChatGPT launched by OpenAI) allow to be optimistic that many of them will be solved well enough to build an efficient social robots.

For the social robot it is important to do provide all these functionalities in a way that builds a trustful relationship between the user and the robot. To achieve it, many factors must be taken into account: the robot should have anthropomorphic form (Sweeney, 2022), all the components of the robot should work well enough and provide high accuracy and performance (Robinette et al., 2017), user should be able to understand how the Inference engine works and what is stored in the Knowledge base, both built-in and learned knowledge, the robot should be able to communicate well and explain its actions (Setchi et al., 2020).

Another important problem is related to the processing power of the robot's computer. Because wireless, broadband communication is becoming more and more available, some computations can be delegated to a computational cloud (Saha & Dasgupta, 2018). Such solution allows to run much more complex algorithms but has also disadvantages. Sharing the data by the robot may result in "out of control" data collection and privacy problems (Pagallo, 2013). Connection to the Internet has also consequences related to cybersecurity (Yaacoub et al., 2021). Especially remote control of a robots by some hacker may result in financial losses, privacy problems, and may be even dangerous to the health or life of people around. Last but not least, dependance on the cloud resources may lead to problems with autonomy of the robot. If connection is lost, the robot will not be able to run advanced computation and it usability will be limited, which may result in reduction of the trust of its user. Therefore, robot should be still useful, even without connection to the Internet.

6.2 Reasoning and learning

Crucial modules of a social robot are reasoning engine, knowledge base, and machine learning modules, which are responsible for processing facts and knowledge, storing it in the repository, learning new and updating the existing knowledge. There are many methods that can be used for these purposes. They may be divided into two main classes: symbolic and non-symbolic AI.

6.2.1 Symbolic approach

The symbolic approach assumes that all the knowledge and processing are based on symbolic knowledge representation. It is often based on formal first order logic, but other formalisms can be also used, for example, fuzzy logic, reasoning under time constraints, planning algorithms or ontologies. To present the idea of symbolic representation, logic-based approach is described in the following.

If formal logic is used in Knowledge base and Reasoning engine, it allows to describe facts using logic formulas. Predicates can be also used to represent history of interactions, knowledge in a form of rules (implications) allowing to infer new facts about the environment, to make plans and choose actions. A convenient way to explain how logic may be used for reasoning is to consider a simplified version of such formulas in first order logic in a scene, in which robot observes a desk with boxes (Figure 6.2 a).

The robot can describe a simplified scene (Figure 6.2 b) using formulas representing observed objects and their coordinates with observed (object, x, y) predicate, which means that *object* is observed at *x* and *y* coordinates:

observed(t, 1, 1).
observed(a, 1, 3).
observed(b, 1, 2).

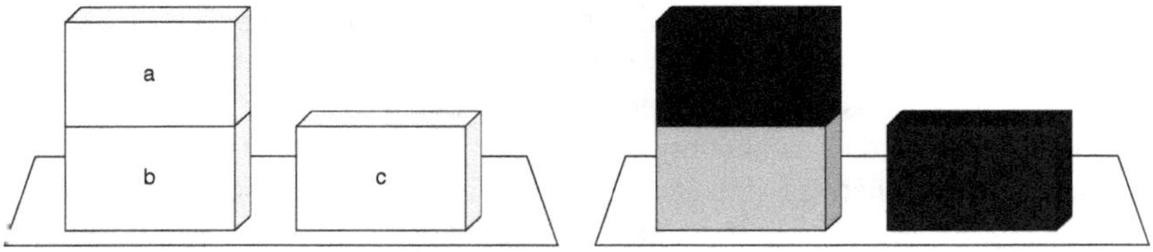

Figure 6.2 Environment observed by the robot – boxes on the table (a) and its simplified representation (b), low-resolution transformation of the image (c)

observed(t, 1, 1).
observed(c, 2, 2).

In these examples PROLOG logic programming language notation is used. Argument names starting with small letter represent constant symbols representing entities. Discovered types of objects can be described using type(object, category) formulas meaning that *objects* belongs to the *category*:

type(t, table).
type(a, box).
type(b, box).
type(c, box).

To describe properties of objects, for example, their color, formula color(object, name) may be applied. It means that *object* has a color *name*:

color(t, white).
color(a, grey).
color(b, dark).
color(c, black).

Relationships between boxes and the table may be represented with use of on(top, bottom) formulas meaning that *top* object is lying on *bottom*:

on(a, b).
on(b, t).
on(c, t).

Such a description may be created automatically from image registered by the robot's camera. The image should be processed by an object recognition software. Currently, for this purpose deep neural networks are usually applied (Francies et al., 2022). Another deep neural network can be used to extract spatial relationships between objects (Lee et al., 2022). How neural networks work is explained in the next section.

Such a description is a set of facts that should be next processed by a reasoning engine. Symbolic representation allows to store rules in the knowledge base and use them for inferencing new facts or invoking actions (Merschformann et al., 2019; Lazzeri et al., 2018). In formal logic rule is represented by implication *premise* → *conclusion* which can be also written as:

IF premise THAN conclusion

Rules can be used to represent and apply properties of relations. For example, the following rule can be used to represent transitivity of the *on* relation:

IF on(X, Y) AND on(Y, Z) THEN on(X, Z).

Capital letters represent variables that match any constant symbol. If it is applied to *X=a*, *Y=b* and *Z=t*, formula on(*a*, *t*) can be inferred from the formulas presented above.

Rule can be also used to infer new facts, using new relation, e.g. above:

IF on(X, Y) THEN above(X, Y).

If it is applied to *a* and *t* it is possible to deduce above(a, t).

Rules can be also used to make plans and choose action for execution. For such a purpose, there should be a predicate representing an action in a conclusion of a rule, for example:

IF goal(take(X)) AND type(X, box) AND NOT on(Y, X) THEN action(grab, X).

It means that if a goal of the robot is to take some box (*X*) and nothing is placed on this box, than robot should execute action grab to take the box.

Having sets of facts and rules, Reasoning engine can perform inference using forward chaining like in rule-based programming language CLIPS (www.clipsrules.net/), which was successfully applied in a control systems for a cognitive architecture for social robots (Lazzeri et al., 2018) or backward chaining, like in PROLOG, that was applied in Matyasik et al. (2007) to build embedded real-time system controlling a mobile robot. Forward chaining checks in a loop which rules have premises satisfied. For such rules their conclusions are added to the knowledge base. The loop continues until some goal fact is added, for example, representing the action to execute. Backward chaining starts with a goal, for example, formula representing action choice, and checks if the goal is already in the knowledge base or can be inferred using some rule (it can be matched to its conclusion). In the latter case, satisfaction of formulas in the premise of the rule needs to be confirmed. They should be in the knowledge base or they can become new levels of inference goals and the process may continue recursively.

Similar results can be obtained by application of other methods, for example, fuzzy logic, which combines sets with fuzzy boundaries with rules. Fuzzy controllers, based on such rules, can be used to control intelligent robots (Chen et al., 2017). They are simpler than rule-based systems but can be used to control part of the behaviors of the robot, for example, its driving or navigation component (Samsudin et al., 2011; Štefek et al., 2021).

Ontologies are logic-based formalisms, in which concepts of objects, categories, properties, and relations between them are predefined. They are usually used for storing and searching information, reasoning and exchange of information. They may be also applied to take control of an intelligent robot (Sun et al., 2019), where ontology is used to represent spatio-temporal, continuous, and discrete information. Rules defined in the Semantic Web Rule Language are applied to choose the tasks for robot in a given context.

Another method that is gaining more and more attention is based on Behavioral Trees (Colledanchise & Ögren, 2018), which allow to hierarchically arrange nodes representing conditions, actions, or control logic. This structure can be used to execute actions under defined conditions in parallel or in a sequence. Behavior Trees are highly modular and allow to easily add more behaviors.

The main advantage of symbolic representation in the context of trust is that both knowledge stored and reasoning process can be easily understood by humans. It is crucial during designing and programming of the social robot, as it allows for verification of facts and rules. It is also very important during usage of the robot because its behavior can be analyzed by the user. It is possible to explain what robot knows by presenting its knowledge base or describing facts using natural language. It is also possible to explain how a certain conclusion was inferred. Inference engine can track what rules were applied to infer given formula and robot may present the reasoning path to the user. It is also possible to answer "why" question explaining the purpose of action of the robot, especially when backward chaining reasoning is applied. If some action is chosen by the reasoning engine, the answer would be that the direct reason for it is the current goal of the backward reasoning. The next level reason is the previous inference goal. For example, if the robot is grabbing block *a* and user asks why, the answer can be that the current goal is to clear top of the block *b*. If user would like to know why it should be clear, the answer could be that the robot needs to grab block *b* and to do this, nothing should be stored on it.

Unfortunately, there is also huge disadvantage of symbolic representation. The rules and knowledge has to be usually hand coded, which is a very hard problem. In some cases it is also possible to learn rules from data using induction algorithms (Inuzuka et al., 2000). Rule induction can even replace reinforcement learning (explained in the following) and learn strategy faster, from smaller amounts of interactions (Sniezynski, 2015). It may provide lifelong learning necessary for a social robot. However, due to complexity of such algorithms, it can work only in low-dimension domains, in which entities are described using dozens of features, or they may be applied for parts of the domain.

6.2.2 Non-symbolic approach

In non-symbolic approach algorithms perform some calculations on numerical representation of the facts and knowledge. Result of these calculations represents the solution. Good examples of such methods are evolutionary algorithms, reinforcement learning, and neural networks.

Evolutionary computations are example of soft-computing methods. They are based on random applications of operators to entities representing whole robots, like in Howard (2019) or their control systems, for example, arms – like in Pena et al. (2023). Operators are usually the following: selection (to choose the best solution), variation (to modify the solution), and succession (to create entities inheriting properties of their ancestors). Review of such methods can be found in Doncieux et al. (2015).

During the past years, more and more attention was given to reinforcement learning applications in robotics. The basic idea is simple. Robot automatically learns its strategy by interaction with the environment, which may be not known, nondeterministic, and changing. Training information is given by rewards reflecting the quality of actions executed by the robot. Therefore, it is learning by trial and error. A robot changes its behavior to establish a strategy providing it as high expected rewards as possible. Idea of reinforcement learning is presented in Figure 6.3.

In the case of a very simple environment, strategy may be represented by a table of triples (*state*, *action*, *expected reward*) triples and in a given *state* the robot may choose an *action* with the highest *expected reward* and the best state in which it will be after the action execution. Q-learning and SARSA are classical examples of reinforcement learning algorithms that can be used in robotics (Saadatmand et al., 2020; Wen et al., 2022). There are also many extensions of these algorithms. In more complex environments, instead of such table, neural networks may be used. To process many input signals, for example, related to image, deep neural network may be applied and modifications to the learning algorithm should be introduced giving algorithms like Deep Reinforcement Learning (Ibarz et al., 2021).

Neural networks work well even in complex domains, in which situation is described with many features. The basic idea of how the artificial neuron works is based on biological neuron concept. In nature, the neuron collects input nerve impulses arriving to its dendrites, integrates them (some are excitatory, others are inhibitory), and if the level of integrated input is higher than a threshold, it generates neural impulse, which is sent through the axon. Artificial neuron has similar architecture and behavior (see Figure 6.4 a). As the input, it receives a signal in the form of a vector of real numbers $X = (x_1, x_2, \ldots, x_n) \in \Re^n$, and at the output, it returns the signal $\hat{y} \in \Re$, which is also a real number. Each element of the input vector x_i is associated with the weight of this element $w_i \in \Re$. Excitation of neuron *e* is calculated on the basis of inputs and weights:

$$e = \sum\nolimits_{i=1}^{n} x_i w_i + w_0. \qquad (6.1)$$

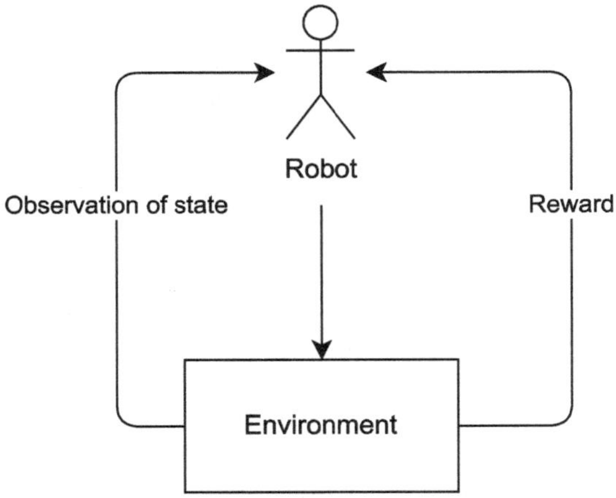

Figure 6.3 Idea of reinforcement learning.

The additional weight $w_0 \in \mathfrak{R}$ allows for the modification of the excitation by a fixed value, independent of the input. The output is calculated from the formula:

$$\hat{y} = f(e), \tag{6.2}$$

where $f : \mathfrak{R} \to \mathfrak{R}$ is the activation function (e.g., tanh), non-linearly transforming the excitation of neuron *e*.

Since a single neuron has little capability, in practice system of many neurons needs to be used. They are arranged in layers that form a network. In the case of a multilayer perceptron (Figure 6.4 b), the output of each neuron of the previous layer is the input of each neuron of the next layer. Using the network, it is possible to compute for a given input $X \in \mathfrak{R}^n$ the output signals $\hat{Y} = (\hat{y}_1, \hat{y}_2, \ldots, \hat{y}_m) \in \mathfrak{R}^m$.

A crucial issue for neural networks is learning, which allows for the determination of connection weights in a way that the output value $\hat{Y}$ for a given input X is correct. For this purpose a training data in the form of pairs of input signals and expected output signals is needed: $D = \{(X, Y) \in \mathfrak{R}^n \times \mathfrak{R}^m\}$. The learning algorithm modifies the connection weights so as to minimize the difference between computed $\hat{Y}$ and the grand true Y. A typical learning method is the Backpropagation of Errors algorithm (Goodfellow et al., 2016).

A good example of neural network capabilities is image analysis. For such application input image from a camera (Figure 4.2 b) is often down-scaled to low resolution (Figure 4.2 c), especially when the movement of objects is taken into account by stacking consequent images and analyzing several of them. Picture is stored as an array of numbers, which represent the brightness or RGB values

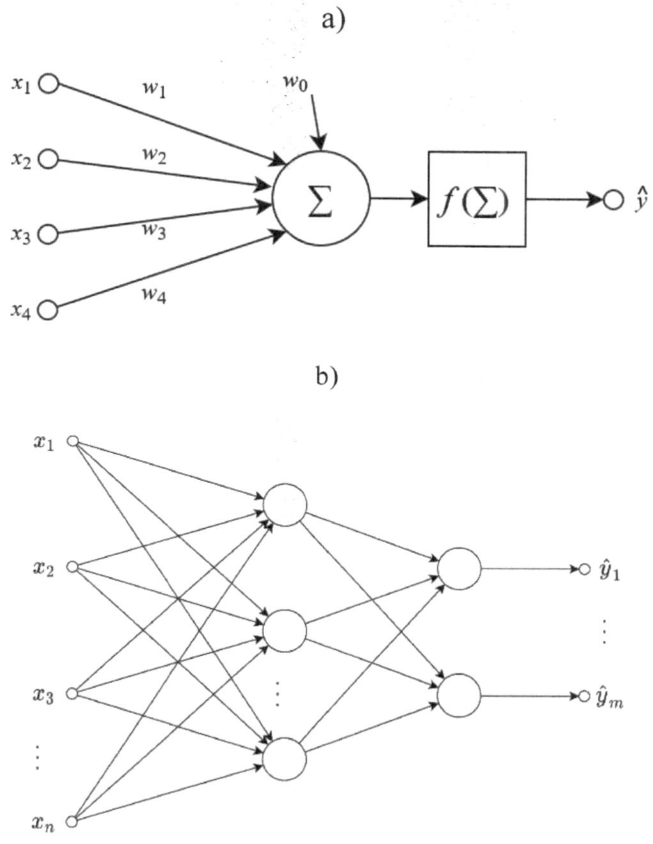

Figure 6.4 Architecture of the artificial neuron (a) and neural network (b).

of every pixel (Figure 4.2 d). To process high number of input signals, many layers of neurons are needed. Hence, deep neural networks are applied. Also, the network architecture may be modified to achieve better results. Therefore, convolutional neural networks (Patil & Rane, 2021) or vision transformers (Chen et al., 2021) are currently used for this purpose.

a) b)

255	255	255	255	255	255
255	255	221	0	0	0
255	221	0	0	0	0
255	221	0	0	0	0
255	221	0	0	0	0

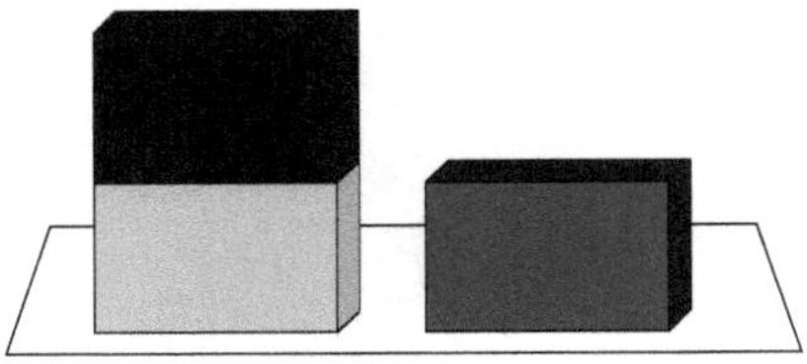

Figure 6.5 Environment observed by the robot – low-resolution transformation of the image

Storing the knowledge in the form of connection weights helps to process high-dimensional, noisy data but is also a key disadvantage of this type of non-symbolic representation. The problem is that it is difficult to understand what exactly is stored, and, as a consequence, how a given conclusion was inferred. This may be particularly important in critical applications or in social robotics, when the user needs to trust the robot and needs an explanation. Therefore, a lot of efforts have been made in the area of explainability of neural networks and the results are very promising. However, symbolic representations are still easier to interpret.

Big neural networks need a lot of training data to learn a huge number of weights. It may be a problem in the case of a social robot that needs to learn or update its strategy online from several interactions with a user. To solve this problem transfer learning can be applied. The network is pretrained using large training set and fine-tuned on user data (Tsitos & Dagioglou, 2022). Another solution is the integration of symbolic and non-symbolic methods.

6.2.3 Integration of symbolic and non-symbolic approaches

To combine the advantages of both approaches, symbolic representation may be used for high-level robot control (Reasoning engine) to infer facts and plan actions, and non-symbolic approach can be used in Perception components to process images and voice signals or execute complex movements of robot's actuators.

It is also possible to integrate both approaches in one inference engine. In Sniezynski (2014), algorithm combining logic inference rules, machine learning operators creating set of rules and database or web search operators is proposed. It is based on Michalski's idea that inference and learning can be considered special cases of knowledge transmutations (Alkharouf & Michalski, 1996). This idea may be extended to cover other complex operators, like asking questions to the user, applying neural networks to process signals, learning neural network, or using reinforcement learning. Backward chaining is applied to find an answer for a given hypothesis. The inference algorithm builds the proof using knowledge transmutations to infer the answer. Knowledge transmutation can be represented as inference rules with additional action:

IF *p* THEN c/a.

where *p* are premises or preconditions, *c* is a consequence representing pattern of formula(s) that can be inferred or generated and *a* is an additional action (empty for simple transmutations) representing algorithm that should be executed to generate consequence if premises are true according to the knowledge base (e.g., execution of a rule induction algorithm).

Four types of knowledge transmutations can be defined:

- logical (logic proof rules) – action *a* is empty here, and consequence *c* is just a logical conclusion of premises;
- learning (e.g., rule induction algorithms or learning a neural network) – *a* is a rule induction algorithm execution, *c* represents a rule pattern that can be learned and *p* allows to check if there are enough facts in the Knowledge base to create training set;
- question (database or web searching or asking a question to a user) – *c* is a formula that represents question goal; for example, if robot needs to know where to move, c=current_destination(*X*) may be used. *a* is asking question or search procedure, and *p* may represent the availability of the user or database or web;
- neural (application of a neural network) – *p* represents inputs of the neural network, *c* is its output and *a* represents calculations needed to compute the output;
- rl-action (one step of reinforcement learning algorithm – application of a strategy learned and update of the strategy) – *p* represents state description, *c* represents an action, *a* is computation to determine *c* (look-up to the action-value table or execution of neural network).

Every transmutation has its cost assigned. The cost should represent its computational complexity and (or) other important resources that are consumed (e.g., asking the user should have higher cost than searching the web). Usually, simple transmutations have a low cost, search transmutations have a moderate cost and complex ones have a high cost. Inference algorithm is based on AUTOLOGIC system developed by Morgan (Morgan, 1985). To limit the number of nodes and to generate optimal inference chains, algorithm A* (Hart et al., 1968) may be used. More details about the reasoning algorithm can be found in Sniezynski (2014). Such an integration allows for explainability like in logic-based approach. It also makes the reasoning engine simple because all types of knowledge transmutations are represented in a uniform way.

6.3 Summary

In this chapter, technological challenges related to the software developed for social robots have been discussed. To provide trustful relationship between a social robot and its user, the robot performance should be high enough, it should be able to explain its behavior, it should be anthropomorphic and communicate with the user in a natural way. Most attention was given to knowledge representation, reasoning, and learning taking into account the explainability of knowledge and reasoning. Two approaches were described: symbolic and non-symbolic methods. In the former usage of the first order logic was discussed. In the latter, neural networks were presented. Integration of these two approaches was also presented.

References

Alkharouf, N. W., & Michalski, R. S. (1996). *Multistrategy task-adaptive learning using dynamically interlaced hierarchies: A methodology and initial implementation of interlace*. Proceedings of the Third International Workshop on Multistrategy Learning.

Barreto-Cubero, A. J., Gómez-Espinosa, A., Escobedo Cabello, J. A., Cuan-Urquizo, E., & Cruz-Ramírez, S. R. (2021). Sensor data fusion for a mobile robot using neural networks. *Sensors*, *22*(1), 305.

Bono, A., Augello, A., Pilato, G., Vella, F., & Gaglio, S. (2020). An ACT-R based humanoid social robot to manage storytelling activities. *Robotics*, *9*(2), 25.

Chen, C. F. R., Fan, Q., & Panda, R. (2021). *Crossvit: Cross-attention multi-scale vision transformer for image classification*. Proceedings of the IEEE/CVF International Conference on Computer Vision, pp. 357–366.

Chen, C. H., Wang, C. C., Wang, Y. T., & Wang, P. T. (2017). Fuzzy logic controller design for intelligent robots. *Mathematical Problems in Engineering*. https://www.hindawi.com/journals/mpe/2017/8984713/

Colledanchise, M., & Ögren, P. (2018). *Behavior trees in robotics and AI: An introduction*. CRC Press.

Doncieux, S., Bredeche, N., Mouret, J. B., & Eiben, A. E. (2015). Evolutionary robotics: What, why, and where to. *Frontiers in Robotics and AI*, *2*(4).

Francies, M. L., Ata, M. M., & Mohamed, M. A. (2022). A robust multiclass 3D object recognition based on modern YOLO deep learning algorithms. *Concurrency and Computation: Practice and Experience*, *34*(1), e6517.

Goodfellow, I., Bengio, Y., & Courville, A. (2016). *6.5 Back-propagation and other differentiation algorithms. Deep learning* (pp. 200–220). MIT Press.

Hart, P. E., Nilsson, N. J., & Raphael, B. (1968). A formal basis for the heuristic determination of minimum cost paths. *IEEE Transactions on Systems Science and Cybernetics*, *4*(2), 100–107.

Howard, D., Eiben, A. E., Kennedy, D. F., Mouret, J. B., Valencia, P., & Winkler, D. (2019). Evolving embodied intelligence from materials to machines. *Nature Machine Intelligence*, *1*(1), 12–19.

Ibarz, J., Tan, J., Finn, C., Kalakrishnan, M., Pastor, P., & Levine, S. (2021). How to train your robot with deep reinforcement learning: Lessons we have learned. *The International Journal of Robotics Research*, *40*(4–5), 698–721.

Inuzuka, N., Onda, T., & Itoh, H. (2000). Learning robot control by relational concept induction with iteratively collected examples. In *Advances in Robot learning: 8th European workshop on learning robots, EWLR-8 Lausanne, Switzerland, September 18, 1999 Proceedings 8* (pp. 71–83). Springer.

Jarosz, M., Nawrocki, P., Sniezynski, B., & Indurkhya, B. (2021). Multi-platform intelligent system for multimodal human-computer interaction. *Computing & Informatics*, *40*(1).

Kopp, S., & Hassan, T. (2022). The fabric of socially interactive agents: Multimodal interaction architectures. In *The handbook on socially interactive agents: 20 years of research on embodied conversational agents, intelligent virtual agents, and social robotics volume 2: Interactivity, platforms, application* (pp. 77–112). https://dl.acm.org/doi/10.1145/3563659.3563664

Lazzeri, N., Mazzei, D., Cominelli, L., Cisternino, A., & De Rossi, D. E. (2018). Designing the mind of a social robot. *Applied Sciences*, *8*(2), 302.

Lee, J. H., Yao, Y., Özdemir, O., Li, M., Weber, C., Liu, Z., & Wermter, S. (2022). Spatial relation learning in complementary scenarios with deep neural networks. *Frontiers in Neurorobotics*, *16*.

Matyasik, P., Nalepa, G. J., & Zięcik, P. (2007, September 10–13). *Prolog-based real-time intelligent control of the hexor mobile robot*. KI 2007: Advances in Artificial Intelligence: 30th Annual German Conference on AI, KI 2007 Proceedings 30. Springer, pp. 485–488.

Merschformann, M., Lamballais, T., De Koster, M. B. M., & Suhl, L. (2019). Decision rules for robotic mobile fulfillment systems. *Operations Research Perspectives*, *6*, 100128.

Morgan, C. G. (1985). Autologic. *Logique et Analyse*, 28(110/111), 257–282.

Moulin-Frier, C., Fischer, T., Petit, M., Pointeau, G., Puigbo, J. Y., Pattacini, U., Low, S. C., Camilleri, D., Nguyen, P., Hoffmann, M., Chang, H. J., Zambelli, M., Mealier, A. L., Damianou, A., Metta, G., & Verschure, P. F. (2017). DAC-h3: A proactive robot cognitive architecture to acquire and express knowledge about the world and the self. *IEEE Transactions on Cognitive and Developmental Systems*, *10*(4), 1005–1022.

Pagallo, U. (2013). Robots in the cloud with privacy: A new threat to data protection? *Computer Law & Security Review*, *29*(5), 501–508.

Patil, A., & Rane, M. (2021). Convolutional neural networks: An overview and its applications in pattern recognition. *Information and Communication Technology for Intelligent Systems: Proceedings of ICTIS 2020*, *1*, 21–30.

Pena, A., Tejada, J. C., Gonzalez-Ruiz, J. D., Sepúlveda-Cano, L. M., Chiclana, F., Caraffini, F., & Gongora, M. A. (2023). An evolutionary intelligent control system for a flexible joints robot. *Applied Soft Computing*, 110043.

Riek, L. D. (2010). *The social co-robotics problem space: Six key challenges*. http://www.chitsazlab.org/robotics/rcv2013/papers/paper11.pdf

Robinette, P., Howard, A. M., & Wagner, A. R. (2017). Effect of robot performance on human–robot trust in time-critical situations. *IEEE Transactions on Human-Machine Systems*, *47*(4), 425–436.

Ruiz-del-Solar, J., Loncomilla, P., & Soto, N. (2018). *A survey on deep learning methods for robot vision*. arXiv preprint arXiv:1803.10862.

Saadatmand, S., Azizi, S., Kavousi, M., & Wunsch, D. (2020, January). Autonomous control of a line follower robot using a Q-learning controller. In *2020 10th Annual computing and communication workshop and conference (CCWC)* (pp. 0556–0561). IEEE.

Saha, O., & Dasgupta, P. (2018). A comprehensive survey of recent trends in cloud robotics architectures and applications. *Robotics*, *7*(3), 47.

Samsudin, K., Ahmad, F. A., & Mashohor, S. (2011). A highly interpretable fuzzy rule base using ordinal structure for obstacle avoidance of mobile robot. *Applied Soft Computing*, *11*(2), 1631–1637.

Setchi, R., Dehkordi, M. B., & Khan, J. S. (2020). Explainable robotics in human-robot interactions. *Procedia Computer Science*, *176*, 3057–3066.

Sniezynski, B. M. (2014). *Integration of inference and machine learning as a tool for creative reasoning*. 2014 AAAI Fall Symposium Series.

Sniezynski, B. M. (2015). A strategy learning model for autonomous agents based on classification. *International Journal of Applied Mathematics and Computer Science*, *25*(3), 471–482.

Stange, S., Hassan, T., Schröder, F., Konkol, J., & Kopp, S. (2022). Self-explaining social robots: An explainable behavior generation architecture for human-robot interaction. *Frontiers in Artificial Intelligence*, *87*.

Štefek, A., Pham, V. T., Krivanek, V., & Pham, K. L. (2021). Optimization of fuzzy logic controller used for a differential drive wheeled mobile robot. *Applied Sciences*, *11*(13), 6023.

Sun, X., Zhang, Y., & Chen, J. (2019). High-level smart decision making of a robot based on ontology in a search and rescue scenario. *Future Internet*, *11*(11), 230.

Sweeney, P. (2022). Trusting social robots. *AI and Ethics*, 1–8.

Tsitos, A. C., & Dagioglou, M. (2022). *Enhancing team performance with transfer-learning during real-world human-robot collaboration*. arXiv preprint arXiv:2211.13070.

Wen, S., Jiang, Y., Cui, B., Gao, K., & Wang, F. (2022). A hierarchical path planning approach with Multi-SARSA based on topological map. *Sensors*, *22*(6), 2367.

Yaacoub, J. P. A., Noura, H. N., Salman, O., & Chehab, A. (2021). Robotics cyber security: Vulnerabilities, attacks, countermeasures, and recommendations. *International Journal of Information Security*, 1–44.

7 The role of trust in human-machine interaction

Cognitive science perspective

Artur Gunia

7.1 Introduction

Intelligent machines based on artificial intelligence systems play an increasingly important role in our lives and are used in more and more fields, both in private life and in professional relationships. When the user realizes how much it affects her/his daily life, the question quickly arises: should I trust its suggestions or decisions? It is obvious that only an affirmative answer guarantees that the system will be successful. Building trust in artificial intelligence systems is a complex task with many aspects and is also one of the key challenges of the Fourth Industrial Revolution. The most important but also the most difficult part is developing a communication channel between the IT system and the real user. Therefore, in this process, the user understands the decision-making process and the machine (especially social robots) could become a trustworthy partner. The resolution of this problem requires an interdisciplinary approach. We need not only efficient IT systems, but also a multifaceted understanding of the process of building trust, the perspective of economic sciences, psychology, cognitive science, and neuroscience.

It can be practically said that at the dawn of time we trust machines and above all their constructors because otherwise we would not get on a train or plane. The development of information technology, including artificial intelligence, makes the relationship with the machine more personal; thus, trust can be built on many levels. In recent research, the question of machine trust has been explored on many fronts. Human safety seems to be of particular importance. Therefore, we want systems that would cause damage to our health and life even in the smallest way. But we also want machines that are reliable and friendly to us, so that they affect our well-being. Building a trust-based human-machine interaction is a multifaceted problem.

Therefore, the article seeks to answer the following questions: 1) What is the mental model of trust shaped in the human–human relationship, as well as in the human–machine relationship (artificial intelligence system, robots)? 2) What are the short-term and long-term trust factors in a man–machine relationship?

DOI: 10.4324/9781003311409-8

3) What factors in the machine influence the strengthening of human trust in the machine? Many technologies based on artificial intelligence are considered in this chapter, but special attention has been paid to social robots. Therefore, the main objective is to make developers, managers, and users aware that their interactive systems with AI modules increase or decrease the level of trust of users.

This chapter is organized into an introductory section with an emphasis on the role of trust in personal and professional relationships with human and non-human agents, four main sections, and a conclusion section. Section 2 illustrates how trust plays an important role in the personal and professional life of humans. A particularly important issue is the attempt to model trust. In addition, it focuses on factors that are important in building trust in the short and long term. Specifying these issues in the relations of people will make it possible to relate them to the relations with machines. Section 3 outlines the perspective of trust toward systems that are equipped with artificial intelligence and the explainable action of its action to build trust between the user and the system. These issues are focused on the disembodied agent, because this problem wants to appear in the systems themselves and not, for example, in their appearance. The most important issue of trusting an embodied agent is presented in Section 4. Robots become our daily companions as well as business partners, and so for them to be effective, the user should trust them. The essential factors for effective and trustworthy interaction with robots are presented in Section 5. Factors that play a role in building and increasing trust in robots are:

1. *reliability*, which concerns how many mistakes the robot makes and what possibilities it has to correct them,
2. *appearance*, which concerns the unchanging look of the robot,
3. *behavior*, which concerns the actions performed by the robot,
4. *artificial cognition*, which concerns learning important issues about the user by the robot.

In Section 6, Conclusion, this problem is wide because it concerns software developers, who are often not aware of the psychological aspects of the systems they build, management staff, which could lead to manipulation based on trust, and the user, who should be aware that the relationship of trust with the machine should not be the same as a relationship of trust with another person.

7.2 Trust in human–human interaction

7.2.1 From philosophy of trust to model of trust

Like many other abstract concepts, trust does not have a single definition in the literature. However, we cannot be indifferent to it; trust is one of the main factors determining the proper functioning of a social group. Trust in people close to us affects our bond with them, and trust in other people or institutions facilitates the achievement of our goals.

In the 1960s, psychologist Julian Rotter embarked on interpersonal trust and defined it as a

> *"generalized expectancy" that "the verbal statements of others can be relied upon."*
>
> (Rotter, 1971)

From social science, trust can be defined as an entity's (i.e., the trustor's) willingness to be vulnerable to another entity (i.e., the trustee). By taking this risk, the trustor assumes that the trustee will act in a manner conducive to the trustor's well-being, despite the trustee's actions being outside the trustor's control (Schilke et al., 2021). Or, simply a trustor is the person doing the trusting; a trustee is a person or system that is being trusted. In the interaction of human-human trust, the question arises of whether a human agent is willing to use the potential vulnerability of a human agent on another, unintentionally due to a lack of ability or intentionally due to a lack of moral integrity (Malle & Ullman, 2021). Undoubtedly, trust is a value that affects our overall quality of life. By trusting the other person, we judge them to have relevant competence, motivation, and opportunity (de Fine Licht & Bru¨lde, 2021).

Trust is important from a philosophical point of view. It is due to trust that we can love someone fully, we can ask someone for advice or help with a task, or entrust someone or something to another person. Especially when we know that no outside force compels them to give us these things. For philosophers, trust is a kind of reliance, although it is not a mere reliance. So people can rely on other people, artifacts, intuitions, and nature, and sometimes they have to even rely on themselves. So, let us give some examples:

> *one neighbor relies on another to keep an eye on her house when her family is out of town; a student relies on her lab partner to complete his task on time. We rely on artifacts as well: you rely on your watch to tell the correct time; I rely on the bridge not to collapse under the weight of my car. And we rely on natural phenomena: you rely on the sunrise to wake you up each morning; I rely on bodily pains to let me know when I should schedule a visit to the doctor.*
>
> (Goldberg, 2020)

At this point, we can propose the first trust-based model related to reliance. Richard Holton (1994) characterizes reliance according to the supposition that one is willing to act: where X is a person, artifact, or natural process, and φ is an action, behavior, or process, relying on X to φ is to act on the supposition that X will φ. We also note that trust is based on reliance, which in turn should be understood as, plus some extra factor, that can be identified with a positive view of the motives of the trusted person (Hawley, 2014). In philosophical analyses, when it comes to agents in the trust process, it is analogous to sociological analysis. Russell Hardin (2002) treats trust as a three-part relationship between a trustor, a trustee, and something that the trustor expects the trustee to do. However, based on Annette Baier (1986) we can say that the trustor expects the trustee to care for things. Although the three-part relationship is a popular model in the literature, some authors focus on the role of risk in trust (Baier, 1986; Becker, 1996; Mayer et al., 1995).

The obvious issue with the emerging risk associated with trust is its loss, which is associated with distrust. The following metaphor is often used in the context of trust and lack of trust, but it seems that this is a much broader problem.

> *Trust is commonly described using the metaphor of an invisible "social glue" that is conspicuous only when it is absent. It is initially tempting to think of distrust as the absence of the "glue" of trust. But this way of thinking oversimplifies the conceptual relationship between trust and distrust. Not trusting a person is not tantamount to distrusting a person.*
>
> (D'Cruz, 2020)

What is important is that distrust is usually accompanied by feelings of uncertainty, cynicism, contempt, or fear, which separates it from the agnostic "wait and see" mode (Hardin, 2001). From an analytical point of view, distrust has the following features: 1) someone cannot at the same time trust and distrust someone about the same matter (Ullmann-Margalit, 2004); 2) distrust is "not mere non-reliance" (Hawley, 2014) – someone may not rely on someone, for example, because they are busy, not because they distrust them; 3) distrust is normally a kind of non-reliance, just as trust is a kind (or many kinds) of reliance. Distrust involves "action tendencies" of avoidance or withdrawal (D'Cruz, 2019).

Another risk associated with building trust is the intention with which trust is built. Even if the level of trust in someone or something is high, confidence can be useful for various other purposes, including persuasion and reputation management (O'Neill, 2020) – and what can be considered a positive phenomenon. However, building trust can also be based on manipulation to achieve private benefits (Baier, 1986; Holton, 1994). In this case, the trustor expects something from the trustee, although this one inspires confidence; however, in the long run, the trustor does not obtain the positive effects of trust or is unaware of the negative effects of this process.

In the context of trust, it should be noted that it is associated with responsibility, and the loss of trust or distrust has its consequences, for example, moral, social, or legal. So, in this matter, entrusting is the assignment of the responsibility of doing something to someone (T. Law & Scheutz, 2021). However, to be able to entrust some behavior, someone must inspire trust, for example, through their authoritative figure, knowledge, skills, or competencies (Frost-Arnold, 2020; McMyler, 2020). Therefore, trust translates into action, entrusting something that both the trustor and the trustee bear the consequences.

All of the aforementioned explanations of trust, mainly based on philosophical analyses, are important because they allow for the presentation of a functional model of trust in the human–human, human–institution, human–nature, or human–artifact relationship. In order to then be able to try to implement it in relation to intelligent agents, or in these agents. Let us look at the basic trust model in Figure 7.1. The human–human interaction will usually be a two-way relationship. In order to be successful, both people must trust each other. If I entrust someone with a task, I trust them to do it. However, this person trusts me that he will receive, for example, payment for his performance. The problems arising in this interaction are mainly of a communicative and psychological nature. An extension of the human–human relationship is a social relation of human–institution. In this interaction, we trust not individuals, but groups of individuals who often create abstract rules or regulations. The relationship is usually one-sided, although each individual can influence the group. The loss of trust here will be associated with the lack of professionalism expected from the group or with the establishment of rules that may lead to abuses of certain people. The next two relationships are only one-sided (unless the element of the human-nature relationship is involved; we will consider the relationship with

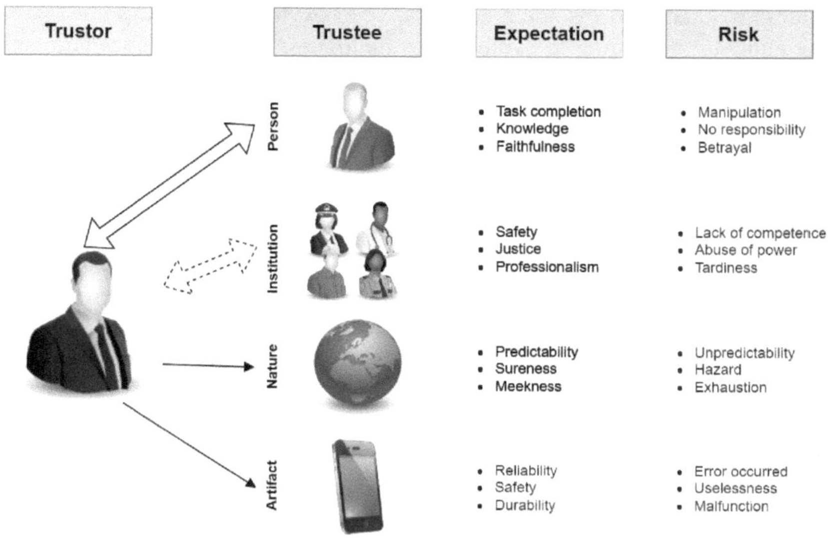

Figure 7.1 Basic model of trust between trustor and trustee, and examples of expectations and risks.

the animal, which can be received as double-sided). Trust in nature is primarily its repetition. The human-artifact interaction is one-sided, although in relation to an artifact, there may be trust in its creator or people (institution) who set the rules for using a given artifact. First of all, we expect reliability from the artifact. However, emerging embodied artificial intelligence technologies, such as robots, make us expect more from them than from any other thing. Although robots will not *per se* trust users, users will look for signs of trust that are characteristic of human–human interactions. To be able to cope with this, it would be necessary to look at the trust process in detail.

7.2.2 *Neuro-cognitive aspects of trust*

Based on the methodological aspects of trust, it is necessary to consider the mechanism behind the fact that an individual can trust another individual, often one she/he does not even know. Some solutions give us cognitive science which is not a unitary discipline, but a cross-disciplinary research domain. Thus, this science will allow you to start from a neurobiological basis toward functional mechanisms that I can trust another agent, both human and nonhuman.

Trust is evolutionarily rooted, so it is a factor responsible for the formation of groups and social relationships, which we can already see in simple animal species. The main role in trust is played by oxytocin, a neurotransmitter and hormone that also affects the stimulation of milk secretion and the initiation of labor. Research shows that in some mammals, oxytocin facilitates the cooperation of individuals and vasotocin, a derivative of oxytocin, also plays this role in other animals. According to evolutionary biologists, vasotocin appeared about 100 million years ago in fish and was designed to weaken the ovulating female's natural fear of males and thus facilitate reproduction. Vasotocin has evolved into oxytocin and arginine vasopressin, which are found in mammals. In the late 1970s, rodent studies showed that oxytocin induces protective behavior in females. Other studies have shown that oxytocin and arginine vasopressin play a role in social behavior in voles (Zak, 2008). Furthermore, studies with human subjects showed that oxytocin reduces anxiety and neuroendocrine responsiveness to social stressors, indicating that it acts as a central regulator of social behavior that protects against stress (Heinrichs et al., 2003).

Empirical studies based on economic games showed that an increase in oxytocin levels appeared in people who trusted other people. Studies have shown that the level of oxytocin increased in people which was a result of trusting another person, and not, for example, because of satisfaction with getting rich. Researchers also found that higher levels of oxytocin were associated with greater dependability. This is due to the action of dopamine, which causes a sense of satisfaction. A study of the brain using magnetic resonance imaging (MRI) showed that when trust is reciprocated, precisely those areas of the midbrain where dopamine binds are activated. An increase in the level of oxytocin causes a greater tendency to trust. However, also an increase in the level of oxytocin in the brain causes some people to lessen the natural fear of interacting with strangers. Research also shows differences in how women and men respond to distrust. In the body of men with whom others did not trust, there was an increase in the level of dihydrotestosterone (DHT), a derivative of testosterone, responsible for physical changes during puberty in men and for aggression tendencies (Kosfeld et al., 2005; Zak, 2008; Zak et al., 2009). Therefore, these physiological indicators, such as oxytocin-related measures as an objective measure of trust, can be used in the human-machine interaction to develop a trust model that is independent of the many parameters that affect trust (Khavas et al., 2020). Although some studies indicate that you can get analogous results from elevated oxytocin when the agent that is supposed to inspire trust is simulated (Anumandla et al., 2011).

The neurobiological basis of trust explains the mechanism of creating a trust-based relationship, but it also requires answering what affects it. Emotions play an important role in trust. Several scholars even recognize trust as one of the emotions, which, however, is an overinterpretation because emotions determine how we perceive the world in a direct manner, how we think, and what judgments we make on matters of fact and evaluate some aspects of the world (Lahno, 2020). Many theories of trust show the idea that trust is nothing but belief based on the information given to the trustor, while information is often subject to emotional attitude. So emotions will be a confidence booster when someone or something makes us happy. When we have positive emotions, we are more likely to trust. But emotions are important mediators of trust decisions. Specifically, betrayal aversion – that evokes negative emotions such as fear, anger, or disgust – which is a form of social anxiety, has been postulated to reduce the propensity to trust relative to matched situations Engelmann and Fehr (2017). Thus, emotions are an important stimulator in social decision-making processes (Dunning et al., 2012; Guo et al., 2019; Krueger & Meyer-Lindenberg, 2019). As I have already indicated, the problem is multi-threaded; positive emotions can push us to excessive and premature trust. As a consequence, in the long run, this can lead to distrust, which also changes emotional attitude. On the other hand, too much fear of potential consequences can lead to not trusting someone or something, or to significantly delaying trust.

Although it seems that emotions will primarily accompany social human-human interaction. After all, if we are happy, we often want it to affect other people, while when we are sad, we expect consolation from a trusted person.

In a one-sided interaction with the artifact, this seems impossible. However, the development of affective computing allows for very good recognizing of emotions from the user, and a quite faithful simulation of emotions by digital agents, which would have an impact on strengthening trust (Calvo et al., 2015; Devillers, 2020).

Another important aspect is to consider trust in terms of other mental states. First, from a cognitive perspective, consider what Castelfranchi and Falcone (2020) pointed out.

> *(a) trust does not involve a single and unitary mental state, (b) trust is an evaluation that implies a motivational aspect, (c) trust is a way to exploit ignorance, (d) trust is, and is used as, a signal, (e) trust cannot be reduced to reciprocity, (f) trust combines rationality and feeling, (g) trust is not only related to other persons but can be applied to instruments, technologies, etc.*
> (Castelfranchi & Falcone, 2020)

Furthermore, trust in the authors mentioned earlier (Castelfranchi & Falcone, 2020) should be established as follows:

1. *Trust based on beliefs*. Belief refers to the attitude that we have, roughly, whenever we take something to be the case or regard it as true (Schwitzgebel, 2021). Therefore, by analyzing trust as a belief, we can consider the following cases. Beliefs about the future, so trust is a positive expectation, whereas an expectation is a combination of a motivational mental state together with a set of beliefs. Trust as a belief in someone's abilities, qualities, willingness, self-confidence, etc. And beliefs about risks, so trust enables us to deal with uncertainty and risks. The trustor must have beliefs about the severity and probability of risks.
2. *Trust as a goal*. Therefore, it is crucial to specify the purpose for which a trustor trusts trustee. The goal is to delegate to others and rely on them to achieve goals; and in the case of the formulation of an "intention" and the execution of an "intentional" action, which are strictly based on self-efficacy, efficacy beliefs, on positive expectation about our own choice, persistence, skills.
3. *Trust as a form of subjective probability*. "Trust is the subjective probability by which an individual X expects that another individual Y performs a given action on which its welfare depends" (Gambetta et al., 2000).
4. *Trust as action and signal*. Apart from understanding trust as a relation, it can be understood as communicative action. If we trust someone, we communicate to someone our positive evaluations of her through our delegation to and reliance on her. Moreover, this action also signals to others our appreciation of someone.
5. *Trust as a norm*. We expect that someone with whom we have a relationship will not kill us or that some food we would like to eat is not toxic. Therefore, norms, such as trust, provide us with uncertainty reduction, predictability, and reliability, and can be the basis for trusting someone or something.
6. *Trust and reciprocity*. This approach can be instrumentally perceived as an expectation of reciprocal help. But it also makes you take the risk of not reciprocating it.

These are only a few examples of the cognitive aspects of trust. However, it is especially worth considering trust in two pairs: 1) short-term and long-term occurrence of trust, and 2) affective and rational trust.

An important question is how much time we need to trust someone or something. Neuroimaging studies using MRI say it takes a few seconds to fall in love with someone (Ortigue et al., 2010). Love can be considered one of the highest levels of trust. As I have already mentioned, trust cannot be considered equally in all cases. Depending on who or what they are concerned with and on the given situation, the level of trust may vary. Depending on the situation, the desire to achieve a given goal, and the emerging risk, there may be different times to achieve trust. For example, in a tourist information office that I am visiting for the first time, I trust the person working there to show me the right way. Although the situation lasts for a while, my trust can be earned by analogy to other institutions of this type. Another case of short-term trust is in emergency situations. In the event of an earthquake (loss of trust in the predictability of nature), I will trust anyone who wants to help me. Short-term trust is often associated with affective trust or emotional trust. Affective trust is the emotional counterpart of a cold and reasoning-based decision. In this way, there are no judgments, no reasons, but simply intuition, attraction/repulsion, sympathy/antipathy, activated affective responses, or evoked somatic markers (Castelfranchi & Falcone, 2020). Just as emotions are spontaneous, so will trust be spontaneous. Hence, often the first impression, appearance, the occurrence of positive emotions will be conducive to trust.

In contrast, we are dealing with long-term trust. In this case, trust in someone or something is built over days, weeks, and even years. In addition, loss of trust in this case has significant consequences, such as divorce in the event of a lack of trust between spouses or breaking a contract between business partners. Building trust is based on rational premises, often on calculated and meticulous calculations. So, it is based on our cognitive abilities, including our knowledge. Therefore, according to rational trust, I can trust someone to speak truthfully due to evidence of their reliability (Pedersen et al., 2014). As will be seen later also in the context of digital agents, we can demonstrate short-term and emotional trust, as well as long-term and rational trust.

7.2.3 Trust in business

Subsections 2.1 and 2.2 summarize the essence of trust. On the other hand, trust is an important success factor both in business and in state institutions. The development of the Fourth Industrial Revolution, whose determinants are the integration of systems and the creation of extensive networks accounts for the main determinant of the changes occurring within the latest trend. At the same time, the physical world and virtual world are being interwoven in dynamically developed cyber-physical systems, in which both people and machines integrate through the Internet and other information technologies. As a result, it is possible to communicate quickly in real time, which translates directly into process optimization. So, the key issue is the complexity of management in the conditions of the Fourth Industrial Revolution, which should be confirmed with trust in many aspects.

So trust goes beyond the gates and local zone of a given organization, trust perspective must be global, and when building it, the needs of different people from different cultures should be taken into account. Trust must be placed in Internet services, which must be reliable and constantly available to the recipient. IT systems should also inspire confidence through their reliability. However, when looking at future solutions, such as artificial intelligence communicating in natural language with the user or social robots that are everyday companions or business partners, trust should be based on certainty, freedom, and lack of suspicion toward these systems.

Obvious trust plays a key role in classical sociological and economics and management theories; therefore, most academic publications focus on these areas and refer to the practical possibility of inspiring trust, especially at work or with business partners (Schilke et al., 2021). But, as in the context of philosophical and cognitive issues, there is a difficulty in defining trust. This is due to the fact that trust occurs at various levels of functioning of persons/entities, where there is a cause-and-effect relationship. Thus, we can talk about the gradual expansion of concentric circles of trust: from the most concrete interpersonal relationships to a more abstract reference to social structures and institutions, or vice versa (Sztompka, 2007).

In the economic context, the concept of trust is closely related to social capital. Robert Putnam (1993) emphasizes that trust is its basic component, and defining social capital, he indicates that these are such features of society as trust, norms, and connections that can increase efficiency by facilitating coordinated actions. Low or no trust is a significant barrier not only in interpersonal relationships, but above all in business relationships. Today, the value of companies is largely composed of trust-based intangible factors, as is trust capital (Castelfranchi & Falcone, 2010; Sztompka, 2007). The growing importance of trust in business relations is also related to the increasing access to information about products and services, greater choice, and faster and cheaper communication with competing companies. Additionally, trust, due to its properties, can create a permanent competitive advantage in organizations, especially those based on knowledge (Casimir et al., 2012).

The multiplicity of research areas dealing with trust makes the concept vague. Therefore, it is worth considering the levels of trust in the economic context, which can be considered on a macroeconomic scale and microeconomic scale (organizational trust) (Kenning, 2008), as well as in the dimension of individual professional relationships (which are the most important from the point of view of the introduction of intelligent agents). At the highest macroeconomic level, trust affects indicators on a macro scale, that is, economic growth (Algan & Cahuc, 2014; Beugelsdijk et al., 2004), income level and inequality index (Elgar & Aitken, 2011; Stephany, 2017), democratic stability and government action (Blind, 2007; Inglehart, 1999), or crime rate (Messner et al., 2004). At the microeconomic level, the focus is on interorganizational trust (Harris & Zaheer, 2006), for example, trust in marketing channels, supply chain, or organization networks (Chow & Chan, 2008; Fawcett et al., 2012; McEvily et al., 2021; Seppanen et al., 2007); and intraorganizational trust (Bieńkowska et al., 2018): interpersonal in relation to coworkers (horizontal trust), between superiors and subordinates (vertical trust) (Agbejule et al., 2021; Guinot & Chiva, 2019) and trust in organizations (Vanhala, 2019; Vanhala & Ahteela, 2011). In the macroeconomic and microeconomic context, research on trust in technology within and outside the organization is also important (Grodzinsky et al., 2020; Kok & Soh, 2020; X. Li et al., 2008).

In contrast, in personal professional relationships, trust is the expectation of a partner to maintain and act predictably and honestly on their commitments (Potter, 2020). So trust is the trustor's expectation and belief that the partner will act in the common interest, which is associated with a certain level of dependence and risk on his/her behavior (Whitener et al., 1998). According to Tzafrir and Eitam-Meilik (2005), it is a willingness to invest one's resources in a relationship with another entity resulting from positive expectations resulting from previous mutual interactions. It also emphasizes the aspect of voluntary dependence that is the basis of trust, and that trust is the result of expectations resulting from previous positive experiences (Brockner et al., 1997).

There are multiple issues related to trust in personal and professional relationships; among them, the issue of affective and rational trust (also called emotional and cognitive trust) is discussed in the previous paragraph. Rational trust is, in this context, a person's confidence or willingness to rely on the competence and reliability of a service provider. It results from accumulated knowledge that provides an opportunity to make judgments with a certain degree of confidence with regard to the likelihood that the focal partner will meet their obligations. Although rational trust is driven by knowledge, the need for trust implies an incomplete state of knowledge. A state of complete certainty regarding a partner's future actions implies that risk is eliminated and trust is redundant (Johnson & Grayson, 2005; Punyatoya, 2018). In other words, rational trust consists of the process that the customer follows to assess an organization's intentions and ability to meet promises by identifying guarantees in terms of competence and predictiveness of behavior. Rational trust would include the following aspects: knowledge, competence, ability, reliability, predictability, creditability, and dependability. Affective trust is the confidence given to a partner based on the feeling generated by the level of care and concern shown by the partner. It is characterized by feelings of security and the perceived strength of the relationship. The essence of affective trust is the reliance on a partner based on emotions and is closely related to the perception that the partner's actions are intrinsically motivated (Johnson & Grayson, 2005; Punyatoya, 2018). In other words, affective trust is based on the process the customer uses to evaluate a company according to the qualities and characteristics that show concern and care as well as their willingness to compromise beyond the profit motive. Affective trust would include the following aspects: empathy, feelings of security, benevolence, goodwill, personal beliefs, and altruism. So, if people want to build an interaction with the machine, these two aspects and their determinants should be taken into account.

7.3 Trust toward intelligent agents

In the previous section, we discuss interactions between a human and a human or a group of people. Therefore, facets of trust such as intentionality, belief, hope, and reliance, facets that come into play when the trustor and the trustee are both humans, or in trust relationships that involve at least one person, were highlighted. However, the development of computer science, and above all artificial intelligence and machine learning techniques, has been throwing a new relationship between a human and an intelligent (artificial) agent for some time now. And it is not a simple one-way human-artifact relationship. As trust in personal and business relationships is often built from scratch, so is trust between the user and the agent system. We can achieve this through positive user experiences using the artificial intelligence system.

But let us start by defining who an artificial agent is, who an intelligent agent is, what manifestations of artificial intelligence should be considered, and what interactions we are dealing with in this case. In the definition by Grodzinsky et al. (2020):

> *In general, an AA [Artificial Agent] is a machine entity designed and constructed by people to run without direct human intervention for long periods (days, not seconds). Its design and construction allow an AA to change its internal state based on its interaction with the environment over time. When we talk about an AA changing its internal state, we are talking about changing the information it has recorded in its table (T) and that it is going to use to direct its next decision. This basic AA has the feature that if at some point in the future the AA has the same internal state, its next decision will be exactly the same as it was the last time it was in this internal state.*

Including artificial intelligence techniques in this concept, we are dealing with an intelligent agent, which is anything that perceives its environment, takes actions autonomously to achieve goals, and may improve its performance with learning or use knowledge (Russell, 2010). What researchers are looking for in these systems is that they are equipped with sensors that take information from the environment. Hence, based on Kaplan and Haenlein (2019), they can be defined as:

> *A system's ability to correctly interpret external data, to learn from such data, and to use those learnings to achieve specific goals and tasks through flexible adaptation.*

The intelligent agent runs through the cycle of perceiving, thinking, and acting. In the context of artificial agents, we can consider: software agent that has file contents, keystrokes, and received network packages that function as sensory input, then act on those inputs, displaying the output on a screen, and robotic agents that have cameras and infrared range finders that act as sensors, and various servos and motors perform as actuators. Importantly, these systems are equipped with artificial intelligence techniques, such as computer vision, natural language processing, data mining, reinforcement learning, supervised and unsupervised learning, decision support or recommendation systems, and many others. We use them ourselves every day, because many smartphone applications are based on this architecture, as specific examples can be listed here: personal virtual assistants such as *Alexa*, *Siri*, *Google Assistant*, or *Cortana*, assistants for self-driving vehicles, recognition systems in augmented and virtual reality, real-time translators, cybersecurity system, wearables, ambient intelligence tools for smart houses, and of course robots.

Recently, artificial intelligence technologies have been increasingly used to support business and daily tasks. Unfortunately, there is still a lack of full trust from both users and entrepreneurs who want to improve their services with AI. Artificial intelligence undoubtedly raises problems, the solution of which is necessary to build trust between users and the system. Among other things, the ability to make decisions in such a way that people will consider them fair. The assistants were conscious and, according to accepted human values and the way they were taken, explained clearly. There are a lot of fears about artificial intelligence that move away from the trust, for example, the issues of huge amounts of data processing for fear of their privacy. Other issues include the black-box nature of some AI approaches, the possible discriminatory decisions that AI algorithms may make, and the accountability and responsibility when an AI system is involved in an undesirable outcome (Rossi, 2018). We are also concerned about security, but also about decisions made by artificial intelligence, because even if they are right, will they be beneficial to us (Gillath et al., 2021).

Understanding that user trust is critical for the development and success of a given product, it is worth analyzing aspects during the planning and implementation process that have the potential to increase the credibility of AI systems. Some of the factors that are specifically applied to robots will be presented in Section 7.5.

7.3.1 Explainability

In everyday life, we trust fairly easily. We trust that the doctor will prescribe the appropriate medicines for us, the taxi driver will take us safely through the city, and the financial advisor will give us valuable advice. We usually base our trust on the assumption that these people have developed their skills through learning. AI systems have similar capabilities in this context; they learn from a set of data and can use their knowledge in practice. So, how do we make our system as reliable as a specialist? Trust in business is built primarily on two pillars: observing that a given consideration works and receiving an explanation of how and why the solution works. Continuing the example of a taxi driver – if he leaves the route without saying a word, we will get the impression that he is trying to cheat us. However, if during a change of route he says that he knows that the main street is closed today, he will no longer lose credibility. To build trust, it is not enough to simply show that the system fulfills its role. Showing good performance in a few cases does not guarantee reliability. Only when the user understands how the system works will he be able to trust it. To build trust between the user and the AI, communication between them is necessary. By definition, AI has a different, more complex, but narrower perception of the world than a human. Often, a decision or result obtained by, for example, machine learning methods seems unjustified to a human. If the decision-making process is a black-box system for the user, it is very hard to believe that it works well. AI has a much greater ability to detect patterns and find connections in available data, but in this process, there is no human-readable interpretation. If all the system does is return the result of matching for specific conditions, the user is deprived of the ability to understand his motives. Therefore, it is hard to trust that the system works properly and that the reasons for making a specific decision are rational. Therefore, it is necessary to implement a real-world interpretation model in the system, which will allow us to understand its operation. In summary, the user of the system must know the mechanisms and processes behind its operation. Many current systems are a kind of black box, where they are not clearly informed about the factors that influenced the decision. The same challenge is explainable artificial intelligence that humans can understand the decisions or predictions made by AI. This is currently one of the biggest challenges of AI systems and is the subject of much research (Samek & Mu¨ller, 2019; Siau & Wang, 2018; Tjoa & Guan, 2020; Vilone & Longo, 2021).

7.3.2 Sustainability

A clearly defined positive impact on reality is an important factor in the AI system that influences trust. The user will not be willing to use the system if it does not bring him or the environment any benefits. When developing AI systems, developers need to be sure that AI decisions will benefit people or the environment. For this, systems must be aligned with human principles and values. Therefore, the goals of artificial intelligence must be in line with human values and focus on improving the quality of human life. This is related to the conscious design approach.

> *Conscious design comprises both a design awareness of the potential long-term and unintended consequences of what we design and a continuous experimentation of our design process to build more sustainable products and services. It is a first step towards building circular economies and transition design.*
>
> (Anderson & Ng, 2020)

Following this approach seems obvious at first glance, but sometimes, when creating AI applications with good intentions, we still violate privacy by collecting large amounts of confidential data. It is absolutely important to design applications that are not too invasive and that use effective security protocols to protect sensitive data. It is imperative that the system is both highly functional and secure. In terms of data protection, transparency of its use is equally important. When asking the user to provide what data, the purpose and conditions under which the system will use them should be clearly defined (Larsson et al., 2019).

7.3.3 Values

The factor influencing trust in others is the level of compliance with the declared values: It is much easier to make a decision for a person with similar views because they have a similar view of the world (Lahno, 2020). Translating this into AI systems, those that can distinguish views have a chance to adapt to the user and create a more personalized decision-making model, enjoying a better level of user trust. In terms of personalizing the model to the user, it is extremely important to be aware of our diversity. For the system to work well, it is necessary to obtain data with the widest cross-section. It is important to realize that narrow data sets can generate biased results that can lead to discrimination against certain social groups. One way to avoid such problems is to ensure that the development team consists of a variety of people. Thus, there is a need for Human-Centered AI (HCAI) that amplifies and augments rather than displaces human abilities. HCAI seeks to preserve human control in a way that ensures that artificial intelligence meets our needs while also operating transparently, providing equitable results, and respecting privacy (Riedl, 2019). Therefore, personalization in AI is essential for sustainability in AI (Mhlanga, 2022).

7.3.4 Integrity

The basis of trust in the AI system is making the right decisions using it. However, a particular concern is that the AI system is getting out of hand. Integrity is the assurance that the systems produce the output according to the operational and technical parameters predefined by the developer. If the system is integral, we can be sure that it works as intended. An element of integrity may also be some set limits that can be used to regulate the use of AI, which will contribute to a better user experience. Therefore, if the system has some constraints, it increases the sense of control over the results (Bostrom, 2017).

7.3.5 Prejudice and bias

It is difficult to establish a trusting relationship with someone if we are insulted, discriminated against, or our dignity is compromised. If the AI system evokes such feelings in us, it means that the data are of poor quality. The data used to train AI systems are one of the main causes of bias. Deep neural networks used for image classification are often trained using data from ImageNet. It is a collection of more than 14 million images with a description that until recently did not have enough representatives of a given race, ethnic group, or gender (Yang et al., 2020). In natural language processing, standard algorithms are trained on collections of billions of words. Researchers typically create data sets from websites such as Google News or Google Images using queries from readily available sources such as Wikipedia (Schmahl et al., 2020). Although the quality is constantly improved, many sources are not always created by competent people. These methods can unintentionally collect data based on beliefs related to gender, ethnicity, or cultural bias. Bias can be inadvertently introduced into the system by improper selection of the training set, for example, lack of appropriate cultural diversity in the emotion detection system. It is very important to support developers creating systems based on artificial intelligence by raising awareness of current opportunities, thanks to numerous bias metrics, concepts of fairness, and algorithms for detecting and minimizing bias in the system. We will certainly trust such systems if they do not perpetuate certain stereotypes and prejudices (Noor, 2020).

7.3.6 Security and privacy protection

Operational security and data protection are two important factors that influence trust in technology. People are unlikely to trust anything that is too risky to operate. Data security is important because machine learning relies on large data sets, making privacy a concern (Hengstler et al., 2016; Siau & Wang, 2018). If we are aware that someone or something is making every effort to provide us with a sense of security, trust in them grows.

7.3.7 Usability and reliability

Performance includes the capability of AI to complete tasks and complete these tasks consistently and confidently. The AI application should be designed to operate easily and intuitively. There should be no unexpected downtime or crashes. Usability and reliability contribute to continuous trust (Siau & Wang, 2018). Usability must go hand in hand with the aforementioned factors, such as explaining (Dieber & Kirrane, 2022).

7.3.8 Positive impact

Today's intelligent agents can recognize many social events, such as social distance between persons, the wrong crossing of the street, or a surge of negative emotions. The architecture is based on sensors that can collect data from the environment to recognize some relevant events for the mandated behavior. Artificial agents are capable of recognizing inappropriate and unsafe human behaviors; if so, can they influence the user to correct this behavior? This assumption fits the concept of the nudge theory. We can define nudge as any aspect of choice architecture that changes people's behavior in a predictable way, without forcing restrictions, prohibiting alternative options, or significantly changing people's economic motivations (Thaler & Sunstein, 2009). Many digital nudges can be used to increase the effectiveness of the working or learning process (Hummel et al., 2018). Important nudges were not intrusive and seem to be even more effective when they rely on metaphors to influence human behavior (Ervas et al., 2022). So if technology has a positive impact on us and we can appreciate this impact, our trust in it will also increase.

The trustworthiness of AI systems and intelligent agents is an extremely complex process that is constantly being improved. When designing a system, factors that increase this trust should be taken into account. In interpersonal relationships, we trust each other quite easily. To improve trust in human intelligent agents relations, it is worth considering what makes us trust another human being and try to adapt these aspects to the system, which will ultimately translate into possible greater profit from a given system, which will ultimately translate into a possible higher profit from a given system.

7.4 Trust in human-robot interaction

However, the studies belonging to the latter provide the first evidence that humans feel such mental states as empathy, trust, and emotional states for robots. Therefore, the researcher identifies several distinguishable factors that evoke and influence trust in robots, such as reliability, robot appearance, behavior, and cognitive abilities of the robot. Of course, the greatest success will be achieved when all three factors are implemented properly.

However, in considering the issue of human-machine interaction, it is crucial to properly distinguish the categories of robots, because the ways of trust will be at different levels depending on the purpose of the robot. Of particular importance is the transition from a machine to a robot. Machines created en masse from the beginning of the industrial revolution were usually supposed to replace people in simple repetitive tasks. They were seen as physical systems designed to perform physical actions in the physical world. However, in the second half of the twentieth century, there was a significant change in the way of thinking about constructing machines. They began to be perceived as systems to manipulate information encoded in an appropriate way (Hor′akov′a & Kelemen, 2009). So robot were mechanical devices that perform automatically programmed tasks. In the 1950s, the robots constructed were machines with simple software, incapable of real control over the way tasks were performed, and very often they did not even have the ability to provide feedback to humans. With each subsequent decade of the second half of the twentieth century, robots became capable of taking new actions. Their appearance changed, their flexibility in the way they perform tasks, and most importantly, they enabled communication and interaction with people (Gasparetto & Scalera, 2019).

Mostly, robots were used to help people do jobs they would rather not do, so the main group of robots is industrial robots. Traditional industrial robots consist of a manipulator's arm designed to perform repetitive tasks. They are in this category we got from small CNC machines (computer numerical control), to large production lines. Therefore, it is generally applied to perform tasks such as picking and placing, welding, painting, packaging and labeling, palletizing, and product inspection, in order to achieve industrial automation (Ji & Wang, 2019). Building trust with these robots is long-term. Therefore, it will be based on the reliability of these machines in continuous operation and the provision of safety components for employees and the production process.

The miniaturization of robotic technologies, as well as the reduction of robot production costs, meant that robots that were previously intended for factory purposes can now be found in our households. Household robots, also called domestic, consumer, or house robots doing your chores (Sahin & Guvenc, 2007). In this group of robots, we deal with vacuum cleaners (like *Roomba*), robots for home monitoring and security (like *Amazon Astro*), floor washing (like *Braava Jet M6*), and lawn mowing robots (like *Husqvarna Automower*). Although the devices continue to perform routine tasks, they must show a much greater degree of automation. One of the important tasks is mapping the area in which they will move and identifying and classifying three-dimensional objects (e.g., an object that can/cannot be vacuumed) (Rusu et al., 2007). Another issue is how the user commands such devices; research focuses mainly on verbal messages (Ferru′s & Somonte, 2016; Hoffner et al., 2022), but also on gaze and gesture commands (Alsharif et al., 2016) or the ability to read intentions, for example, from the user's emotions (Zhong et al., 2021). As with industrial robots, reliability will be an important factor in building interaction and trust with these robots. However, factors such as: 1) precision of the task being performed, 2) intuitive way of communication, and 3) ambient character – that is, whether they will not disturb the user's attention with their work, will also have an impact.

Medical robots are another important group from the point of view of society and economy. Medical robotics is poised to transform all aspects of medicine, from surgical interventions to targeted therapy, rehabilitation, and hospital automation. Key areas include the development of robots for minimally invasive intervention (Beasley, 2012; Troccaz et al., 2019). Some futuristic studies refer to micro/nanorobots operating within the human body for precise and targeted medical interventions at the cellular level (Soto et al., 2020). These systems are rather characterized by limited autonomy; hence, they are manipulators controlled by medical personnel. Their primary purpose is to support perception, decision, and action during medical procedures and also to enable telemedicine. Currently, the main application of medical robots we have is in the following areas: neurosurgery (robots like *neuromate, CyberKnife*), laparoscopy (like *da Vinci, i-Snake*), endoluminal (like *Niobe, Magellan*), and orthopedics (like *Navio, Mako*) (Troccaz et al., 2019). Trust in these robots must be shown both in medical staff and in the patient. From the medical staff's point of view, the important factors will be reliability and thus the certainty that not even the slightest error will occur during the procedure. The second factor is precision, so the feeling that, by using a robot, a given procedure will be performed with greater precision than with conventional methods. From the patient's point of view, the most important factor will be safety, to assure the patient that the procedure with the use of a robot will be successful (e.g., information about fewer blood losses during surgery).

Another group of robots is the system that will never inspire trust at first. Military robots and drones are autonomous, unmanned, or remotely controlled mobile robots designed for military applications, from transport to search, rescue, and attack. Therefore, such machines will not only be able to support combatants, but are capable of taking our place in war (Kahn, 2017). Here, we have remotely controlled drones for kamikaze attacks (such as the Iranian drone *Shahed-136*) or neutralizing enemy units (such as the Turkish *Bayraktar TB2*). Other solutions are remotely operated vehicle robots designed for missions ranging from reconnaissance to combat (such as US *Foster-Miller TALON*), on their platforms can be placed rifles, machine guns, or grenade launchers. On the other hand, a more peaceful solution will be robots that support sappers, which will allow them to disarm explosives (such as the Polish *PIAP IBIS*). Although it is difficult to talk about trust in the context of military robots, because autonomous systems that allow killing raise many ethical doubts (Borenstein, 2008; Hellstrom, 2013; Noorman & Johnson, 2014) and at the same time violate the basic laws of robotics proposed by Isaac Asimov in his 1942 short story "Runaround":

> *A robot may not injure a human being or, through inaction, allow a human being to come to harm.*
>
> (Asimov, 1942)

However, trust in these machines should be perceived, especially through a sense of respect, and thus as a preventive factor against a greater escalation of conflicts.

When considering different types of robots, one should bear in mind machines that at first glance do not evoke associations with robots. An important category will be autonomous vehicles (also known as self-driving cars or robotic cars). We can list here current solutions such as driver assistance systems that support the driver, as well as fully automated vehicles, which means a motor vehicle that has been designed and constructed to move autonomously without any driver supervision (EU, 2019). So trust will be based on security and reliability as before. Furthermore, it is important that these systems are equipped with moral modules that could make rational decisions in dangerous situations (Awad et al., 2018; Martinho et al., 2021). In a similar way, we can consider planetary rovers that must be characterized by a high degree of autonomy because, due to the large distances, they cannot be remotely controlled by operators (e.g., sending a signal from Mars to Earth takes between 5 and 20 minutes[1]). Building trust should therefore be based on autonomous decisions in new, unfamiliar situations.

Finally, we have to consider the group of social and humanoid robots. From the point of view of the development of robotics and the impact on the economy, this type of robot will have an impact on Rev 4.0. Therefore, building interaction and trust with them will be multilevel because we will be dealing with not only an automaton that repeats certain actions, but a machine that resembles a human in appearance and behavior. Let us start with a humanoid robot, otherwise an android, which is a device that automatically performs certain tasks, the shape of which resembles the human body. However, the main group of works whose integration should be considered are both humanoid and non-humanoid social robots. Robots designed for social purposes are called social robots. Social robots are autonomous robots that are distinguished by the ability to establish and maintain interactions with people in a natural way for humans, taking into account established social and cultural norms. Social robots have the characteristics necessary to work with people in everyday settings, such as hospitals, healthcare centers, museums, or schools (Belpaeme et al., 2018; Breazeal et al., 2008; Logan et al., 2019). They are usually designed to be visually likable for people and to be able to participate in simple or more complex human-robot interactions, for example, by communicating with people in dialogues or expressing and perceiving emotions (Hegel et al., 2009). Sarrica et al. (2019) have identified several key features of social robots that are repeated across multiple sources, and they are:

1. be an autonomous system;
2. have a physical body;
3. sense and respond to environmental cues;
4. interact with humans (or other robots); and
5. understand and follow social rules.

Instead, Li et al. (2011) exchange the basic skills of social robots that need to be designed during their development:

1. recognizing human presence by sight, touch, or sound;
2. engaging in physical contact such as holding, touching;
3. using physical movements and gestures;
4. expressing and/or perceiving emotions; and
5. participating in the conversation.

Some special cases of social are sex robots, which are anthropomorphic robotic sex dolls that have a humanoid form, human-like movement or behavior, and some degree of artificial intelligence. So, they are supposed to be companions of erotic pleasures. However, a disturbed relationship can lead to a more emotional relationship, in extreme cases, even to falling in love with a robot. For this to happen, a high degree of user trust in the robotic agent is needed (Devlin, 2020).

But let us get back to the essential social robots. The capabilities of social robots will increase, and they themselves have the potential to perform various tasks in our society. Among other things, social robots can help us deal with emergencies, teach our children, care for people who are close to us, or become full members of our teams. Also in the professional context, they will protect our assets, communicate with our clients or contractors, and accompany us during the conclusion of contracts. Sometimes we will spend only a moment with a given robot, other times the relationship will be permanent and long-term. For all of these roles, the issue of trust in robotic agents will be crucial. For example, we are in a difficult health situation that requires hospital intervention. A social robot sits at the hospital reception and its task would be to admit to the hospital ward. The interaction with the robot will be reasonably short and spontaneous, without the need to establish a lasting relationship. In order to achieve human-machine trust, the robot will be expected to empathize with the more difficult situation in which I found myself. The clarity, simplicity, and precision of the information provided by the agent will also be important. The appearance of the robot, which should be friendly, will also be of great concern. But also his behavior, such as appropriate voice modulation, supporting the discussion with nonverbal messages (e.g., pointing to the right door of the ward with his arm), or the willingness to repeat or explain. In such a situation, the person expects sympathy, and not necessarily a cold machine message.

But let us also consider a second example of a professional long-term relationship. This time, the social robot sits at the bank's reception desk, while we are regular customers of this bank, where we deposit and withdraw cash in various currencies. Therefore, the interaction is continued and long-lasting. In order to achieve human-machine trust, first of all, the robot must be effective and reliable; it should understand our commands, provide support, and quickly withdraw cash in the indicated currency. Appearance does not play such an important role anymore, because we have gotten used to it. However, higher cognitive abilities, such as learning, seem to be important. It is enough for small talk to appear, in which the robot will remember our name or the effects of the previous conversation. These small issues will significantly enrich the interaction with the robot. The aim of designing human-robot interaction should be to minimize distrust to establish a real and effective interaction. However, it should not be forgotten that too much trust can lead to manipulation. Man cannot give up his/her instinct for self-preservation in favor of a machine, whether through convenience, ignorance, or stupidity. In human-robot interaction, it is good if trust appears, but one cannot deprive yourself of the feeling that you are not dealing with a machine.

7.5 Human-robot interaction enhancement factors

7.5.1 Reliance in human-robot interaction as a relationship based on trust

In recent years, the social nature of the interaction between humans and robots has been intensively researched (Deng, Mutlu, Mataric et al., 2019; Luria et al., 2018; Mieczkowski et al., 2019; Mirnig et al., 2017; Smedegaard, 2019). We also note the development of science dealing with the study of phenomena occurring between humans and robots, Human-Robot Interaction (HRI), which grew out of the study of human-computer interaction (HCI) (Heuer & Stein, 2019; Weiss & Manfred, 2010; Young et al., 2011). Depending on what the robot is used for, its appearance, speech, behavior, and features are created that are supposed to evoke specific feelings in a human. In turn, Kristin K. Schaefer (2013) mentions that one of the most important challenges in developing effective cooperation with robots and effective human-robot interaction will be to develop trust in them.

By analyzing research on the issue of trust in human-robot interaction, Hancock et al. (2011) modeled trust in human-robot interactions by dividing trust factors into three main groups:

1. Human-related factors, such as engagement, competency, awareness of the situation, and previous experience.
2. Robot-related factors, such as behavior, dependability, robot reliability, predictability, level of automation, failure rates, robot personality, adaptability, robot type, and anthropomorphism.
3. Environmental factors such as culture, communication, shared mental model, complexity of tasks, and physical environment.

Then, in a meta-analysis of research on trust in human-robot interactions and automated machines, K.E. Schaefer et al. (2016) updated the previous model and created a new one (Table 7.1). Among the factors that affect trust in human-robot interactions, one of the most common themes appearing in the literature is

Table 7.1 Descriptive model of human-robot trust based on K (Schaefer, 2013)

Human		*Robot*		*Environment*	
States	*Traits*	*Features*	*Capability*	*Task*	*Team*
Workload	Personality	Level of Automation	Behavior	Risk	Role Interdependence
Stress	Ethnicity	Intelligence	Reliability	Physical Environment	Team Composition
Fatigue	Gender	Robot Type	Errors	Task Type	Shared Mental Models
Attentional Control	Age	Anthropomorphism	Quality	Multitasking	Culture
		Robot Personality	Accuracy		Societal Impact
		Mode of Communication	Feedback		

those related to behavior, ways of reacting, and reliability and making mistakes. Behavior factors will be discussed in Section 5.3. The reliability of social robots is an important factor in the context of trust, and the results show that its increase affects the increase of trust in the context of human-robot interaction (Bailey & Scerbo, 2007). In turn, the low level of error made by the robot has an impact on the development of trust. In overreliance, failure of a high automation level may lead to more serious safety issues than low levels of automation. It may therefore lead to overreliance on automation (Donmez et al., 2006).

The reliability of the robot is an important factor of trust for at least two reasons. First of all, robots make mistakes and will make them, especially in the first stages of implementing them in our daily life. The mistakes of the robot are supposed to be something unintentional, something over which designers and engineers have no direct impact. However, they are undoubtedly going to have a negative impact on our trust in robots. A study conducted by Salem et al. (2015) shows interaction with household social robot. The test consisted of two conditions, the correct one where the robot correctly and smoothly navigated the participant to the target, while the second incorrect condition where the robot moved inconsistently, did not remember the user's choice, and rotated around itself from time to time. It was shown that people tended to trust the robot more and perceive it as more reliable in the first correct condition. The second reason for the importance of reliability is the fact that the robot's mistakes will cause a breach of trust in the first place; therefore, in research, we should also focus on developing methods to rebuild it (Kok & Soh, 2020).

Building trust in human-robot interaction based on reliability requires an understanding of possible errors and failures. Honig and Oron-Gilad (2018) proposed a classification of failures occurring during human-robot interaction, where they distinguish two main types: technical failures and interaction failures. Technical failures can be caused by hardware problems or software system problems. In contrast, the causes of interaction failures can be environmental uncertainties or human behavior. Each failure can be further characterized by the following attributes:

1. Functional Severity: criticality of the failure to the robot's functioning (non-critical, recoverable, terminal).
2. Social Severity: criticality of the failure to future acceptance of the robot's services (non-critical, recoverable, unrecoverable).
3. Relevance: relevance of the fault to different robot systems, which can be high (relevant to almost all robotic systems), medium (relevant only to some robotic systems), or low (highly specialized failures).
4. Frequency: how often the failure occurs (never, sporadic, regularly, frequently).
5. Condition: the context in which the fault and failure occurred.
6. Symptoms: indicators used to identify the failure.

(Honig & Oron-Gilad, 2018)

However, the most common group of failures are technical failures, such as:

1. failure by the robot to perform a given task;
2. performing a wrong action or colliding with an obstacle;
3. crush;
4. problems with correct expression;
5. repetitions without the need for any action;
6. behave in an unpredictable way;
7. making a mistake due to lack of knowledge on a given subject;
8. questions for human assistance.

But we can also present several strategies aimed at mitigating the effects of mistakes made and rebuilding trust by the robot, for example:

1. informing users about the capabilities of the robot and warning them that they may make some mistakes;
2. a courtesy strategy, that is, an apology for making a mistake;
3. informing the user about the cause of a given failure;
4. compensation for a mistake;
5. asking for human help to correct the mistake;
6. re-executing a task that the robot performed incorrectly;
7. presenting an alternative solution to the problem.

Conducted research (Cameron et al., 2021; Hamacher et al., 2016; Lee et al., 2010) in which robots made mistakes and tried to mitigate them showed that apology positively influenced the assessment of the robot as likable, while negatively influenced the assessment of its competence, while explaining how the error was detected positively influenced its perceived competence. Therefore, the studies showed that trust based on perceived liking for the robot had a much greater impact on willingness to use it than trust based on perceived capabilities.

Research on this topic of reliability shows that making any attempt to rebuild trust is an approach worth using as part of human-robot interaction. Research shows that even the occurrence of errors can be easily eliminated. Important further research in this area was conducted under natural conditions. Reliability and correcting your mistakes are important factors that influence trust, but it is worth looking at the cognitive aspects that affect the improvement or reduction of trust in human-robot interaction.

7.5.2 Robot's appearance

Short-term and emotional trust is based on positive first impressions of robots. In this context, the main factor in trustworthiness is physical appearance. In human-human interaction, the visual look is important; even if we later rationalize our experiences, the perception imposes positive or negative feelings on the other person. What we intuitively realize is also confirmed by scientific research: physical attractiveness allows social interaction, especially in people of opposite sex in heterosexual people (Reis et al., 1982). In a professional relationship, the appearance of the physician matters in trust, for example, the preference of patients for doctors and their staff to dress professionally (Sams, 2002). The appearance will also be important in interaction with the artificial agent; it will determine how we will treat the robot, and whether it will be able to trust it in a short time.

Therefore, trust with the robot is based on short perceived trust, which refers to an individual's first impressions or an assessment of how much trust should be attributed to the robot trustee. This factor is usually dependent on the trustor's personal preferences and preconceptions in relation to the appearance of the robot (Khalid et al., 2021). Appearance includes the physical characteristics of the robot, such as the shape of the robot, its size, facial features (if the robot has a face), having arms, the presence and location of LEDs, or the degree of freedom in expressing movements. In this case, the configuration and design possibilities are very limited. The appearance of the robot is designed only once; it is not possible to change the appearance of the robot during its operation. In a few cases, there are some configuration options for the appearance, for example, the ability to use tablets in place of the robot's head (a robot such as *Misty 2* design by *Misty Robotics*) or on the torso (a robot such as *Pepper* design by *Softbank Robotics*); in the case of more advanced robots, it is possible to replace different types of grippers in the arm (a robot such as *TIAgo* design by *PAL robotics*), while in contact with sex robots, it is possible to change the hairstyle or genitals (such an option offers *Robot Companion Sex Dolls*). However, in most cases, the appearance of robots is very static.

Trust will therefore be based on how we perceive robots. Already in the early work on social robotics, Bartneck et al. (2009) distinguished the levels of how we perceive robots:

1. anthropomorphization of robots means the attribution of a human form, human characteristics, or human behavior to nonhuman things.
2. animacy of robots, experience how inanimate things resemble living organisms.
3. likeability, is positive first impressions toward robots,
4. perceived robot intelligence – the occurrence of rational behavior during interaction with the robot
5. feeling of trust and safety in the robot's company – important in the perception of robots, ensuring that the robot will not harm us and that we will be able to rely on it in a specific situation.

The first two dimensions are specifically related to the appearance of the robot. However, let us focus on the most important dimension in this aspect:

anthropomorphization or the similarity of a simple robot to a human is one of the main domains of trust in the human-robot interaction. Multiple studies show that people prefer technologies with anthropomorphic characteristics (Miesler, 2012; Riek et al., 2009; Waytz et al., 2014); therefore, people also trust a more humanoid robot over a less humanoid robot, when robots assume the role of caretaker (Erebak & Turgut, 2019). Designing even such subtle features of the robot as simple facial expressions affects trust. People are more trusting of the robot with a socially motivated facial expression compared to a robot with a neutral expression or one that simply mimics (Gonsior et al., 2011).

Of course, we cannot design one universal robot appearance that inspires the most trust in people, as it depends on the context and social space. In studies in child-robot interaction, it was observed that little boys prefer robots that resemble men or boys in appearance (Lu¨cking et al., 2016; Sandygulova & O'Hare, 2016) and when the robot was supposed to act as a tutor, it was supposed to resemble a teacher for credibility (van Straten et al., 2020). In the context of robots in the museum space, it was important to look like a guide and have arms that allowed gesticulation. This appearance caused more interest in a given exhibition (Gasteiger et al., 2021). In turn, the use of a BellaBot robot that resembles a cat in the shopping space attracts new customers with its cute look and fulfills the marketing purpose, and people also trust the robot recommendation (Dabrowska-Cydzik, 2022). The seal-like *PARO* robot has successfully performed a therapeutic role in nursing homes for the elderly. Its animal appearance, including its soft fur, gave it the feel of a real pet, without the negative consequences of having pets, the elderly were happy to be in his company (Shibata, 2012).

As research shows, anthropomorphic or animal appearance inspires people's trust and attachment to robots. Even if some robots do not resemble human shapes, and especially faces, people often see them in robots. People often look for faces in robots, Wodehouse et al. (2018) propose a scale facial phenomena in robots: 1) functional robots, usually industrial machines without anthropomorphic features, 2) robot-assistant, acts as a helper. It differs in appearance from anthropomorphism, but can take zoomorphic or biomorphic forms to appear friendly, 3) humanoid – the form resembles a very simplified, geometric human figure, 4) android – is characterized by greater complexity of form and functionality than a humanoid, while remaining clearly a mechanical robot, and 5) uncanny – the robot's form imitates the human one, while remaining noticeably artificial. It should be noted that too much similarity in the appearance of a robot to a human can result in a phenomenon called the Uncanny Valley (Mori et al., 2012). When the agent has become very realistic, but not yet perfectly humanlike, trustworthiness drops, and humans become rather anxious and uncomfortable in continuing interaction with the robot (Ghazali et al., 2018).

Therefore, appearance is an important factor in building trust. However, this is a factor only for short-term and emotional trust, in order to achieve long-term trust, it is necessary to implement appropriate robot behavior and cognitive modules.

7.5.3 Robot's behavior

It should be remembered that today's social robots are primarily automatic and autonomous agents. The operation of robots should be independent of any human control (although we can include controlling methodology such as Wizard-of-Oz, however, in the wide application of robots this methodology will not be applicable), while designing and programming robots should take into account many expected and unexpected events. In the event of their occurrence, the robot must behave appropriately.

However, anthropomorphism does not necessarily have to be manifested in the appearance of the robot. Instead, the behavior or movements of the robot can give it human-like characteristics. If the robot behaves in accordance with the adopted social code, it will be conducive to building trust in the robot, including long-term trust (Fink, 2012; M.V. Law et al., 2019). As already mentioned, the behavior of the robot must be reliable, that is, free from technical errors, failures, long reaction times, or crushes, to ensure trust. The effectiveness of individual behaviors is also important. In any case, these are technical reliability issues. On the other hand, especially for social and domestic robots, social behavior seems to be particularly important here. Therefore, behavioral aspects, including repertoire of hand and body gestures, gaze, and making eye contact, facial expressions, or speech-based behaviors (e.g., prosody and whining), or behaviors that can only be performed by robots, that is, LED lighting, displaying messages on screens, playing special sounds, or transforming (reshaping) your components (body). In the context of behavior, performing behaviors perceived as social, such as social codes, expressing emotions, gesturing, etc. makes the robot more trustworthy (Rossi, 2018; van den Brule et al., 2014).

When analyzing movements, you need to relate them especially to arms, hands, or grippers. In assessing behavior, it is important to how precise the movements are, whether they are slow or rapid movements, what the effect of a given movement (whether it allows you to move an object, if so, with what weight or with what delicacy) and also whether movements and gestures are culturally accepted. In terms of efficiency, it will be important to perform tasks quickly, that is, fast movements by the robot. However, some research found that participants tended to trust robots that performed tasks more slowly than those that performed tasks quickly (Bahner et al., 2008). So it all depends on the purpose of the robot, in the case of an industrial or cleaning household robot, speed of movement will be a desirable and trustworthy feature, while in the case of humanoid social robots we would expect rather calm movements, otherwise fast movements could be perceived as dangerous. However, in the context of speed of operation, the information provided by the robot increases awareness of the situation of the person interacting, thus influencing their trust (Wang et al., 2010). Another study has shown that prompt feedback from a robot is essential to maintaining trust when interacting with a human (Tsui et al., 2010).

In human-human face-to-face communication to reach personal honesty, competence, and reliability, and so about their trustworthiness, evidence is provided by the context of speaking, facial expressions, and gestures of the person (O'Neill, 2020). But also, imitation of human gestures has the effect of humanizing robots, so people would respond to the nonverbal behavior of agents in the same way as they would respond to other people; therefore, similar mental models are created with respect to the reception of nonverbal communication in human-human and human-robot interactions (Khalid et al., 2021; Washburn et al., 2021). Studies show that participants during human-robot interaction under gesture conditions felt greater social interaction, enjoyment, and participation over the course of three weeks than participants under no gesture conditions (Kim et al., 2013); therefore, in the long term, gestures influence trust factors. Gestures are so important because it allows us to manifest cognitive aspects like emotions that will be described in Section 5.4.

The ability to continuously perform robot tasks with expressive and personalized behaviors also helps build trust. Current research also explores social robot architectures for gaze-mediated human-robot interactions. The gaze of the eye is an important mode of communication. It allows people to better understand each other's intentions, desires, interests, etc. (Jarosz et al., 2019). In terms of human-robot interaction design, the issue of maintaining eye contact requires the use of relatively simple algorithms to detect a human face and then, in a humanoid robot, move its head to follow the human gaze (Admoni & Scassellati, 2017). The gaze of the robot can also be referred to as joint attention because it involves sharing the focus of attention with a common object, so this interaction between the robot and the human user directs its gaze to a common object of interest, giving the impression of a more realistic interaction (Huang & Thomaz, 2010; Moore et al., 2014). However, wrong or too intrusive design of the gaze modules in robots may occur, the gaze aversion which is the intentional redirection away from the face of an interlocutor. Therefore, a human user shifts gaze away from the main direction of gaze, which is typically a partner's face (Andrist et al., 2014). Thus, each occurrence of a factor causing discomfort will reduce trust toward robot.

Speech also affects trust. Speech programming seems to be important, not only in the content spoken by the robot, but in the way the robot communicates, so what is the modulation, accent, and timbre of the robot's voice (Torre and White, 2021)? For example, the Pepper robot in its starting configuration has a sexless, childish voice, which can make it seem trustworthy in casual interactions and one we can sympathize with. However, in professional relationships, such voice modulation may seem too unreliable. However, in this case, robots, as well as intelligent agents in general, have a significant advantage over humans. Voice perception will affect emotional intelligence. If the human voice of the interlocutor does not suit us, it can lead to irrational prejudices, in the case of a robot, with a small configuration, we can change the speech modulator or even adjust the tone of speech to the user's preferences.

7.5.4 Robot's cognition

The behavior of the robot is therefore relatively easy to program. Usually, a certain course of activities that the robot is to perform is predetermined. After a longer interaction, people are able to pick up certain rules on which the robot works, and this will lead to fatigue and lower trust in the robot. Thus, modern social robotics faces the challenge of designing cognitive modules based on advanced methods of artificial intelligence.

Cognitive aspects, including the ability to remember information about a particular user from past interactions or the ability to learn about individual user behaviors. This also applies to the ability to read the internal states of the user, such as his affective feelings. Designing cognitive modules is therefore a challenge in terms of programming, and it often requires the use of not only an individual robot but also numerous peripheral tools (e.g., smartphones, smartwatches, cameras, information from sensors from other places, such as cars, and in the near future data from cyborg technologies inside our bodies), which will be combined with a robot thanks to the architecture of the Internet of Things. But it is also a huge undertaking in the context of cognitive science, which requires understanding, reading, and modeling human emotions, modules for making ethical decisions or creating mental models that can be implemented in artificial agents.

The ability to learn new phenomena is one of the main challenges of artificial intelligence. In relation to already embodied robots, this aspect primarily concerns the ability to distinguish and remember individual users, but also applies to complex phenomena, such as remembering past events by the robot and, based on them, forming new interactions so that they are adequate to the past and current event. Simply remembering the user's name will significantly improve future interaction with the robot.

Another issue related to cognitive aspects is to recognize internal human states, especially human emotions. As we mentioned earlier, the role of emotion is in conjunction with the affective dimensions of trust. From the late 1990s, affective computing began to develop, with the goal of being able to read and process human emotions by information systems. In particular, it concerns the following areas:

1. Methods of recognizing the emotional states of users of computers, mobile devices, and robots on the basis of various characteristics (facial expressions, body posture, physiological parameters, voice, text, behavioral patterns);
2. designing communication channels, taking into account affective and cognitive states, based on multimodal information channels;
3. creating techniques to assess frustration, stress, and mood indirectly, through natural interaction and conversation;
4. the use of emotional intelligence mechanisms in information technology, which would particularly respond to negative emotions and moods of users of these systems;

5. developing technologies to improve self-awareness of the emotional state and the selective ability to limit certain emotional states;
6. increasing understanding of how affects and emotions affect personal health through self-tracking systems and wearable technologies;
7. simulations of emotional states for virtual characters and robots;
8. research on ethical issues in affective computing.

(Calvo et al., 2015; Picard, 2000; Tao & Tan, 2005)

Affective computing has proper application in the field of social robotics, and the field of artificial emotions focuses on developing robots capable of mimicking the human vocabulary of affective communication, from nod and gesture to gaze, tone of voice, etc. Research in this regard focuses on the use of computer vision techniques to read emotions, especially from the micro-expression of the human face, based on Ekman's model, we can read six basic emotions (anger, disgust, fear, happiness, sadness, and surprise) (Ekman, 2004), but also from facial expressions we can read the valence and arousal of the emotional states. Robots that react to people's emotions in a society-accepted way appeared to be more friendly and credible (Blazejowska et al., 2023; Oh et al., 2020; Schouten et al., 2022).

But there are numerous concerns about robotic expressions of emotion. Sullins (2012) identifies the simulation of emotions as a profoundly unethical trick, because, as we can be easily fooled through such displays into believing, indeed, feeling on our part that the machine somehow has emotion and so responding in kind with emotions of our own. This is especially true of sex robots with whom someone can establish a very close relationship, thereby destroying personal relationships with other people. In turn, Charles Ess (2020) is even more critical:

> *Building AIs and social robots that seek to evoke our trust in part by mimicking the relevant emotive signals of trust is certainly possible, but given that these signals derive from solely artificial emotions, such "design for affective trust" (my phrase) would be the height of deception and so a complete violation of any extant trust relationship.*

Therefore, common sense must be used when modeling emotional modules because too faithful mapping of the characteristics of human emotions will trigger the Uncanny Valley phenomenon, while too strong an impact of emotional modules on a person may be perceived as manipulation.

The cognitive aspects of robot architecture also incorporate ethical situational or contextual awareness. This allows the robot's behavior to be adapted not only to the emotional state of the human interaction partner, but also to the current situation and context, resulting in the robot exhibiting the most appropriate and effective reaction among the given context factors. Such problems have been illustrated by Pandey et al. (2017); for example, a robot designed to greet a repeat visitor to a mall with a message such as "You bought those running shoes last time, I hope they are comfortable" could make personal connections with visitors. But this might not be socially prudent and may even backfire if the visitor is male, the bought object is a piece of jewelry, and the visitor is with a lady friend who was not the recipient of the jewelry.

Aspects are the biggest challenge, not only in technical terms but also in terms of social and ethical implications. Poorly designed modules may violate established cultural codes, may lead to privacy violations, and other abuses. On the other hand, a multifaceted and natural conversation with a robot is crucial for building a relationship based on trust.

7.6 Conclusion

When robots begin to appear closer and closer to us, becoming social subjects, trust in them may become a factor that has a real impact on the quality of our lives. That is why research in this field of human-robot interaction research is so important, so that people are not disappointed by them, not so much at the stage of implementation, but at the stage of designing robots for everyday use.

An important issue to consider is the problem of excessive trust in robots, in particular when robots will accompany us in emergency and dangerous situations. For example, in a study by Booth et al. (2017), people ignored an emergency exit sign during a fire hazard simulation to follow a robot that had been operating inefficiently before the fire broke out. In another study, investigating human-robot trust during high-risk situations, participants were not reluctant to let an unfamiliar robot into restricted rooms. Overtrust occurs when people take too much risk and fear an entity that is trusted to mitigate this risk. This raises a pressing question: in what way a robot must be defective before participants stop following its instructions (Robinette et al., 2016)? These examples were intended to show that only an appropriate level of trust in robots will allow us to use them properly (Kok & Soh, 2020).

Therefore, when implementing advanced technologies equipped with artificial intelligence systems that very faithfully resemble the relationship with another human being, it should be taken into account whether, in the name of building trust between man and machine, it will not consciously or unknowingly cause a feeling of harm. The Fourth Industrial Revolution is focused on the development of technology, but is not indifferent to the observance of ethical issues. So the proper development of technology is only possible with the multifaceted social forecast about the consequence of the use of intelligent machines in society.

7.7 Acknowledgment

This chapter was supported by a grant from the Priority Research Area Digi-World PSP: U1U/P06/NO/02.30 under the Strategic Programme Excellence Initiative at Jagiellonian University.

Note

1 https://mars.nasa.gov/mars2020/spacecraft/rover/communications/

References

Admoni, H., & Scassellati, B. (2017). Social eye gaze in human-robot interaction: A review. *Journal of Human-Robot Interaction*, *6*(1), 25–63.

Agbejule, A., Rapo, J., & Saarikoski, L. (2021). Vertical and horizontal trust and team learning: The role of organizational climate. *International Journal of Managing Projects in Business*. https://www.emerald.com/insight/content/doi/10.1108/IJMPB-05-2020-0155/full/html

Algan, Y., & Cahuc, P. (2014). Trust, growth, and well-being: New evidence and policy implications. In *Handbook of economic growth* (Vol. 2, pp. 49–120). Elsevier.

Alsharif, S., Kuzmicheva, O., & Gr¨aser, A. (2016). Gaze gesture-based human robot interface. In *Technische Unterstu¨tzungssysteme, die die Menschen wirklich wollen* (p. 339). https://www.researchgate.net/publication/313896309_Gaze_Gesture-Based_Human_Robot_Interface

Anderson, W., & Ng, K. (2020, June). Conscious design manifesto and principles, a willwai perspective. *Medium*. https://medium.com/@willwai/conscious-design-manifesto-and -principles-a-will-wai-perspective-203b47cdb629

Andrist, S., Tan, X. Z., Gleicher, M., & Mutlu, B. (2014). *Conversational gaze aversion for humanlike robots*. 2014 9th ACM/IEEE International Conference on Human-Robot Interaction (hri), pp. 25–32.

Anumandla, S. R., Bray, L. C. J., Thibeault, C. M., Hoang, R. V., Dascalu, S. M., Harris, F. C., & Goodman, P. H. (2011). *Modeling oxytocin induced neurorobotic trust and intent recognition in human-robot interaction*. The 2011 international joint conference on neural networks, pp. 3213–3219.

Asimov, I. (1942). Runaround. *Astounding Science Fiction*, *29*(1), 94–103.

Awad, E., Dsouza, S., Kim, R., Schulz, J., Henrich, J., Shariff, A., Bonnefon, J.-F., & Rahwan, I. (2018). The moral machine experiment. *Nature*, *563*(7729), 59–64.

Bahner, J. E., Hu¨per, A.-D., & Manzey, D. (2008). Misuse of automated decision aids: Complacency, automation bias and the impact of training experience. *International Journal of Human-Computer Studies*, *66*(9), 688–699.

Baier, A. (1986). Trust and antitrust. *Ethics*, *96*(2), 231–260.

Bailey, N. R., & Scerbo, M. W. (2007). Automation-induced complacency for monitoring highly reliable systems: The role of task complexity, system experience, and operator trust. *Theoretical Issues in Ergonomics Science*, *8*(4), 321–348.

Bartneck, C., Kuli´c, D., Croft, E., & Zoghbi, S. (2009). Measurement instruments for the anthropomorphism, animacy, likeability, perceived intelligence, and perceived safety of robots. *International Journal of Social Robotics*, *1*(1), 71–81.

Beasley, R. A. (2012). Medical robots: Current systems and research directions. *Journal of Robotics*. https://www.hindawi.com/journals/jr/2012/401613/

Becker, L. C. (1996). Trust as noncognitive security about motives. *Ethics*, *107*(1), 43–61.

Belpaeme, T., Kennedy, J., Ramachandran, A., Scassellati, B., & Tanaka, F. (2018). Social robots for education: A review. *Science robotics*, *3*(21), eaat5954.

Beugelsdijk, S., De Groot, H. L., & Van Schaik, A. B. (2004). Trust and economic growth: A robustness analysis. *Oxford Economic Papers*, *56*(1), 118–134.

Bieńkowska, A., Walecka-Jankowska, K., Zabl ocka-Kluczka, A., & Zimmer, J. (2018). Influence of intra-organizational trust on organizational outcomes. *Operations Research and Decisions*, *28*.

Blind, P. K. (2007). Building trust in government in the twenty-first century: Review of literature and emerging issues. In *7th global forum on reinventing government building trust in government* (Vol. 2007, pp. 26–29). https://www.almendron.com/tribuna/wp-content/uploads/2016/11/building-trust-in-government-in-the-twenty-first-century.pdf

Booth, S., Tompkin, J., Pfister, H., Waldo, J., Gajos, K., & Nagpal, R. (2017). *Piggybacking robots: Human-robot overtrust in university dormitory security*. Proceedings of the 2017 ACM/IEEE International Conference on Human-Robot Interaction, pp. 426–434.

Borenstein, J. (2008). The ethics of autonomous military robots. *Studies in Ethics, Law, and Technology*, *2*(1).

Bostrom, N. (2017). *Superintelligence*. Dunod.

Breazeal, C., Takanishi, A., & Kobayashi, T. (2008). *Social robots that interact with people*. https://www.researchgate.net/publication/227252198_Social_Robots_that_Interact_with_People

Brockner, J., Siegel, P. A., Daly, J. P., Tyler, T., & Martin, C. (1997). When trust matters: The moderating effect of outcome favorability. *Administrative Science Quarterly*, 558–583.

Błażejowska, G., Gruba, Ł., Indurkhya, B., & Gunia, A. (2023, January). A study on the role of affective feedback in robot-assisted learning. *Sensors*, *23*(3), 1181. doi:10.3390/s23031181

Calvo, R. A., D'Mello, S., Gratch, J. M., & Kappas, A. (2015). *The Oxford handbook of affective computing*. Oxford Library of Psychology.

Cameron, D., de Saille, S., Collins, E. C., Aitken, J. M., Cheung, H., Chua, A., Loh, E. J., & Law, J. (2021). The effect of social-cognitive recovery strategies on likability, capability and trust in social robots. *Computers in Human Behavior*, *114*, 106561.

Casimir, G., Lee, K., & Loon, M. (2012). Knowledge sharing: Influences of trust, commitment and cost. *Journal of Knowledge Management*, *16*, 740–753. https://doi.org/10.1108/13673271211262781

Castelfranchi, C., & Falcone, R. (2010). *Trust theory: A socio-cognitive and computational model*. John Wiley & Sons.

Castelfranchi, C., & Falcone, R. (2020). Trust: Perspectives in cognitive science. In *The Routledge handbook of trust and philosophy* (pp. 214–228). Routledge.

Chow, W. S., & Chan, L. S. (2008). Social network, social trust and shared goals in organizational knowledge sharing. *Information & Management*, *45*(7), 458–465.

Dabrowska-Cydzik, J. (2022, October). *Carrefour i pepsico ponadprzecietnie zadowolone z robota kerfu's*. www.wirtualnemedia.pl/artykul/kerfus-robot-jak-dziala-gdziezobaczyc

D'Cruz, J. (2019). Humble trust. *Philosophical Studies*, *176*(4), 933–953.

D'Cruz, J. (2020). Trust and distrust. In *The Routledge handbook of trust and philosophy* (pp. 41–51). Routledge.

de Fine Licht, K., & Bru¨lde, B. (2021). On defining "reliance" and "trust": Purposes, conditions of adequacy, and new definitions. *Philosophia*, *49*(5), 1981–2001.

Deng, E., Mutlu, B., & Mataric, M. J. (2019). Embodiment in socially interactive robots. *Foundations and Trends® in Robotics*, *7*(4), 251–356.

Devillers, L. (2020). Human-robot interactions and affecting computing: The ethical implications. *Dagstuhl Reports*, *10*(1), 19, ISSN 2192–5283.

Devlin, K. (2020). *Turned on: Science, sex and robots*. Bloomsbury Publishing.
Dieber, J., & Kirrane, S. (2022). A novel model usability evaluation framework (muse) for explainable artificial intelligence. *Information Fusion*, *81*, 143–153.
Donmez, B., Boyle, L. N., Lee, J. D., & McGehee, D. V. (2006). Drivers' attitudes toward imperfect distraction mitigation strategies. *Transportation Research Part F: Traffic Psychology and Behaviour*, *9*(6), 387–398.
Dunning, D., Fetchenhauer, D., & Schlosser, T. M. (2012). Trust as a social and emotional act: Noneconomic considerations in trust behavior. *Journal of Economic Psychology*, *33*(3), 686–694.
Ekman, P. (2004). Emotions revealed. *BMJ*, *328*(Suppl S5).
Elgar, F. J., & Aitken, N. (2011). Income inequality, trust and homicide in 33 countries. *European Journal of Public Health*, *21*(2), 241–246.
Engelmann, J. B., & Fehr, E. (2017). The neurobiology of trust and social decision-making: The important role of emotions. In *Trust in social dilemmas* (pp. 33–56). Oxford University Press.
Erebak, S., & Turgut, T. (2019). Caregivers' attitudes toward potential robot coworkers in elder care. *Cognition, Technology & Work*, *21*(2), 327–336.
Ervas, F., Gunia, A., Lorini, G., Stojanov, G., & Indurkhya, B. (2022). Fostering safe behaviors via metaphor-based nudging technologies. In *International conference on software engineering and formal methods* (pp. 53–63).
Ess, C. M. (2020). Trust and information and communication technologies. In *The Routledge handbook of trust and philosophy* (pp. 405–420). Routledge.
EU, E. U. (2019). *Regulation (eu) 2019/2144 of the European parliament and of the council of ministers*. European Commission Brussels.
Fawcett, S. E., Jones, S. L., Fawcett, A. M. (2012). Supply chain trust: The catalyst for collaborative innovation. *Business Horizons*, *55*(2), 163–178.
Ferru´s, R. M., & Somonte, M. D. (2016). Design in robotics based in the voice of the customer of household robots. *Robotics and Autonomous Systems*, *79*, 99–107.
Fink, J. (2012). Anthropomorphism and human likeness in the design of robots and human-robot interaction. In *International conference on social robotics* (pp. 199–208).
Frost-Arnold, K. (2020). Trust and epistemic responsibility. In *The Routledge handbook of trust and philosophy* (pp. 64–75). Routledge.
Gambetta, D., et al. (2000). Can we trust. *Trust: Making and Breaking Cooperative Relations*, *13*(2000), 213–237.
Gasparetto, A., & Scalera, L. (2019). A brief history of industrial robotics in the 20th century. *Advances in Historical Studies*, *8*(1), 24–35.
Gasteiger, N., Hellou, M., & Ahn, H. S. (2021). Deploying social robots in museum settings: A quasi-systematic review exploring purpose and acceptability. *International Journal of Advanced Robotic Systems*, *18*(6), 17298814211066740.
Ghazali, A. S., Ham, J., Barakova, E. I., & Markopoulos, P. (2018). Effects of robot facial characteristics and gender in persuasive human-robot interaction. *Frontiers in Robotics and AI*, *5*, 73.
Gillath, O., Ai, T., Branicky, M. S., Keshmiri, S., Davison, R. B., & Spaulding, R. (2021). Attachment and trust in artificial intelligence. *Computers in Human Behavior*, *115*, 106607.
Goldberg, S. C. (2020). Trust and reliance 1. In *The Routledge handbook of trust and philosophy* (pp. 97–108). https://www.taylorfrancis.com/chapters/edit/10.4324/9781315542294-8/trust-reliance-1-sanford-goldberg

Gonsior, B., Sosnowski, S., Mayer, C., Blume, J., Radig, B., Wollherr, D., & Ku¨hnlenz, K. (2011). *Improving aspects of empathy and subjective performance for hri through mirroring facial expressions. 2011 ro-man* (pp. 350–356). https://scholar.google.dk/citations?view_op=view_citation&hl=ja&user=WGdQIlEAAAAJ&citation_for_view=WGdQIlEAAAAJ:9yKSN-GCB0IC
Grodzinsky, F., Miller, K., & Wolf, M. J. (2020). Trust in artificial agents. In *The Routledge handbook of trust and philosophy* (pp. 298–312). Routledge.
Guinot, J., & Chiva, R. (2019). Vertical trust within organizations and performance: A systematic review. *Human Resource Development Review*, *18*(2), 196–227.
Guo, L., Liang, J., Zhu, Y., Luo, Y., Sun, L., & Zheng, X. (2019). Collaborative filtering recommendation based on trust and emotion. *Journal of Intelligent Information Systems*, *53*(1), 113–135.
Hamacher, A., Bianchi-Berthouze, N., Pipe, A. G., & Eder, K. (2016). *Believing in Bert: Using expressive communication to enhance trust and counteract operational error in physical human-robot interaction*. 2016 25th IEEE International Symposium on Robot and Human Interactive Communication (ro-man), pp. 493–500.
Hancock, P. A., Billings, D. R., Schaefer, K. E., Chen, J. Y., De Visser, E. J., & Parasuraman, R. (2011). A meta-analysis of factors affecting trust in human-robot interaction. *Human Factors*, *53*(5), 517–527.
Hardin, R. (2001). Distrust. *Bulletin & Review*, *81*, 495.
Hardin, R. (2002). *Trust and trustworthiness*. Russell Sage Foundation.
Harris, J., & Zaheer, A. (2006). Interorganizational trust. In *Handbook of strategic alliances* (pp. 169–197). https://www.darden.virginia.edu/sites/default/files/inline-files/Zaheer_Harris_2006.pdf
Hawley, K. (2014). Trust, distrust and commitment. *Nouˆs*, *48*(1), 1–20.
Hegel, F., Muhl, C., Wrede, B., Hielscher-Fastabend, M., & Sagerer, G. (2009). *Understanding social robots*. 2009 2nd International Conferences on Advances in Computer-Human Interactions, pp. 169–174.
Heinrichs, M., Baumgartner, T., Kirschbaum, C., & Ehlert, U. (2003). Social support and oxytocin interact to suppress cortisol and subjective responses to psychosocial stress. *Biological Psychiatry*, *54*(12), 1389–1398.
Hellstrom, T. (2013). On the moral responsibility of military robots. *Ethics and Information Technology*, *15*(2), 99–107.
Hengstler, M., Enkel, E., & Duelli, S. (2016). Applied artificial intelligence and trust – the case of autonomous vehicles and medical assistance devices. *Technological Forecasting and Social Change*, *105*, 105–120.
Heuer, T., & Stein, J. (2019). *From HCI to HRI: About users, acceptance and emotions*. International Conference on Human Systems Engineering and Design: Future Trends and Applications, pp. 149–153.
Hoffner, S., Porzel, R., Hedblom, M. M., Pomarlan, M., Cangalovic, V. S., Pfau, J., Bateman, J., & Malaka, R. (2022). Deep understanding of everyday activity commands for household robots. *Semantic Web*(Preprint), 1–15.
Holton, R. (1994). Deciding to trust, coming to believe. *Australasian Journal of Philosophy*, *72*(1), 63–76.
Honig, S., & Oron-Gilad, T. (2018). Understanding and resolving failures in human-robot interaction: Literature review and model development. *Frontiers in Psychology*, *9*, 861.

Hor´akov´a, J., & Kelemen, J. (2009). Artificial living beings and robots: One root, variety of influences. *Artificial Life and Robotics*, *13*(2), 555–560.
Huang, C.-M., & Thomaz, A. L. (2010). *Joint attention in human-robot interaction*. 2010 AAAI Fall Symposium Series.
Hummel, D., Toreini, P., & Maedche, A. (2018). *Improving digital nudging using attentive user interfaces: Theory development and experiment design*. 13th International Conference on Design Science Research in Information Systems and Technology (Desrist).
Inglehart, R. (1999). Trust, well-being and democracy. *Democracy and Trust*, *88*, 88–120.
Jarosz, M., Nawrocki, P., Placzkiewicz, L., Sniezynski, B., Zielinski, M., & Indurkhya, B. (2019). Detecting gaze direction using robot-mounted and mobile-device cameras. *Computer Science*, *20*.
Ji, W., & Wang, L. (2019). Industrial robotic machining: A review. *The International Journal of Advanced Manufacturing Technology*, *103*(1), 1239–1255.
Johnson, D., & Grayson, K. (2005). Cognitive and affective trust in service relationships. *Journal of Business Research*, *58*(4), 500–507.
Kahn, L. (2017). Military robots and the likelihood of armed combat. In *Robot ethics 2.0: From autonomous cars to artificial intelligence* (pp. 274–287). https://academic.oup.com/book/2320/chapter-abstract/142471563?redirectedFrom=fulltext
Kaplan, A., & Haenlein, M. (2019). Siri, Siri, in my hand: Who's the fairest in the land? on the interpretations, illustrations, and implications of artificial intelligence. *Business Horizons*, *62*(1), 15–25.
Kenning, P. (2008). The influence of general trust and specific trust on buying behaviour. *International Journal of Retail & Distribution Management*. https://www.emerald.com/insight/content/doi/10.1108/09590550810873938/full/html
Khalid, H. M., Helander, M. G., & Lin, M.-H. (2021). Determinants of trust in human-robot interaction: Modeling, measuring, and predicting. In *Trust in human-robot interaction* (pp. 85–121). Elsevier.
Khavas, Z. R., Ahmadzadeh, S. R., & Robinette, P. (2020). Modeling trust in human-robot interaction: A survey. In *International conference on social robotics* (pp. 529–541).
Kim, A., Han, J., Jung, Y., & Lee, K. (2013). *The effects of familiarity and robot gesture on user acceptance of information*. 2013 8th ACM/IEEE International Conference on Human-Robot Interaction (Hri), pp. 159–160.
Kok, B. C., & Soh, H. (2020). Trust in robots: Challenges and opportunities. *Current Robotics Reports*, *1*(4), 297–309.
Kosfeld, M., Heinrichs, M., Zak, P. J., Fischbacher, U., & Fehr, E. (2005). Oxytocin increases trust in humans. *Nature*, *435*(7042), 673–676.
Krueger, F., & Meyer-Lindenberg, A. (2019). Toward a model of interpersonal trust drawn from neuroscience, psychology, and economics. *Trends in Neurosciences*, *42*(2), 92–101.
Lahno, B. (2020). Trust and emotion. In *The Routledge handbook of trust and philosophy* (pp. 147–159). Routledge.
Larsson, S., Anneroth, M., Fell¨ander, A., Fell¨ander-Tsai, L., Heintz, F., & ˚Angstr¨om, R. C. (2019). *Sustainable ai: An inventory of the state of knowledge of ethical, social, and legal challenges related to artificial intelligence* (Tech. Rep.). AI Sustainability Center. https://lup.lub.lu.se/search/files/62833751/Larsson et al 2019 SUSTAINABLE AI web ENG 05.pdf

Law, M. V., Jeong, J., Kwatra, A., Jung, M. F., & Hoffman, G. (2019). *Negotiating the creative space in human-robot collaborative design*. Proceedings of the 2019 on Designing Interactive Systems Conference, pp. 645–657.
Law, T., & Scheutz, M. (2021). Trust: Recent concepts and evaluations in human-robot interaction. In C. Nam & J. Lyons (Eds.), *Trust in human-robot interaction* (pp. 27–57). Elsevier. https://hrilab.tufts.edu/publications/law2020trust.pdf
Lee, M. K., Kiesler, S., Forlizzi, J., Srinivasa, S., & Rybski, P. (2010). *Gracefully mitigating breakdowns in robotic services*. 2010 5th ACM/IEEE International Conference on Human-Robot Interaction (Hri), pp. 203–210.
Li, H., Cabibihan, J.-J., & Tan, Y. K. (2011). Towards an effective design of social robots. *International Journal of Social Robotics*, *3*(4), 333–335.
Li, X., Hess, T. J., & Valacich, J. S. (2008). Why do we trust new technology? A study of initial trust formation with organizational information systems. *The Journal of Strategic Information Systems*, *17*(1), 39–71.
Logan, D. E., Breazeal, C., Goodwin, M. S., Jeong, S., O'Connell, B., SmithFreedman, D., Heathers, J., & Weinstock, P. (2019). Social robots for hospitalized children. *Pediatrics*, *144*(1).
Lücking, P., Rohlfing, K., Wrede, B., & Schilling, M. (2016). *Preschoolers' engagement in social interaction with an autonomous robotic system*. 2016 Joint IEEE International Conference on Development and Learning and Epigenetic Robotics (icdl-epirob), pp. 210–216.
Luria, M., Forlizzi, J., & Hodgins, J. (2018). *The effects of eye design on the perception of social robots*. 2018 27th IEEE International Symposium on Robot and Human Interactive Communication (Ro-man), pp. 1032–1037.
Malle, B. F., & Ullman, D. (2021). A multidimensional conception and measure of human-robot trust. In *Trust in human-robot interaction* (pp. 3–25). Elsevier.
Martinho, A., Herber, N., Kroesen, M., & Chorus, C. (2021). Ethical issues in focus by the autonomous vehicles industry. *Transport Reviews*, *41*(5), 556–577.
Mayer, R. C., Davis, J. H., & Schoorman, F. D. (1995). An integrative model of organizational trust. *Academy of Management Review*, *20*(3), 709–734.
McEvily, B., Zaheer, A., & Soda, G. (2021). Network trust. In *Understanding trust in organizations*. Taylor & Francis.
McMyler, B. (2020). Trust and authority. In *The Routledge handbook of trust and philosophy* (pp. 76–87). Routledge.
Messner, S. F., Rosenfeld, R., & Baumer, E. P. (2004). Dimensions of social capital and rates of criminal homicide. *American Sociological Review*, *69*(6), 882–903.
Mhlanga, D. (2022). Human-centered artificial intelligence: The superlative approach to achieve sustainable development goals in the fourth industrial revolution. *Sustainability*, *14*(13), 7804.
Mieczkowski, H., Liu, S. X., Hancock, J., & Reeves, B. (2019). *Helping not hurting: Applying the stereotype content model and bias map to social robotics*. 2019 14th ACM/IEEE International Conference on Human-Robot Interaction (Hri), pp. 222–229.
Miesler, L. (2012). Product choice and anthropomorphic designs: Do consumption goals shape innate preferences for human-like forms? *The Design Journal*, *15*(3), 373–392.
Mirnig, N., Stollnberger, G., Miksch, M., Stadler, S., Giuliani, M., & Tscheligi, M. (2017). To err is robot: How humans assess and act toward an erroneous social robot. *Frontiers in Robotics and AI*, *21*.

Moore, C., Dunham, P. J., & Dunham, P. (2014). *Joint attention: Its origins and role in development*. Psychology Press.
Mori, M., MacDorman, K. F., & Kageki, N. (2012). The uncanny valley [from the field]. *IEEE Robotics & Automation Magazine, 19*(2), 98–100.
Noor, P. (2020). Can we trust ai not to further embed racial bias and prejudice? *BMJ, 368*.
Noorman, M., & Johnson, D. G. (2014). Negotiating autonomy and responsibility in military robots. *Ethics and Information Technology, 16*(1), 51–62.
Oh, S., Lee, J.-Y., & Kim, D. K. (2020). The design of CNN architectures for optimal six basic emotion classification using multiple physiological signals. *Sensors, 20*(3), 866.
O'Neill, O. (2020). Questioning trust. In *The Routledge handbook of trust and philosophy* (pp. 17–27). Routledge.
Ortigue, S., Bianchi-Demicheli, F., Patel, N., Frum, C., & Lewis, J. W. (2010). Neuroimaging of love: FMRI meta-analysis evidence toward new perspectives in sexual medicine. *The Journal of Sexual Medicine, 7*(11), 3541–3552.
Pandey, A. K., Gelin, R., Ruocco, M., Monforte, M., & Siciliano, B. (2017). *When a social robot might learn to support potentially immoral behaviors on the name of privacy*. Proceedings 2017 Conference Human-Robot Interaction (Workshop on Privacy-Sensitive Robotics), pp. 1–4.
Pedersen, N. J. L. L., Ahlstrom-Vij, K., & Kappel, K. (2014). Rational trust. *Synthese, 191*(9), 1953–1955.
Picard, R. W. (2000). *Affective computing*. MIT Press.
Potter, N. N. (2020). Interpersonal trust. In *The Routledge handbook of trust and philosophy* (pp. 243–255). Routledge.
Punyatoya, P. (2018). *Effects of cognitive and affective trust on online customer behavior*. Marketing Intelligence & Planning.
Putnam, R. (1993). The prosperous community: Social capital and public life. *The American Prospect, 13*(4).
Reis, H. T., Wheeler, L., Spiegel, N., Kernis, M. H., Nezlek, J., & Perri, M. (1982). Physical attractiveness in social interaction: 2. Why does appearance affect social experience? *Journal of Personality and Social Psychology, 43*(5), 979.
Riedl, M. O. (2019). Human-centered artificial intelligence and machine learning. *Human Behavior and Emerging Technologies, 1*(1), 33–36.
Riek, L. D., Rabinowitch, T.-C., Chakrabarti, B., & Robinson, P. (2009). *How anthropomorphism affects empathy toward robots*. Proceedings of the 4th ACM/IEEE International Conference on Human Robot Interaction, pp. 245–246.
Robinette, P., Li, W., Allen, R., Howard, A. M., & Wagner, A. R. (2016). *Overtrust of robots in emergency evacuation scenarios*. 2016 11th ACM/IEEE International Conference on Human-Robot Interaction (Hri), pp. 101–108.
Rossi, F. (2018). Building trust in artificial intelligence. *Journal of International Affairs, 72*(1), 127–134.
Rotter, J. B. (1971). Generalized expectancies for interpersonal trust. *American Psychologist, 26*(5), 443.
Russell, S. J. (2010). *Artificial intelligence a modern approach*. Pearson Education, Inc.
Rusu, R. B., Blodow, N., Marton, Z., Soos, A., & Beetz, M. (2007). *Towards 3d object maps for autonomous household robots*. 2007 IEEE/RSJ International Conference on Intelligent Robots and Systems, pp. 3191–3198.

Sahin, H., & Guvenc, L. (2007). Household robotics: Autonomous devices for vacuuming and lawn mowing [applications of control]. *IEEE Control Systems Magazine*, *27*(2), 20–96.

Salem, M., Lakatos, G., Amirabdollahian, F., & Dautenhahn, K. (2015). *Would you trust a (faulty) robot? effects of error, task type and personality on human-robot cooperation and trust*. 2015 10th ACM/IEEE International Conference on Human-Robot Interaction (Hri), pp. 1–8.

Samek, W., & Muller, K.-R. (2019). Towards explainable artificial intelligence. In *Explainable ai: Interpreting, explaining and visualizing deep learning* (pp. 5–22). Springer.

Sams, W. M. (2002). Physician appearance is a matter of trust and responsibility. *Archives of Dermatology*, *138*(4), 518–518.

Sandygulova, A., & O'Hare, G. M. (2016). *Investigating the impact of gender segregation within observational pretend play interaction*. 2016 11th ACM/IEEE International Conference on Human-Robot Interaction (Hri), pp. 399–406.

Sarrica, M., Brondi, S., & Fortunati, L. (2019). How many facets does a "social robot" have? A review of scientific and popular definitions online. *Information Technology & People*. https://link.springer.com/article/10.1007/s43154-020-00035-0

Schaefer, K. E. (2013). *The perception and measurement of human-robot trust* (Doctoral dissertation). University of Central Florida. https://stars.library.ucf.edu/cgi/viewcontent.cgi?article= 3688&context=etd

Schaefer, K. E., Chen, J. Y., Szalma, J. L., & Hancock, P. A. (2016). A meta analysis of factors influencing the development of trust in automation: Implications for understanding autonomy in future systems. *Human Factors*, *58*(3), 377–400.

Schilke, O., Reimann, M., & Cook, K. S. (2021). Trust in social relations. *Annual Review of Sociology*, *47*, 239–259.

Schmahl, K. G., Viering, T. J., Makrodimitris, S., Jahfari, A. N., Tax, D., & Loog, M. (2020). *Is Wikipedia succeeding in reducing gender bias? Assessing changes in gender bias in Wikipedia using word embeddings*. Proceedings of the 4th Workshop on Natural Language Processing and Computational Social Science, pp. 94–103.

Schouten, A. P., Portegies, T. C., Withuis, I., Willemsen, L. M., & Mazerant-Dubois, K. (2022). Robomorphism: Examining the effects of telepresence robots on between-student cooperation. *Computers in Human Behavior*, *126*, 106980.

Schwitzgebel, E. (2021). Belief. In E. N. Zalta (Ed.), *The Stanford encyclopedia of philosophy* (Winter 2021 ed.). Metaphysics Research Lab, Stanford University. https://plato.stanford.edu/archives/win2021/entries/ belief/.

Sepp¨anen, R., Blomqvist, K., & Sundqvist, S. (2007). Measuring interorganizational trust – a critical review of the empirical research in 1990–2003. *Industrial Marketing Management*, *36*(2), 249–265.

Shibata, T. (2012). Therapeutic seal robot as biofeedback medical device: Qualitative and quantitative evaluations of robot therapy in dementia care. *Proceedings of the IEEE*, *100*(8), 2527–2538.

Siau, K., & Wang, W. (2018). Building trust in artificial intelligence, machine learning, and robotics. *Cutter Business Technology Journal*, *31*(2), 47–53.

Smedegaard, C. V. (2019). *Reframing the role of novelty within social Hri: From noise to information*. 2019 14th ACM/IEEE International Conference on Human-Robot Interaction (Hri), pp. 411–420.

Soto, F., Wang, J., Ahmed, R., & Demirci, U. (2020). Medical micro/nanorobots in precision medicine. *Advanced Science*, *7*(21), 2002203.
Stephany, F. (2017). Who are your joneses? socio-specific income inequality and trust. *Social Indicators Research*, *134*(3), 877–898.
Sullins, J. P. (2012). Robots, love, and sex: The ethics of building a love machine. *IEEE Transactions on Affective Computing*, *3*(4), 398–409.
Sztompka, P. (2007). *Zaufanie: fundament spo leczen´stwa*. Wydawnictwo Znak.
Tao, J., & Tan, T. (2005). Affective computing: A review. In *International conference on affective computing and intelligent interaction* (pp. 981–995).
Thaler, R. H., & Sunstein, C. R. (2009). *Nudge: Improving decisions about health, wealth, and happiness*. Penguin.
Tjoa, E., & Guan, C. (2020). A survey on explainable artificial intelligence (xai): Toward medical xai. *IEEE Transactions on Neural Networks and Learning Systems*, *32*(11), 4793–4813.
Torre, I., & White, L. (2021). Trust in vocal human–robot interaction: Implications for robot voice design. In *Voice attractiveness* (pp. 299–316). Springer.
Troccaz, J., Dagnino, G., & Yang, G.-Z. (2019). Frontiers of medical robotics: From concept to systems to clinical translation. *Annual Review of Biomedical Engineering*, *21*, 193–218.
Tsui, K. M., Desai, M., & Yanco, H. A. (2010). *Considering the bystander's perspective for indirect human-robot interaction*. 2010 5th ACM/IEEE International Conference on Human-Robot Interaction (Hri), pp. 129–130.
Tzafrir, S. S., & Eitam-Meilik, M. (2005). The impact of downsizing on trust and employee practices in high tech firms: A longitudinal analysis. *The Journal of High Technology Management Research*, *16*(2), 193–207.
Ullmann-Margalit, E. (2004). *Trust, distrust, and in between*. Russell Sage Foundation.
van den Brule, R., Dotsch, R., Bijlstra, G., Wigboldus, D. H., & Haselager, P. (2014). Do robot performance and behavioral style affect human trust? *International Journal of Social Robotics*, *6*(4), 519–531.
Vanhala, M. (2019). Trust as an organizational knowledge sharing enabler– validation of the impersonal trust scale. *VINE Journal of Information and Knowledge Management Systems*. https://www.emerald.com/insight/content/doi/10.1108/VJIKMS-12-2018-0119/full/html
Vanhala, M., & Ahteela, R. (2011). The effect of HRM practices on impersonal organizational trust. *Management Research Review*. https://www.emerald.com/insight/content/doi/10.1108/01409171111152493/full/html
van Straten, C. L., Peter, J., & Ku¨hne, R. (2020). Child–robot relationship formation: A narrative review of empirical research. *International Journal of Social Robotics*, *12*(2), 325–344.
Vilone, G., & Longo, L. (2021). Notions of explainability and evaluation approaches for explainable artificial intelligence. *Information Fusion*, *76*, 89–106.
Wang, L., Rau, P.-L. P., Evers, V., Robinson, B. K., & Hinds, P. (2010). *When in Rome: The role of culture & context in adherence to robot recommendations*. 2010 5th ACM/IEEE International Conference on Human-Robot Interaction (Hri), pp. 359–366.
Washburn, A., Matsumoto, S., Riek, L. D. (2021). Trust-aware control in proximate human-robot teaming. In *Trust in human-robot interaction* (pp. 353–377). Elsevier.

Waytz, A., Heafner, J., & Epley, N. (2014). The mind in the machine: Anthropomorphism increases trust in an autonomous vehicle. *Journal of Experimental Social Psychology, 52*, 113–117.

Weiss, A., & Manfred, T. (2010). Special issue on robots for future societies: Evaluating social acceptance and societal impact of robots. *International Journal of Social Robotics, 2*(4), 345–346.

Whitener, E. M., Brodt, S. E., Korsgaard, M. A., & Werner, J. M. (1998). Managers as initiators of trust: An exchange relationship framework for understanding managerial trustworthy behavior. *Academy of Management Review, 23*(3), 513–530.

Wodehouse, A., Brisco, R., Broussard, E., & Duffy, A. (2018). Pareidolia: Characterising facial anthropomorphism and its implications for product design. *Journal of Design Research, 16*(2), 83–98.

Yang, K., Qinami, K., Fei-Fei, L., Deng, J., & Russakovsky, O. (2020). *Towards fairer datasets: Filtering and balancing the distribution of the people subtree in the image net hierarchy*. Proceedings of the 2020 Conference on Fairness, Accountability, and Transparency, pp. 547–558.

Young, J. E., Sung, J., Voida, A., Sharlin, E., Igarashi, T., Christensen, H. I., & Grinter, R. E. (2011). Evaluating human-robot interaction. *International Journal of Social Robotics, 3*(1), 53–67.

Zak, P. J. (2008). The neurobiology of trust. *Scientific American, 298*(6), 88–95.

Zak, P. J., Kurzban, R., Ahmadi, S., Swerdloff, R. S., Park, J., Efremidze, L., Redwine, K., Morgan, K., & Matzner, W. (2009). Testosterone administration decreases generosity in the ultimatum game. *PLoS One, 4*(12), e8330.

Zhong, J., Ling, C., Cangelosi, A., Lotfi, A., & Liu, X. (2021). On the gap between domestic robotic applications and computational intelligence. *Electronics, 10*(7), 793.

8 Robot ethics and artificial morality

Artur Gunia, Mariusz Sołtysik and Szymon Jarosz

8.1 Introduction

The importance of ethics in the organization is that ethical behavior (i.e., all decisions are made and performed in a fair, reliable, credible manner and without accepting or giving illegal benefits, and equal and fair toward all employees and contractors) reflects the results of the organization, adds value and strengthens brand assets and reputation (Brickley et al., 2002). In addition, ethical behavior in modern organization results in benefits such as a positive image and anti-discrimination and ensuring equality (Choi & Rainey, 2014; Grigoropoulos, 2019). An ethical organization is more likely to develop a positive reputation, which can pay dividends over time (Hooker, 2003). On the other hand, unethical actions result in the company losing market share. As such, public organizations must consider at least three of the following four elements of the ethics function in organizational performance: (a) ethics contributes to employee engagement and trust; (b) ethics contribute to investor loyalty; (c) ethics contribute to public satisfaction and trust; and (d) ethics contribute to the creation of public value (PV) or profit (Anshari et al., 2022).

A more positive point of view, however, is that an organization's ethical practices have a positive impact on an organization's profits, and ethical behavior can have a significant impact on competitive advantage (McMurrian & Matulich, 2011). It is indicated that ethical practice is a guiding principle for the long-term success of the organization (Graafland, 2002). A high level of organizational ethics can help increase the profitability of an organization by lowering transaction costs, building stakeholder trust, fostering exceptional teamwork, and maintaining the social capital that is an integral part of an organization's market identity (McMurrian & Matulich, 2011).

Visions of the future depict a factory floor where humans, collaborative robots, and autonomous agents form dynamic teams capable of responding to changing needs in the production environment. Human actors have personally defined roles based on their current skills, but they can constantly develop their skills and thus can change their roles in the team. Similarly, autonomous agents

DOI: 10.4324/9781003311409-9

and collaborative robots can learn using advanced supervised and unsupervised learning techniques. All actors are in constant interaction, communicating, collaborating, and coordinating their duties. How can such a dynamic entity be designed? Of course, after the initial design and implementation, it begins to develop on its own, because both people learn from their own experiences and knowledge of new possibilities, and intelligent machines learn them based on historical data, which then can use them in new situations (Anshari et al., 2022).

1. Actor-network theory focuses on describing social engineering networks and interactions through evidence-based empirical analyses. This is promising because it treats human and non-human actors equally. The actor-network theory can help you understand how a dynamic human-machine team works and how it evolves. This can support design and development activities.
2. The concept of operations is a promising method and design tool that provides the means to describe different actors and their interdependencies. Compared to previous model-based methods, it better supports both the dynamic nature of the overall system and collaborative design and development activities with relevant stakeholders.
3. Human-machine teams raise ethical doubts, apart from the question of replacing man with machine, they are related to such aspects as task allocation, decision-making by machines, and human roles. A gradually evolving common system may introduce new ethical issues not identified in the original design. Therefore, an ethical point of view should be an integral part not only of the initial design but also of the continuous development of man-machine teams.

Smart devices are being used to generate human-computer interactions, but little effort has been made to make these devices behave socially and ethically. Various approaches to making AI responsible have been presented in the literature, but they focus primarily on individual intelligent devices, not collectives networks without human intervention. Zhu et al. (2022) focused on three challenges related to human-AI interaction, which are the hard-to-implement ethical principles of artificial intelligence (AI), the general idea of trust versus trustworthiness, and product/process support for trust/trustworthiness. In the context of the ethical principles of AI and responsible AI, the study highlighted missing elements in the operationalization of ethical AI concepts and potential solutions, using the example of predicting agricultural yields. However, beyond trust and credibility, the study did not address other aspects of ethical standards.

Intelligent solutions based on collaborative robots and systems with implemented AI have great potential in facilitating tasks that require physical work as well as intellectual/mental/logical/abstract abilities. However, nowadays, these kinds of solutions usually provide employees with a twofold experience: on the one hand, employees may feel that work has become a passive and boring monitoring task, on the other hand, they describe overwhelming challenges when they have to solve failures of intelligent machines (Kaasinen, Anttila, & Heikkilä, 2023). There is a clear need to develop work allocation and teamwork in human-machine teams so that workers feel they are in the loop and human work remains meaningful and manageable.

There are still many tasks where humans are better than machines. Some manual tasks are too difficult to automate, and there is little scope for human know-how to automate, not to mention intuition that cannot be replaced by the analytical capabilities of AI. Artificial intelligence learns well from historical data, while humans can think "outside the box" and provide creative solutions. Also, tasks that require a sense of empathy and fairness are unlikely to be delegated to machines. In legal judgment or in moral evaluation, we can try to use historical data to build Law AI or Moral AI, but the uniqueness of certain situations requires a broader view that cannot be automated (Bigman & Gray, 2018; Indurkhya, 2019). Integrating these two complementary viewpoints can create a team that is greater than the sum of human and AI capabilities (Chakraborti & Kambhampati, 2018). The introduction of intelligent solutions allows considering the roles of all actors, asking questions such as: What are the new tasks that each team member is responsible for? How should team members collaborate and communicate? How to support the competence development plans of each team member?

When designing human-machine systems, the roles of workers and the associated skill requirements must be considered. This is consistent with the initial value system in social engineering design (Mumford, 2000) while technology and organizational structures may change across the industry, the rights and needs of all workers must always be given a high priority and be relatively permanent. These rights and needs include varied and challenging work, good working conditions, learning opportunities, decision-making, good training and supervision, and the ability to progress. Moreover, in the dynamic environment of Industry 5.0, employees should be able to flexibly change their roles on the fly, based on learning new skills or simply taking turns (Kaasinen, Anttila, & Heikkilä, 2023)

Although sociologists and futurologists see the replacement of human workers in many industries by intelligent machines, for example, Yuval Harari (2019) expresses concern that due to the development of AI and robotics techniques, we will face the problem of global unemployment, other visionaries, such as Raymond Kurzweil (Kurzweil, 2005, 2022) dream that thanks to this development, IT systems, robots, and intelligent agents will relieve us of the need to work. However, it is now worth striving for balance in man-machine work. Stern and Becker point out that many future industrial workplaces portray themselves as human-machine systems where tasks are accomplished through interactions with several workers, production machines, and cyber-physical support systems. An important design decision in these types of systems is the division of tasks between various human and machine actors. Stern and Becker (2019) propose design principles for these types of human-machine systems, focusing on usability, feedback, and support systems. Gräßler et al. (2021) discuss the integration of human factors in the model-based development of cyber-physical manufacturing systems. They argue that human actors are often greatly simplified in model-based design, thus disregarding individual personality and skill profiles. They propose the discipline of Human System Integration (HSI) as a promising approach to designing the interactions between people and technology in such a way that people's needs and abilities are appropriately considered in system design. In their approach, HSI concepts allow for the integration of workers' abilities as a fundamental part of a cyber-physical manufacturing system to enable the successful development of manufacturing systems (Gräßler et al., 2021).

Most research on human-robot interactions focuses on human interaction with a single robot (Jung, Šabanović et al., 2017). As robotics technology advances, robots are becoming more capable of working with humans to perform collaborative work, thus presenting design challenges of interdependence and teamwork (Mingyue et al., 2018). The impact of robots on teamwork was investigated, focusing on task-specific aspects such as situational awareness, common ground, and task coordination. Robots also affect the social functioning of a group: robots evoke emotions as well as can read emotions (Błażejowska et al., 2023; Oh et al., 2020; Spezialetti et al., 2020) and can redirect attention, change communication patterns, and may require changes in routines (Jung, Beane et al., 2017). Communication, coordination, and collaboration can be seen as the cornerstones of human-robot teamwork. Humans may have difficulty creating mental models of robots and managing their expectations of robot behavior and performance, while robots have difficulty recognizing human intentions (Kaasinen, Anttila, & Heikkilä et al., 2022; Mingyue et al., 2018).

8.2 AI ethics

AI ethics overlaps with computer (Internet) ethics, cyber ethics, robot ethics, and cyborg ethics. Their intersecting relationships may seem complicated but looking at them from the sidelines can make them easier to understand. AI ethics should be understood as detailed general issues in the area of infoethics (information ethics), which should be understood as a set of norms and moral judgments characteristic of a given society about the transfer of information from the source of the message to the object of their destination, that is, the recipient. It can be considered that it is an intangible relationship between the source of information and the recipient through the media, which is an unambiguous, unambiguous way to convey this information without accidental or special distortion to distort and cause the effects desired by a given social group, for example, manipulation of information to achieve financial benefits or favorable and positive media reception (Florid, 2010; Smith, 1992) AI ethics, on the other hand, is a system of moral principles aimed at informing about the development and responsible use of solutions using AI. Examples of issues that AI ethics must face are Security of AI systems, Data privacy, Autonomy toward humans, Rights of robots, and Norms of the behavior of artificial agents (Müller, 2021).

The following are examples of applications that can be used in education to study AI ethics (Han, 2022):

- Cases of cyborg ethics: an accident caused by a malfunction of a robotic leg; an exoskeleton worn by an elderly person; a chip equipped with a micro(nano) processor capable of processing AI systems, implanted in the cerebral cortex, would provide the ability to search for information on the Internet and deliver it directly to the recipient, for example, through the use of augmented reality (AR) applications. Tzafestas (2018) emphasized not only issues arising from the improvement of human physical functions, but also issues that may arise as a result of changes like human mental processes caused by the combination of human and machine functions.
- AI robotics ethics cases: the acquisition and collection of sensitive personal data in interactions with social robots; interacting with autonomous vehicles to determine what to do in the event of an accident; illegal personal data breach by self-driving delivery robots (e.g., drones). More examples can be found in the cases of Tzafestas (2018) in the branches of medical robotics, assistive robotics, sociorobot ethics, war robotics, self-driving car ethics, and cyborg ethics.
- AI bot/agent ethics cases: hospital visit chatbot that selects and books only doctors who have paid an advertising fee; smart speakers that recommend services based on biased data; an in-game agent performs an optional attack after considering the player's win rate to promote the purchase of game items.
- Cases of cyber ethics: hacking during a video conference; obscene dialogue or material presented in interactions with other people's avatars in the metaverse; defamation or abuse on SNS; sending and disseminating via the messenger files not allowed due to copyright.

Leslie (2019) defines AI ethics as "a set of values, principles, and techniques that use widely accepted standards of right and wrong to guide moral conduct in the development and application of AI technology." The ethics of AI is related to the ethics of computers, machines, and computation. While computer ethics focuses on the ethical issues arising from human use of computers in machine ethics, a machine can be considered an ethical actor to the extent that it can make decisions that have ethical consequences for human users, and possibly other machines. Machine ethics is considered an extension of computer ethics while Segun (2021) explores machine ethics as a subfield of AI ethics. However, it is not clearly defined whether this concept covers the entire ethics of AI or is part of it (Christoforaki & Beyan, 2022).

The main problem that all computer ethics faces is whether ethical problems, which are qualitative in nature, can be transferred to a quantitative plane that is calculable and more natural to digital systems (Lock & Seele, 2015; Powell, 2020). Computational ethics deals with making ethics computable as far as AI systems, for example, robots or autonomous systems, can make decisions that can have consequences (Segun, 2021). Moor (1995) deals with the question of whether ethics is computable, the main two questions being: (a) whether a machine (or in this case a piece of software) can be considered a moral agent, and (b) how moral judgment is achieved. In this context, the term artificial moral agent (AMA) is used to characterize software or a robot that is capable of engaging in moral behavior or at least avoiding immoral behavior that may be determined by some ethical theory (Cervantes et al., 2020). AMAs are differentiated by Moore into ethical influence agents, covers, and serves as ethical agents. Ethical influencers can have a praiseworthy or reprehensible influence by their very existence and use (or misuse), for example, by replacing a person at work with a machine or giving an advantage to the person who uses it. Hidden ethical agents support ethical behavior or avoid unethical behavior through the way they are constructed, such as when a program enforces safety and security constraints. Explicit ethical actors have clearly defined ethical principles and can make ethical judgments using some form of calculation. Fully ethical agents can make and justify ethical decisions, such as adults with consciousness, intentionality, and free will (Christoforaki & Beyan, 2022).

Three approaches can be used to calculate an ethical decision: top-down, where moral judgment is determined by a philosophical approach; bottom-up, where moral behavior is identified and rewarded so that the system is trained to distinguish right from wrong (essentially a machine learning approach); and finally, a hybrid that combines both (Christoforaki & Beyan, 2022).

When it comes to evaluating artificial agent implementations, recent reviews have noted that there are only a few prototypes that can deal with certain moral issues, and there is no way to add cultural influences or social preferences to existing systems. There is a lack of benchmarks for evaluating existing approaches and no specific tasks to implement, no consensus on what the correct outcome is, and few datasets to use in implementation (Christoforaki & Beyan, 2022). Hence, the practice used for this type of problem is to use the tools of experimental philosophy. Experimental philosophy is a relatively young trend that emerged as a field of philosophy based on the analytic tradition. Using methods characteristic of the social sciences, especially experimental psychology, experimental philosophers systematically collect data on philosophical intuitions shared by non-philosophers (and sometimes also professional philosophers) and try to draw conclusions to philosophical considerations (Joshua, 2012; Knobe, 2007). The introduction of moral modules in AI systems has become very common in many areas, an example being the Moral Machine project for making moral decisions in autonomous cars (Awad et al., 2018) as well as building ethical systems based on the convention of the majority, allows for taking into account cultural differences, which is also shown by research results regarding the preferences of saving individual groups of people in the Moral Machine experiment (Maxmen, 2018). And even if the methods taken from experimental philosophy are not optimal, they allow for the development of more adequate guidelines in the context of ethical issues. Summing up, the moral modules in the machines would be based on the average moral premises of a given community, which were collected in a survey.

8.3 Robot ethics

Bynum (2018) noted that with the development and spread of information technology itself, additional subfields of information and computer ethics emerged: online ethics, agent ethics (robots, softbots), cyborg ethics (part human, part machine), open-source movement, e-government, global information ethics, information technology and genetics, and computer terrorism. *Computer ethics* and *information ethics* were historically the oldest terms encountered by teachers and students, but *cyber ethics* has become more common with the increasing use of videoconferencing platforms and the metaverse. With the development of AI, robot technology, and the proliferation of 5G networks, there have been even more ethical issues related to digital humans, AI agents, robots, and self-driving cars. In response to these developments, Tzafestas (2018) summarized the core concepts of robotics and the twelve issues to be addressed in roboethics, pointing out that there are common issues in computer ethics, information ethics, automation ethics, and bioethics (Han, 2022). To sum up, roboethics should be considered a branch of ethics dealing with the introduction of rules to be followed when using robots or automatic (or autonomous) technologies, for example, for military, industrial, medical, home, or entertainment purposes (e.g., sex-robots). In particular, it is to concern ethical systems that are: built into robots; used by robots; used by engineers during the construction of robots; used by robot users; by robot manufacturers; and how humans treat robots.

Currently, AI ethics is not as clearly defined as other branches of ethics. Additionally, there is a mix of terms in the areas of AI ethics, AI robot ethics, and robot ethics. These terms from different computing platforms can reduce the effectiveness of information technology ethics education, as teachers and students can be confused by the ambiguity of terms, concepts, and boundaries. Bynum stated that in addition to a very broad definition and metaphysical approach to information ethics, teachers and students also need a professional, ethical approach that will enable them to directly or indirectly experience as users and producers (Bynum, 2018). For example, the terms *AI* and *robot* referenced in philosophical literature and in articles discussing information ethics or computer ethics are often used to describe concepts involving programmable softbots and AI agents. Grodzinsky et al. (2010) also presented a model that distinguishes between e-communication (e.g., blogging, Skype) and p-communication (physical or mediated communication, for example, touching, face-to-face talking) in interactions between artificial agents and humans.

According to Tzafestas (2018) the academic history of robot ethics begins with the European Robotic Research Network (EURON). He argued that robotic design and ethics-based legislation are needed through such a research network with experts from various fields (computers/robots/mechanics/automation/AI engineers, cognitive scientists, philosophers, and ethicists) and provided detailed explanations of the branches of roboethics: medical roboethics, assistive roboethics, sociorobot ethics, war roboethics, autonomous car ethics, and cyborg ethics. These branches include robots that can interact physically, but do not include softbots in virtual space. Malle (2016) divided the ethics of robots into two categories: the problem of designing, arranging, and using robots, and the problem of their moral abilities. Reader and Savin-Baden (2020) divided robot ethics into robot laws using a metaphysical perspective and interaction-based ethics from a general point of view.

As more and more robots are used in schools and businesses and in the form of self-driving cars, the ethical issues surrounding them have become more prevalent, but for more than twenty years, robot ethics has mainly revolved around robots that engage in physical activities. Recently, Smakman et al. (2021) investigated the knowledge of parents and policymakers on the ethical issues surrounding the introduction of social robots in classrooms. They found that most people assumed that robot ethics only applied to robots performing physical activity. However, philosophers, ethicists, and some computer scientists hold (Florid, 2010; Grodzinsky et al., 2010) and others believe that robot ethics extends even to programming robots such as chatbots. Furthermore, the question of applying AI ethics or robot ethics to AI-equipped physical robots can also be confusing (Han, 2022).

Robot ethics is a relatively young branch of ethics and is often met with two objections. First, robot ethics has no specific subject of analysis because ethics is not about stocks and stones, that is, objects. Second, even if it is legitimate to include artificial systems in ethical reflection, they do not raise any questions that have not been asked long ago in more traditional ethical debates. However, in response to the first objection, robots may occupy a place in the moral universe, even if we do not want to identify them as moral agents, comparable to the countless (partially) inanimate entities that have value to human eyes – landscapes, ecosystems, planet Earth, and even houses, cars, and smartphones (Loh, 2019).

Robot ethics is a subcategory of machine ethics and represents a relatively new form of ethics used in the so-called Western cultural area (Anderson & Anderson, 2007; Edgar, 2002). All robots are machines, but not all machines are robots. This classification of robot ethics as a subcategory of applied ethics of machine ethics is based on the understanding of ethics as a category of action that is initially specific to humans. The philosophical discipline of ethics, beginning with Aristotle's classical definition, dealt with human customs, traditions and customs, the good life, scientifically reflected on human practices, and evaluated the criteria of good and bad conduct (Aristotle et al., 2009). Many people assume that only humans are acting beings whose actions are not governed by blind instinct and drive, but are shaped by intentions, norms, and reasons (Loh, 2019).

In considering applied ethics, we can consider two approaches. The first concerns those ethical systems that deal with a non-human counterpart. In addition to machine and robot ethics, these ethical systems also include animal, plant, environmental, computer, and technological ethics in general. For example, like robot ethics, animal ethics focuses on normative criteria that play a role in the breeding, domestication, and keeping of animals, animal interactions in general, and human-animal relations, plant ethics. Robot ethicist David Gunkel has already stated (Gunkel, 2012) in *The Machine Question (2012) that robot ethics is related to animal ethics in particular, as "the machine question . . . is the other side of the animal question.*" René Descartes, as Gunkel understands him, initially attributed the same ontological status to animals and machines. It was not until the twentieth century that this ontological equality of animals and machines was abolished in favor of animals. The second considered approach in applied ethics is the creation of ethical systems for specific areas of human life, in which values are represented, norms are enforced, and rules are formulated, which are usually assigned a different status in people's everyday lives. Examples of this form of applied ethics include medical ethics, the ethics of humanitarian intervention, the ethics of war and business, and the ethics of international relations. The latter type of applied ethics is discussed only marginally, if at all, in this article (Loh, 2019).

Robot ethics was referred to earlier as a sub-category of machine ethics because all robots are machines, but not all machines are robots. A machine is an artificial structure that consists of individual parts moved by a drive system (engine, wind, water, etc.) and consumes energy (Canguilhem, 2009; Strandh, 1980). Robots are special machines. Historically, the term "robot" comes from the Czech word "robota" meaning work, compulsory service, and forced labour, and was coined in 1920 by the artist Josef Čapek. His brother Karel Čapek used it in the play *RUR Rossum's Universal Robots* for humanoid devices that provide services to humans. This original understanding is rooted in the idea of robots as artificial slaves (from the Slavic root "rab" meaning "slave") and support systems that relieve humans from tiring, boring (e.g., repetitive) and dangerous work. The first established human domain where robots have been deployed to perform these boring, dangerous, and dirty jobs, namely in industry, reflects the vision that Čapek creates in the said art. It is also the core of Industry 4.0, that is, the technological transformation of the human work environment through digitization and automation. However, Čapek is not a blind tech enthusiast and *RUR* deals with the many challenges that accompany the creation of robots. The plot of his play ultimately boils down to a rebellion of robots that no longer want to submit to their human creators to turn against humans in order to take over the world. But Čapek also poses many other philosophical questions, such as the nature of "human," the responsibility of scientists for their artificial creatures, what it means to form an emotional bond with another being. His play ends with the prospect of a loving relationship that begins to develop between the two robots. Thus, the historical understanding of the robot founded by Čapek creates a broad basis for discussions that should erupt in the next decades (Loh, 2019). Although, as we have mentioned, there have been a lot of publications on roboethics in recent years, it is worth considering the core of this perspective. The robot should be considered as a machine designed for slave labor. The development of AI techniques causes fear that the robot will oppose people through its autonomy, or that robots will be used by a very small group that wants to subjugate other people and will cease to be slaves of people. Thus, many years before robots became commonplace, science fiction author Isaac Asimov formulated the laws of robots. It is also worth mentioning that the term robot first appeared in English in Isaac Asimov's short story Liar (Liar) in 1941. In his short story, Playing in Tag, Asimov (1942) introduced three laws regarding robotics. These read as follows: 1) A robot may not harm a human or, by inaction, allow a human to be harmed; 2) A robot must obey a human's orders unless they conflict with the First Law; and 3) A robot must protect itself as long as it does not conflict with the First or Second Law. Then Asimov, in the story Robots and Empire, added the zero law in the 1980s, which overrides the other three: 0) A robot may not harm humanity or cause harm to humanity by inaction. These laws are not perfect and are often criticized because they apply only to machines and automata with a very low level of autonomy, which are highly specialized devices, but with a very limited range of possible actions (Moravec, 1994; Murphy & Woods, 2009). Despite their shortcomings, these laws have inspired the development of more complex ethical systems for robotics. I wanted to end this part of the lecture on these issues of different perceptions of ethical issues and the face of new technologies. And move on to issues related to information theory.

8.3.1 Artificial empathy

The feeling of sharing this pain is thought to be the source of empathy, assuming that the MNS enables agents to perceive the pain of others. Here we understand empathy, the ability to share the emotional state of another person (Coll et al., 2017), so what will be important in the context of interaction with the robot is also the ability to feel what emotions other people feel, and it will be an adequate response to the occurrence of a given emotional state in another person. Singer et al. conducted a functional empathy imaging study in which subjects observe their loved ones in physically painful situations and found that only parts of the pain network related to its affective characteristics, but not its sensory characteristics, mediate empathy. These parts are the anterior insula (AI) and the rostral anterior cingulate cortex (ACC) (Singer et al., 2004). Importantly, empathy plays an important role in social interactions. It facilitates interaction between people, enabling them to understand what others think and feel, and empathy supports pro-social behavior (Decety et al., 2016). Using these definitions, you can demonstrate what is the purpose of designing empathy modules for social robots. Namely, it is the desire to support human pro-social behavior and to strengthen human experiences around human emotions.

In a review of articles on artificial empathy (Asada, 2015), it was mentioned that many articles on empathy in neuroscience, cognitive science, and psychology have addressed pain as a research target. Designing empathy (artificial empathy) within robots seems very difficult because the very definition of empathy is ambiguous and therefore measuring how much robots empathize with humans is difficult to assess. In addition, even before that, estimating human emotions is another difficulty.

The narrow definition of empathy is simply the ability to create an embodied representation of another person's emotional state while being aware of the causal mechanism that produced that emotional state (Gonzalez-Liencres et al., 2013). This suggests that the empath has an interoceptive awareness of their own bodily states and is able to distinguish themselves from others, a key aspect of the definition of empathy terms from an evolutionary perspective, and these terms are ordered from an evolutionary and developmental perspective. According to the evolutionary process of empathy proposed by (de Waal, 2008), the upper rectangles of empathy-related terms such as emotional contagion, emotional empathy, and cognitive empathy, and the lower rectangles related to imitation are placed in parallel with the developmental process of self/other discrimination. The vertical ellipses indicate the mental functions needed for empathy to emerge. In the case of emotional contagion, "MNS" is the assumption, and "self-awareness" is an acquired mental function and another assumption regarding the emergence of "emotional empathy."

The aim of further research is the possibility of simulating emotions and empathic states by machines. One of the basic questions is: what emotions and what empathic behaviors are to be reproduced by machines or all emotions or only the positive ones? Michael Arbib (Fellous & Arbib, 2005) notes that various kinds of expressions and emotional impressions are possible to simulate on machines. He believes that this is a desirable element in connection with the design of human-computer interfaces. Simulated emotions should be designed so that they can be understood and received unambiguously. The introduction of emotionality will be conducive to establishing communication with machines; therefore, emotionality should be an important feature, especially of social robots, which are autonomous devices whose main task is to communicate with people in accordance with social behavior and roles. The task of these robots is to provide information or care functions, for example, for the elderly.

8.4 Summary

Current technological developments in the field of machine learning mean that humanity will face a machine-driven moral singularity in the not-so-distant future. However, while amoral machines may be problematic, they may actually pose less difficulty than super moral machines, as this drive to eliminate evil may actually lead to misfortune. Today, robots are replacing humans in some of the most dangerous missions in warfare, such as searching tunnels and caves used by terrorists, spying on enemy territory, rescuing wounded soldiers, and even killing enemies. Confirmation of the progress of machine learning is provided by Lin, who points to the fact that while the US had no ground robots deployed in Iraq and Afghanistan in 2003, today the number has increased to over 12. The imperative is that while humans have a control mechanism in society to detect and prevent sociopathic activities, the ethical land mines that face the continued development of AI and the creation of autonomous robots require pragmatic intervention mechanisms (Watson, 2019).

This research builds on the existing literature on human morality, AI, and human relationships. Swiss psychologist Jean Piaget's "Genetic Epistemology" shows how knowledge develops in humans through cognitive development, a series of stages that people go through, from the early sensorimotor stage of basic reflexes to puberty, social interaction, and so on. Piaget suggested that cognitive development was a constant attempt to adapt to the environment in terms of assimilation and accommodation (Oakley, 2004). Lawrence Kohlberg was also interested in the development of the child and sought to use Piaget's idea. His theory of moral reasoning, underpinning ethical behavior, identified six developmental stages grouped into three levels of morality: preconventional, conventional, and postconventional (Kohlberg, 1981). Outlining these different stages, Kohlberg wanted to identify changes in moral reasoning as people age.

Scholars have tried to adapt such theories to the field of AI by relating them to equivalent stages of human development. Rosenberg suggests that Piaget's theory may be particularly relevant to AI because it offers a theoretical and empirical guide to designing programs that learn to solve (Rosenberg, 1980). Several attempts have been made since the 1970s to build programs and computational models to embed Piaget's learning stages, and the process has become increasingly sophisticated in recent times. As Stojanov argues, most of the models used for Piaget's inspiration are based on agent-environment interaction. The main weakness was the lack of a *creative process* in which machines would be able to develop their knowledge and apply it to new fields (Stojanov, 2009).

Although we are now on the verge of great technological advancement, most theorists accept the difficulty of assessing how effective morality can be programmed into machines. Allen et al. argue that computers and robots are part of a materialistic era that is not entirely in line with the ethical values that have emerged from a long historical and spiritual tradition. Nevertheless, they see the task of moral engineering as inevitable (Allen et al., 2005). Some scholars are quite optimistic about the prospect of successful programming. Waser agrees with the view that humans have become social beings, working together to survive and thrive. Similarly, he argues (partly inspired by Kohlberg) that we may be able to develop a universal basis for ethics if we view altruism and morality as a form of survival. Waser proposes a collaborative approach to developing an ethical system that could enable safe AI by controlling self-protection, selfishness, and injustice in machine morality (Watson, 2019).

These studies took a different approach, suggesting that, in fact, human theories of evolutionary logic are difficult to apply to machines. Contrary to Wasser's opinion, I suggest that rather than ensuring survival and a safe transition to AI, there is an inherent danger of significant potential for unintended consequences when attempting to evolve machine morality, which can lead to serious problems. We need to recognize the dangers of super moral machines, and this should inform how AI will develop in the coming years.

References

Allen, C., Smit, I., & Wallach, W. (2005). Artificial morality: Top-down, bottom-up, and hybrid approaches. *Ethics and Information Technology*, *7*(3), 149–155. https://doi.org/10.1007/s10676-006-0004-4

Anderson, M., & Anderson, S. L. (2007). Machine ethics: Creating an ethical intelligent agent. *AI Magazine*, *28*(4), 15. https://doi.org/10.1609/aimag.v28i4.2065

Anshari, M., Syafrudin, M., & Fitriyani, N. L. (2022). Fourth industrial revolution between knowledge management and digital humanities. *Information*, *13*(6), 292. https://doi.org/10.3390/info13060292

Aristotle, Ross, W. D., & Brown, L. (2009). *The Nicomachean ethics*. Oxford University Press.

Asada, M. (2015). Towards artificial empathy. *International Journal of Social Robotics*, *7*(1), 19–33. https://doi.org/10.1007/s12369-014-0253-z

Asimov, I. (1942). Runaround. *Astounding Science Fiction*, *29*(1), 94–103.

Awad, E., Dsouza, S., Kim, R., Schulz, J., Henrich, J., Shariff, A., Bonnefon, J.-F., & Rahwan, I. (2018). The moral machine experiment. *Nature*, *563*(7729), 59–64. https://doi.org/10.1038/s41586-018-0637-6

Bigman, Y. E., & Gray, K. (2018). People are averse to machines making moral decisions. *Cognition*, *181*, 21–34. https://doi.org/10.1016/j.cognition.2018.08.003

Błażejowska, G., Gruba, Ł., Indurkhya, B., & Gunia, A. (2023). A study on the role of affective feedback in robot-assisted learning. *Sensors*, *23*(3), 1181. https://doi.org/10.3390/s23031181

Brickley, J. A., Smith Jr, C. W., & Zimmerman, J. L. (2002). Business ethics and organizational architecture. *Journal of Banking & Finance*, *26*(9), 1821–1835. https://doi.org/10.1016/S0378-4266(02)00193-0

Bynum, T. (2018). Computer and information ethics. In E. N. Zalta (Ed.), *The Stanford encyclopedia of philosophy*. Metaphysics Research Lab, Stanford University.

Canguilhem, G. (2009). Maschine und organismus. *Ders.: Die Erkenntnis Des Lebens. Berlin*, 183–232.

Cervantes, J.-A., López, S., Rodríguez, L.-F., Cervantes, S., Cervantes, F., & Ramos, F. (2020). Artificial moral agents: A survey of the current status. *Science and Engineering Ethics*, *26*(2), 501–532. https://doi.org/10.1007/s11948-019-00151-x

Chakraborti, T., & Kambhampati, S. (2018). Algorithms for the greater good! On mental modeling and acceptable symbiosis in human-ai collaboration. *ArXiv*.

Choi, S., & Rainey, H. G. (2014). Organizational fairness and diversity management in public organizations. *Review of Public Personnel Administration*, *34*(4), 307–331. https://doi.org/10.1177/0734371X13486489

Christoforaki, M., & Beyan, O. (2022). AI ethics – a bird's eye view. *Applied Sciences*, *12*(9), 4130. https://doi.org/10.3390/app12094130

Coll, M.-P., Viding, E., Rütgen, M., Silani, G., Lamm, C., Catmur, C., & Bird, G. (2017). Are we really measuring empathy? Proposal for a new measurement framework. *Neuroscience & Biobehavioral Reviews*, *83*, 132–139. https://doi.org/10.1016/j.neubiorev.2017.10.009

de Waal, F. B. M. (2008). Putting the altruism back into altruism: The evolution of empathy. *Annual Review of Psychology*, *59*(1), 279–300. https://doi.org/10.1146/annurev.psych.59.103006.093625

Decety, J., Bartal, I. B.-A., Uzefovsky, F., & Knafo-Noam, A. (2016). Empathy as a driver of prosocial behaviour: Highly conserved neurobehavioural mechanisms across species. *Philosophical Transactions of the Royal Society B: Biological Sciences*, *371*(1686), 20150077. https://doi.org/10.1098/rstb.2015.0077

Edgar, S. L. (2002). *Morality and machines: Perspectives on computer ethics*. Jones & Bartlett Learning.

Fellous, J.-M., & Arbib, M. A. (2005). Who needs emotions? The brain meets the robot. In J.-M. Fellous & M. A. Arbib (Eds.), *Who needs emotions? The brain meets the robot*. Oxford University Press. https://doi.org/10.1093/acprof:oso/9780195166194.001.0001

Florid, L. (2010). *Handbook of information and computer ethics*. Cambridge University Press.

Gonzalez-Liencres, C., Shamay-Tsoory, S. G., & Brüne, M. (2013). Towards a neuroscience of empathy: Ontogeny, phylogeny, brain mechanisms, context and psychopathology. *Neuroscience & Biobehavioral Reviews*, *37*(8), 1537–1548. https://doi.org/https://doi.org/10.1016/j.neubiorev.2013.05.001

Graafland, J. J. (2002). Profits and principles: Four perspectives. *Journal of Business Ethics*, *35*(4), 293–305. https://doi.org/10.1023/A:1013805111691

Gräßler, I., Wiechel, D., & Roesmann, D. (2021). Integrating human factors in the model based development of cyber-physical production systems. *Procedia CIRP*, *100*, 518–523. https://doi.org/https://doi.org/10.1016/j.procir.2021.05.113

Grigoropoulos, J. E. (2019). The role of ethics in 21st century organization. *International Journal of Progressive Education*, *15*(2), 167–175. https://doi.org/10.29329/ijpe.2019.189.12

Grodzinsky, F. S., Miller, K., & Wolf, M. (2010). Toward a model of trust and e-trust processes using object-oriented methodologies. *Proceedings of the ETHICOMP 2010*, 265–272.

Gunkel, D. J. (2012). *The machine question: Critical perspectives on AI, robots, and ethics*. MIT Press.

Han, J. (2022). An information ethics framework based on ICT platforms. *Information*, *13*(9), 440. https://doi.org/10.3390/info13090440

Harari, Y. (2019). *21 lessons for the 21st century*. Vintage.

Hooker, J. (2003). *Why business ethics?* https://johnhooker.tepper.cmu.edu/ethics/whybizethics.pdf

Indurkhya, B. (2019). Is morality the last frontier for machines? *New Ideas in Psychology*, *54*, 107–111. https://doi.org/https://doi.org/10.1016/j.newideapsych.2018.12.001

Joshua, A. (2012). *Experimental philosophy: An introduction*. Polity Press.

Jung, M. F., Beane, M., Forlizzi, J., Murphy, R., & Vertesi, J. (2017). *Robots in group context: Rethinking design, development and deployment*. Proceedings of the 2017 CHI Conference Extended Abstracts on Human Factors in Computing Systems, pp. 1283–1288. https://doi.org/10.1145/3027063.3051136

Jung, M. F., Šabanović, S., Eyssel, F., & Fraune, M. (2017). *Robots in groups and teams*. Companion of the 2017 ACM Conference on Computer Supported Cooperative Work and Social Computing, pp. 401–407. https://doi.org/10.1145/3022198.3022659

Kaasinen, E., Anttila, A.-H., & Heikkilä, P. (2023). New industrial work: Personalised job roles, smooth human-machine teamwork and support for well-being at work. In C. Röcker & S. Büttner (Eds.), *Human-technology interaction: Shaping the future of industrial user interfaces* (pp. 271–301). Springer International Publishing. https://doi.org/10.1007/978-3-030-99235-4_11

Kaasinen, E., Anttila, A.-H., Heikkilä, P., Laarni, J., Koskinen, H., & Väätänen, A. (2022). Smooth and resilient human–machine teamwork as an industry 5.0 design challenge. *Sustainability*, *14*(5), 2773. https://doi.org/10.3390/su14052773

Knobe, J. (2007). Experimental philosophy. *Philosophy Compass*, *2*(1), 81–92. https://doi.org/10.1111/j.1747-9991.2006.00050.x

Kohlberg, L. (1981). *Essays on moral development, Vol. I: The philosophy of moral development*. Harper & Row.

Kurzweil, R. (2005). *The singularity is near: When humans transcend biology*. Penguin.

Kurzweil, R. (2022). Superintelligence and Singularity. In *Machine learning and the city* (pp. 579–601). Wiley. https://doi.org/10.1002/9781119815075.ch48

Leslie, D. (2019). *Understanding artificial intelligence ethics and safety*. CoRR, abs/1906.05684. http://arxiv.org/abs/1906.05684

Lock, I., & Seele, P. (2015). Quantitative content analysis as a method for business ethics research. *Business Ethics: A European Review*, *24*, S24–S40. https://doi.org/10.1111/beer.12095

Loh. (2019). Responsibility and robot ethics: A critical overview. *Philosophies*, *4*(4), 58. https://doi.org/10.3390/philosophies4040058

Malle, B. F. (2016). Integrating robot ethics and machine morality: The study and design of moral competence in robots. *Ethics and Information Technology*, *18*(4), 243–256. https://doi.org/10.1007/s10676-015-9367-8

Maxmen, A. (2018). Self-driving car dilemmas reveal that moral choices are not universal. *Nature*, *562*(7728), 469–470. https://doi.org/10.1038/d41586-018-07135-0

McMurrian, R. C., & Matulich, E. (2011). Building customer value and profitability with business ethics. *Journal of Business & Economics Research (JBER)*, *4*(11). https://doi.org/10.19030/jber.v4i11.2710

Mingyue Ma, L., Fong, T., Micire, M. J., Kim, Y. K., & Feigh, K. (2018). Human-robot teaming: Concepts and components for design. In R. Hutter Marco & R. Siegwart (Eds.), *Field and service robotics* (pp. 649–663). Springer International Publishing.

Moor, J. H. (1995). Is ethics comptable? *Metaphilosophy*, *26*(1/2), 1–21. www.jstor.org/stable/24439044

Moravec, H. (1994). The age of robots. In M. More (Ed.), *Extro 1, proceedings of the first extropy institute conference on transhumanist thought*. Extropy Institute.

Müller, V. C. (2021). *Ethics of artificial intelligence and robotics* (N. Z. Edward, Ed.). Metaphysics Research Lab, Stanford University.

Mumford, E. (2000). Socio-technical design: An unfulfilled promise or a future opportunity? In DeGoss, J. I., R. Baskerville, & J. Stage (Eds.), *Organizational and social perspectives on information technology: IFIP TC8 WG8.2 international working conference on the social and organizational perspective on research and practice in information technology June 9–11, 2000, Aalborg, Denmark* (pp. 33–46). Springer. https://doi.org/10.1007/978-0-387-35505-4_3

Murphy, R., & Woods, D. D. (2009). Beyond Asimov: The three laws of responsible robotics. *IEEE Intelligent Systems*, *24*(4), 14–20. https://doi.org/10.1109/MIS.2009.69

Oakley, L. (2004). *Cognitive development*. Routledge. https://doi.org/10.4324/978 0203482834

Oh, S., Lee, J.-Y., & Kim, D. K. (2020). The design of CNN architectures for optimal six basic emotion classification using multiple physiological signals. *Sensors*, *20*(3), 866. https://doi.org/10.3390/s20030866

Powell, T. C. (2020). Can quantitative research solve social problems? Pragmatism and the ethics of social research. *Journal of Business Ethics*, *167*(1), 41–48. https://doi.org/10.1007/s10551-019-04196-7

Reader, J., & Savin-Baden, M. (2020). Ethical conundrums and virtual humans. *Postdigital Science and Education*, *2*(2), 289–301. https://doi.org/10.1007/s42438-019-00095-2

Rosenberg, J. K. (1980). *Piaget and artificial intelligence*. Proceedings of the AAAI'80 Proceedings of the First AAAI Conference on Artificial Intelligence, pp. 266–268.

Segun, S. T. (2021). From machine ethics to computational ethics. *AI & SOCIETY*, *36*(1), 263–276. https://doi.org/10.1007/s00146-020-01010-1

Singer, T., Seymour, B., O'Doherty, J., Kaube, H., Dolan, R. J., & Frith, C. D. (2004). Empathy for pain involves the affective but not sensory components of pain. *Science*, *303*(5661), 1157–1162. https://doi.org/10.1126/science.1093535

Smakman, M., Vogt, P., & Konijn, E. A. (2021). Moral considerations on social robots in education: A multi-stakeholder perspective. *Computers & Education*, *174*, 104317. https://doi.org/https://doi.org/10.1016/j.compedu.2021.104317

Smith, M. M. (1992). Infoethics for leaders: Models of moral agency in the information environment. *Library Trends*, *40*.

Spezialetti, M., Placidi, G., & Rossi, S. (2020). Emotion recognition for human-robot interaction: Recent advances and future perspectives. *Frontiers in Robotics and AI*, *7*. https://doi.org/10.3389/frobt.2020.532279

Stern, H., & Becker, T. (2019). Concept and evaluation of a method for the integration of human factors into human-oriented work design in cyber-physical production systems. *Sustainability*, *11*(16), 4508. https://doi.org/10.3390/su11164508

Stojanov, G. (2009). *History of usage of Piaget's theory of cognitive development in AI and robotics: A look backwards for a step forwards*. Proceedings of the 9th International Conference on Epigenetics, pp. 243–244.

Strandh, S. (1980). *Die Maschine. Geschichte – Elemente – Funktion*. Ein enzyklopaedisches Sachbuch.

Tzafestas, S. (2018). Roboethics: Fundamental concepts and future prospects. *Information*, *9*(6), 148. https://doi.org/10.3390/info9060148

Watson, E. N. (2019). The supermoral singularity – AI as a fountain of values. *Big Data and Cognitive Computing*, *3*(2), 23. https://doi.org/10.3390/bdcc3020023

Zhu, L., Xu, X., Lu, Q., Governatori, G., & Whittle, J. (2022). AI and ethics – operationalizing responsible AI. In *Humanity driven AI* (pp. 15–33). Springer International Publishing. https://doi.org/10.1007/978-3-030-72188-6_2

9 The importance of trust in the process of generating innovation

Urszula Bukowska, Małgorzata Tyrańska and Sylwia Wiśniewska

9.1 Generating innovation in process terms

The term "innovation" has a long history, as it appears as early as around 400 AD in Old Latin (classical Latin) as *innovatio*, meaning renewal, change (Marciniak, 2010). This term is the subject of extensive discussions, as evidenced by the rich literature on the subject (Taylor, 2017). Nowadays, it is emphasized that innovations are essential for improving living standards, economic development, and the well-being of society (Zastempowski & Cyfert, 2022).

According to J. A. Schumpeter (1928), the precursor of the theory of innovation in economic sciences, innovations mean a significant change in the production function, consisting of a new combination, that is, combining objects, means, and methods of production. The distinguishing feature of this interpretation is the recognition of innovation as a novelty on a global scale.

Nowadays, in the literature on the subject and economic practice, innovation is not limited to novelties on a global scale but also novelties in a given region, country, or enterprise. In general terms, innovations are understood as the development and use of new ideas, concepts, or behaviors in an organization (Zhou, 2006). Innovations are also defined as intentional and beneficial changes of a pioneer or secondary nature, introduced in the scope of a product, process, organization, or marketing activities, being the result of an innovative process and being a novelty in the world, country, region, or enterprise (Wiśniewska, 2015, p. 19).

When interpreting the concept of innovation, it is worth referring to the essence of innovativeness, that is, the organization's ability to search for, implement, and disseminate new ideas, concepts, and inventions (Pomykalski, 2001, p. 18). In a broad sense, innovativeness is defined as the search for creative, unusual, and new solutions to existing problems and needs. These solutions can be new technologies, processes, products, and services (Dabić et al., 2011). Innovativeness is also understood as the organization's internal tendency, ability to implement innovations, and readiness to take risks inherently related to implementing new ideas, concepts, ideas, and inventions (Pichlak, 2012, p. 36).

It is worth noting that innovativeness is also defined in the context of the innovation process. In this perspective, innovativeness is the ability (readiness,

DOI: 10.4324/9781003311409-10

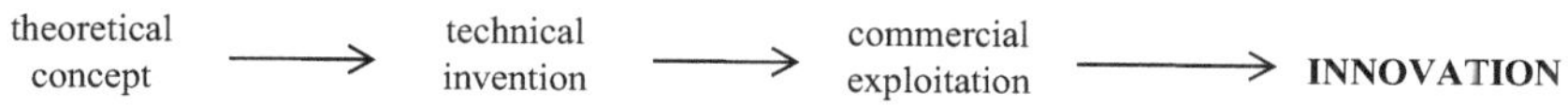

Figure 9.1 Innovation as a process.

Source: Own study based on Pomykalski (2001).

skill, and ability) to effectively implement the innovation process, defined as a set of activities aimed at creating, implementing, and disseminating innovations (Bal-Woźniak, 2004).

Enterprise innovativeness might also be understood as the function of innovative potential, that is, the ability to effectively introduce innovations, such as new products, technologies, organizational methods, or marketing innovations (Poznańska, 1998).

In the literature on management science, it is commonly assumed that generating innovation in an organization is not a one-off event but a continuous process (Lundvall, 2007; Pichlak, 2014). This approach emphasizes that the innovation process includes all development, financial and commercial activities undertaken by a given organization to implement innovations.

Following the presented approach, innovation is defined as a constant process of searching and discovering, resulting in new products, methods, technologies, forms of organization, and markets. It is also emphasized that this process includes the first introduction of a new solution to the market and the diffusion and repeated use of an innovative solution. The presented understanding indicates that innovations are not a single event but a permanent process consisting of many activities (Lundvall, 2007).

Importantly, innovation in the process approach is understood as a comprehensive process including activities related to the creation of a theoretical concept of a new idea, the creation of an invention, the introduction of a new or improved product, service, or process, and their dissemination (Pomykalski, 2001). The approach to innovation as a process is shown in Figure 9.1.

In addition, innovation is a process involving the generation, adaptation, and use of the added value of novelties in the socio-economic sphere, as well as the improvement of products and services, the expansion of markets, the development of new production methods, and the implementation of new management systems. Therefore, a specific innovation results from an innovation process (Crossan & Apaydin, 2010).

Based on the considerations made for this article, three primary stages of the innovation process were adopted (Pichlak, 2014):

- the inventive stage, characterized by activities leading to the identification of needs or problems, as well as the provision of appropriate technical means to start research aimed at meeting these needs or solving existing problems,

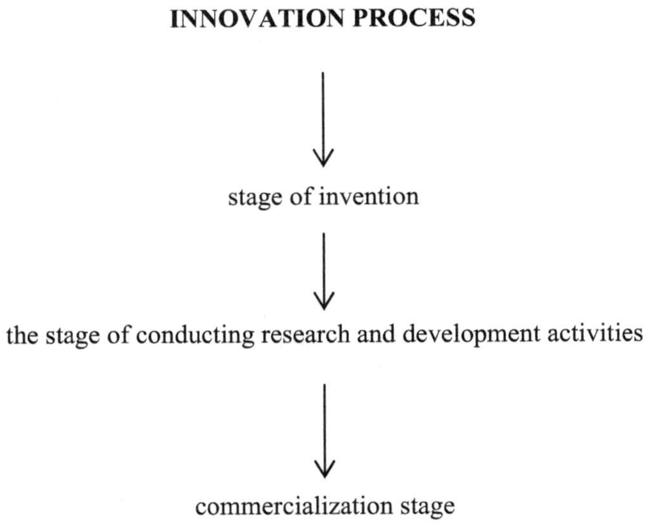

Figure 9.2 Stages of the innovation process.

Source: Own study based on Pichlak (2014).

- the stage of conducting research and development activities, including activities undertaken to create an original solution to an identified problem or need through the implementation of broadly understood research works,
- the commercialization stage of innovations concerning the commercial use of innovations after determining their economic feasibility.

The stages of the innovation process are shown in Figure 9.2.

At the same time, it is worth emphasizing that each innovation, which is a change, may encounter resistance at various stages of the innovation process. An appropriate level of trust in the implemented innovation processes can minimize this resistance. Nowadays, trust is becoming an increasingly valuable intangible resource of an organization, as it supports the generation and implementation of innovative ideas. It becomes essential in organizations focused on increasing innovation, where employees operate in high risk and uncertainty (Krot & Lewicka, 2015, pp. 65–66). Importantly, in organizations implementing innovation processes, it is necessary to trust employees' mutual intentions and competencies (De Jong, 2008, p. 50).

In addition, it is worth adding that the impact of trust on organizational innovation has been confirmed in empirical research (Hoe, 2007; Golipour et al., 2011; Lazányi, 2017; Oei & Pratono, 2020). Research results indicate that trust contributes to the free exchange of information and knowledge, which is the basis for innovation (De Jong, 2008). Moreover, cooperation based on trust enables both the generation and implementation of innovative solutions in business practice (Kraus et al., 2017), which is crucial for the effective implementation of innovation processes.

9.2 Types of innovation and trust

Trust in an object is the knowledge or belief that its actions, future state, or properties will be per our wishes. Trust can be had, possessed, nurtured, or felt for someone or something. Trust is oriented toward the future and usually involves some risk because we are uncertain of the future. By trusting someone or something, we enter into an arrangement with the other party (Zieliński, 2012). Trust refers not only to interpersonal relationships but also to various types of institutions and products or services, especially innovative ones. A. Lipka emphasizes that trust is a feature of relationships. It is an essential element of creating the relationship that builds organizational social capital, constituting the foundation of all team activities in the organization. In particular, it has an impact on knowledge sharing. The literature on the subject emphasizes trust's role in generating innovation, which shows the relationship of trust with the intellectual module and creativity (Lipka, 2022). There is a definition of the cognitive/cognitive dimension of trust (Krot & Lewicka, 2016) in the form of a rational calculation based on previous experience (Krot & Lewicka, 2016) and knowledge (knowledge-based trust).

In 1992, innovation research led to the Oslo Manual's first edition. The Oslo Handbook, created by the Organization for Economic Cooperation and Development (OECD), was developed to provide a framework for defining innovation and related concepts. Currently, it is the largest and most up-to-date collection of research results and terminology in the field of innovation. The classification included in this study divides innovations into two types: technological innovations, which include product and process innovations, as defined in the first edition of the Oslo Manual, and non-technological innovations, which include organizational and marketing innovations, as defined in the second and third editions of the 2005 manual.

Technological innovations cover a wide range of activities affecting the development of the company in terms of products and processes by improving the existing product, technology, processes or introducing entirely new solutions within the company as a response to the currently emerging needs on the market (Stawasz & Niedbalska, 2011).

The concept of non-technological innovation is a combination of organizational innovations introduced in the second edition of the Oslo Manual and marketing innovations presented in the third edition of this manual. Their introduction was aimed at expanding the possibilities of increasing the efficiency of the company and introducing changes, not only in the field of products and processes related to products but also within the organization and in activities on the market that may have an impact on increasing the scale of operations and sales (OECD & Eurostat, 2008, pp. 52–53).

The latest edition of the Oslo Manual presents the updated classification of innovations compared to the previous edition. It is an international standard in the methodology of analysis and statistical measurement of innovation in enterprises. Innovation has been divided into two main categories (OECD & Eurostat, 2018, pp. 70–77):

- product innovations – new or improved products or services introduced to the market that improve one or more properties or performance characteristics,
- innovations in business processes – new or improved business processes introduced in the enterprise for one or more business functions.

Product innovations are characterized by the improvement of functional features affecting the usability of products or services. However, they do not have to be concerned with improving all features of these products. They are often based on new knowledge or technology or use existing knowledge or technology in new ways (OECD & Eurostat, 2018, pp. 70–71).

When interpreting the second category of innovation (innovations in business processes), it is worth emphasizing that business processes should be understood as company functions related primarily to goods and services. They also relate to marketing and sales, administration and management, distribution and logistics, information and communication systems, and the development of products and business processes. Improvements in business functions relate to reliability, resource efficiency, convenience, or usability for all units involved in the business process (OECD & Eurostat, 2018, pp. 72–74).

The research results indicate that the importance of trust is significant for entrepreneurs, regardless of the type of innovation introduced (Danik & Żukowska, 2011, pp. 5–7). In the case of process, marketing, and organizational innovations, trust was mentioned by 16% of respondents, while in the case of marketing innovations – 18%. More significant differences can be observed when analyzing individual cross-sections of enterprises. Regardless of the type of innovation, medium-sized enterprises more often perceive the lack of trust as a significant barrier to cooperation in creating innovations than large enterprises. However, these differences were not significant (19% of medium-sized and 17% of large enterprises considered lack of trust as a significant barrier to product innovations; 17% of medium-sized enterprises considered the lack of trust to be a significant barrier to marketing and organizational innovations; 15% of large enterprises considered it a significant difference in marketing innovations, and 16% of them – in organizational innovations).

The challenge of modern civilization is eco-innovations, which are gaining more and more importance due to the increase in ecological awareness and more significant pressure for the good of the natural environment and the entire globe. Eco-innovations are sometimes called sustainable development innovations aimed at improving the natural environment. The created products often have to meet the standards related to the level of permissible environmental pollution or act pro-ecologically. Therefore, innovations cannot be detached from environmental requirements (Janasz, 2005). Eco-innovation is defined as the implementation for broader use of new technologies, products, and infrastructure devices aimed at protecting air, land, water, fauna and flora, landscape, and most importantly, people against the harmful impact of human activities. Eco-innovations contribute to sustainable development (Białoń, 2010, p. 25).

Creating eco-innovations is supported by the EMAS (Eco-Management and Audit Scheme) eco-management and audit system. It is an EU instrument for environmental protection, operating based on Regulation (EC) No. 1221/2009 of the European Parliament and of the Council of November 25, 2009, on the voluntary participation of organizations in the Community eco-management and audit scheme (EMAS). Its purpose is to encourage enterprises and non-commercial institutions to improve the effects of their activities in environmental protection continuously. It defines the guidelines by which companies create management procedures that minimize the negative impact on the environment. It defines the obligations regarding the initial environmental review, the methodology, the frequency of internal audits, and the supervision of suppliers and subcontractors. This system also emphasizes achieving results as part of conducting environmental activities, ensuring compliance with environmental protection law, employee involvement in implementing environmental policy, and dialogue with interested parties.

The research results showed that the benefits achieved by organizations registered in EMAS in Poland include sustainable resource management. Additionally, a better position to meet the challenges related to climate change, the involvement of all employees in establishing and improving the environmental management system, competitive advantage, and increasing compliance with the law belong to further advantages of participation in EMAS (Krzyczkowski, 2015). As part of EMAS registration, organizations are required to demonstrate continued compliance with legal requirements for environmental protection. The entities thoroughly analyze the legal requirements that apply to their activities and make efforts to ensure compliance with them. To achieve it, the organization introduces procedures in the field of environmental sustainability. An accredited verifier and the registration authority check this element in detail. Thanks to this, organizations present in the EMAS system minimize the risk of penalties for non-compliance with environmental protection law and gain greater trust from public administration. One of the critical elements of business is the ability to build credibility and trust. EMAS helps to create a positive relationship between the company and its stakeholders and thus strengthens credibility. One of the system's requirements is maintaining an open dialogue with the public and other stakeholders, including the local population and customers. Transparency and periodic presentation of environmental information in the form of environmental declarations are fundamental elements that distinguish this system from other environmental management standards, including ISO 14001. Thanks to EMAS, organizations shape their image as reliable and responsible partners. The last of the most frequently defined vital areas of benefits resulting from the registration in the EMAS system is implementing sustainable development and CSR (Corporate Social Responsibility) in the organization. EMAS fits perfectly into the assumptions of corporate social responsibility, which assumes that social and environmental aspects are voluntarily taken into account in business activities and relations with stakeholders. For many organizations, this system becomes a pillar of CSR strategy implementation. Maintaining the balance of the natural environment and the durability of fundamental natural processes creates a unique socio-economic value.

The idea of eco-innovation fits into the category of frugal innovations, which focus on functionality and removing unnecessary product features aiming at reducing not only the selling price but also the cost of using the product. Cost discipline is an integral part of creating an innovative product or service. It is up to the innovators to find a creative way to reduce material and labor costs and to design features that meet the needs of the poor community (Tiwari & Herstatt, 2012). Frugal innovations include newly designed products, services, or organizational solutions adapted to the limited resources of developing economies (Poskrobko & Zielińska, 2015, p. 277). Frugal innovations are characterized by lower resource consumption in the design, production, and consumption phases and adaptation to price-sensitive consumers. They are characterized by creativity and economy, which also benefits the natural environment and, consequently, leads to the construction of a sustainable economy. These innovations have gained popularity among entrepreneurs operating in the markets of less wealthy countries, where capital is highly dispersed (Jasiński et al., 2019).

The development of civilization has led to a new type of innovation, that is, social innovation. They function best in those sectors where existing innovation models fail, prevent the effective use of opportunities emerging in the environment, or are outdated. Social innovations are "new solutions (products, services, models, markets, processes) that meet social needs (are more effective than existing solutions) and lead to new or improved opportunities and relationships, and better use of resources and resources" (Caulier-Grice et al., 2012, p. 42). Social innovations aim to contribute to social change (Cajaiba-Santana, 2014), that is, to create such new solutions that play a significant role in solving vital social problems in education, health care, environmental protection, public finance, public and social services, and in urban planning. Thanks to social innovations, there are new, more effective, more efficient, more durable, or fairer solutions to social problems than existing ones (Jasiński et al., 2019). In addition, the benefits of social innovation accrue to society as a whole, not to individual individuals (Phills et al., 2008).

Social innovation is a formula also developing in EU legal acts and has a growing share when it comes to specific financial activities of its institutions. Social innovations are significant in building a knowledge-based economy, as well as skillfully dealing with the effects of the economic crisis when it becomes necessary to launch social mechanisms, such as social trust or openness to innovative solutions (Kasprowicz & Murzyn, 2014). Social innovations can be an instrument for building social trust because they are created for people and by them. The whole process of creating innovations is social. Openness to sharing ideas and experiences is part of the idea of social innovation. Stimulating new social groups (e.g., previously marginalized) to action improves the awareness of the possibility of influencing the environment and the society's ability to act; new relationships and social roles are created. An example of social innovation in education is the outdoor education method. It is a method of work that shapes interpersonal skills, builds self-esteem, and teaches how to act in and with a group. Outdoor educational activities are based on experience and the pursuit of goals through implementing specific tasks related to human beings in the natural environment. The outdoor education method triggers the process of self-improvement and eliminates boundaries and barriers. Using outdoor methods in teaching and upbringing introduces a new quality into the system of social norms and values and effectively eliminates negative social attitudes. The role of social skills in building civil society is increasing, especially when there is more and more talk about the crisis of trust, lack of authority, and individualization of social life (Skubiak, 2016).

A new category of innovation is open innovation. The term "open" can be analyzed in two ways. Firstly, innovations of this type encourage openness understood in various ways, so it is the creation of a solution that allows for new types of openness, for example, through the prism of knowledge sharing (e.g., online knowledge-sharing platforms, forums, and applications). Thus, the term "openness" focuses, in this case, on the effect of innovation. The second possibility of analyzing the term "open" may be an analysis through the prism of the sources of innovation, which may mean that the innovation was created in a way that involves the organization's external and internal resources (Chrzanowski & Zawada, 2018, p. 18). According to this logic, the more systematic exploration of external and internal sources of knowledge resources, the greater the openness of the organization and its innovative activity. Thus, open innovation is a sustainable and systematic practice based on the commitment to search for and then integrate ideas (suggestions, solutions) from sources beyond the boundaries of the enterprise (Sisodiya et al., 2013). The term "open" refers to the source of innovation, not only to the effect, as in the case of process, product, marketing, organizational, social, or eco-innovations, and open innovations are a kind of meta-innovation. After all, the source of marketing innovation may be external stakeholders. Therefore, it is appropriate (from the point of view of logic) to talk about open marketing innovation. The source of eco-innovation may be the cooperation of the company's internal resources with external research and development centers; thus, it should be said that we are dealing with open eco-innovation (Chrzanowski & Zawada, 2018).

According to H.T. Tsou, C.C. Cheng, and H.Y. Hsu, there are four criteria for selecting partners in creating open innovation: partner reliability, partner complementarity, partner knowledge, and partner compatibility. The selection of partners following these criteria contributes to achieving a better competitive advantage. The primary criterion is the partner's reliability, understood as trust in him and his commitment. Partner complementarity is a set of competencies characteristic of a partner, manifested, among others, in the diversification of owned resources and matching them to the company's resources. The partner's knowledge is interpreted as his abilities, which can strengthen the company's capabilities. On the other hand, partners' compatibility manifests itself in similar goals and values that facilitate cooperation (Tsou et al., 2015).

Trust between enterprises and universities, experts, and public institutions, i.e., partners combining their potentials – being cells of a kind of innovation ecosystem, seeing cooperation as an opportunity for development – is a key value in the process of creating and commercializing innovation, in which high risk is inherent. The entities mentioned earlier, through mutual understanding of their needs and dialogue, condition the correct functioning of the entire innovation ecosystem, ensuring the transfer of scientific research results to the economy. An important factor that builds trust between entities creating innovations is open communication, which determines understanding, openness to other arguments, and cooperation, allowing one to face the challenges arising at various stages of creating and commercializing innovations.

Thus, on the one hand, trust is a prerequisite for creating and commercializing innovation. On the other hand, a specific type of innovation – social innovation – is an instrument for building social trust, shaping attitudes of openness to innovative solutions, and ensuring social and economic development.

9.3 Competence as the basis of trust

Among the numerous definitions of trust presented in publications in management, one can find those that associate trust with competencies. One of them is the definition by K. Blomqvist (1997), indicating that trust is "An actor's expectation of the other party's competence and goodwill." The competencies of the trusted entity are perceived as a source of trust, as presented in Table 9.1.

Competency-based trust means the expectation that the trusted partner will perform at a certain level, possessing the skills and expertise needed to achieve the partnership's objective (Dowell et al., 2013). When trust is given to an "artificial" object, for example, an innovation, these expectations may result from the belief that competent people created this object. The trusting person expects that thanks to the competence of its creator, this object can be relied upon to meet

Table 9.1 Competencies as a source of trust

Author	*Sources of trust*
Butler (1991)	availability, competence, consistency, discreetness, fairness, integrity, loyalty, openness, promise, fulfillment, receptivity
Mayer et al. (1995)	ability, benevolence, integrity
Clark and Payne (1997)	integrity, competence, consistency, kindness, openness
Dowell et al. (2013)	ability/competency, integrity, benevolence
Di Battista et al. (2020)	benevolence, competence

Source: Own study.

needs or serve interests (Barbalet, 2019). What is essential is that expectations are set within specific contextual parameters and existing constraints (Lewicki & Bunker, 1995). These limitations may be caused by, for example, the current knowledge level or financial possibilities related to the created innovation.

The reference to competence is evident in the approach referred to as competence-based trust (Di Battista et al., 2020) and competency trust (Dowell et al., 2013). However, when the essence of competencies is taken into account, namely that they are "an underlying characteristic of a person which results in effective and/or superior performance in a job" (Boyatzis, 1982, p. 21), it can be seen that the approach "skill-based trust" (Mayer et al., 1995) is a narrowing down of the competency-based approach.

Among the components of individual competencies, there are various elements, but the most frequently indicated are knowledge, skills, and attitudes (Wiśniewska, 2021). Others are, for example, psychophysical features, abilities, motivation, character traits, health status, predispositions, and authorizations to act (Wiśniewska, 2021). Interpenetrating, the competencies of employees and associates, together with knowledge and collective memory, competencies taken over from the outside, social competencies (cooperation with the environment, ethics), management competencies, and competencies in the sphere of shaping products and technologies, create the competencies of the organization (Oleksyn, 2018). Organizational competencies "determine the domain of activity, the results of the conducted activity and are a source of competitive advantage" (Tyrańska, 2021, p. 37). It is important that trust, similarly to competence, can be considered at the level relating to the individual and the level relating to the organization (Dowell et al., 2013).

Regarding the variety of elements of the competencies of an individual, competencies were divided into hard and soft. The first includes those elements that determine the correct use of workplace procedures, tools, and methods. Therefore, these are knowledge, skills, and the power to act. They are acquired through learning or practical experience (Lamri, 2021). Soft competencies, in turn, relate to conduct and interpersonal relations. Lamri (2021) noted that they are difficult to define, but they are essential for motivation, organizational culture, competitiveness, ethics, burnout, and trust, especially in this paper. Soft competencies are characterized by a much greater degree of universality when creating innovations than hard competencies, determined by the specificity of this innovation. For example, soft competencies conducive to innovation were identified, such as creativity, communicativeness, resistance to stress, the ability to share knowledge, and the ability to work in a diverse team (Katana, 2016). However, another study confirmed that the following attributes favor individual innovation abilities: discovering, developing, and demonstrating knowledge, oral communication, self-development, and the ability to prioritize and expose knowledge (Galván et al., 2022). These factors can also be classified as soft competencies. At the same time, these competencies emphasize the importance of knowledge and its use when creating innovations.

Researchers who postulated a multi-dimensional view of individual competencies distinguished cognitive competencies (covering primarily knowledge and understanding), functional competencies (including skills), social competencies (mainly including behaviors and attitudes), and meta-competencies (enabling the acquisition of the previously mentioned competencies) (Delamare le Deist & Winterton, 2005, p. 39). The importance of individual competencies as a factor in building trust varies on the stage of the innovation process and the type of innovation. For example, during the first stage of creating social innovations, identifying needs, social competencies such as sensitivity and empathy (also classified as soft competencies) are extremely important. As Lamri (2021) writes, for a person to solve a problem that does not concern him personally, he should be able to put himself in the role of a person who experiences this problem. In the sustaining phase, when the legal, financial, and production bases enabling the implementation of innovations are being developed, cognitive and functional competencies can be essential (Bukowska, 2019).

Boyatzis (1982) pointed out that when considering an individual's competencies, one should refer not only to their type but also their level. Concerning the level of competence, he distinguished the threshold competencies necessary to perform work but not related to cause and effect with excellent results at work. Outstanding competencies are responsible for excellent, above-average results. It can be assumed that distinctive competencies support the creative process, which is an integral part of creating innovation.

When trust refers to competence, it is crucial that the trusted entity not only possesses competencies but also that the trustee perceives them. In other words, the trustee should know that the trusted entity has the necessary competencies to complete the task perfectly. Looking at trust through the prism of how it was established, knowledge-based trust was distinguished (Lewicki & Bunker, 1995). In this case, knowledge is not a component of competence. However, it is a factor that allows for assessing the predictability of behavior and the likelihood of choosing a course of action by a trusted entity. Therefore, knowledge means knowing the partner entity endowed with trust (Grudzewski et al., 2009). Better knowledge of the partner allows for a more accurate behavior prediction. Regular communication and "courtship" are therefore essential for knowledge-based trust. What is needed is constant contact with each other and exchanging information about needs, preferences, and approaches to problems. Without it, one can "lose touch" with the other person – not only emotionally but also in the ability to think similarly and anticipate the other person's reaction. "Courtship" is a behavior specifically geared toward developing a relationship to learn more about a potential partner. It has been explained (Lewicki & Bunker, 1996) that courtship is about interviewing a partner, observing how he behaves in different situations, experiencing the other person in different emotional states, and learning how others perceive this behavior (Lewicki & Bunker, 1996). These activities aim to get to know the partner and his competencies. However, while trust is based on experience, it is always future-oriented and refers to what the person bestowed with it is likely to do in the future (Barbalet, 2019).

Knowledge-based trust understood in this way is usually low in the initial stages of the relationship (Grudzewski et al., 2009). It is worth mentioning, however, that in particular situations, trust can be based on someone else's knowledge, following the principle of transitivity of trust (Grudzewski et al., 2009). The transitivity of trust means that when there is no personal knowledge about the partner, the knowledge of another trusted entity with such knowledge can be used. A specific form of knowledge and credibility resulting from competence is reputation, understood as a "record of past deeds and characteristics of an individual" (Sztompka, 2007, p. 166). "Other people's knowledge," understood as knowledge of the entity undertaking the innovative activity, is therefore of great importance. For example, in the initial stages of the relationship, when the reputation for competence is expressed in recommendations and references (Sztompka, 2007), other people's knowledge may decide to finance innovation.

As Mayer et al. (1995, p. 712) noted, "trust is not a necessary condition for cooperation to occur because cooperation does not necessarily put a party at risk." The decision to trust is made in situations where the following situational parameters occur: ambiguous course of future actions, effects depending on the behavior of others, and more significant consequences of a harmful event than a beneficial one (Lewicki & Bunker, 1995). The course of the innovative activity and its effect are not entirely predictable and, therefore, risky. Trust is not only predictability but self-confidence in the face of risk (Lewicki & Bunker, 1995). Implementing innovative projects is accompanied by various types of risk (Szatkowski, 2016). Due to the nature and area of activity, they can be divided into technical, economic, organizational, transport, legal, and insurance. These risks may be predictable or unpredictable, and their impact may be minor, moderate, or significant. Other types of risk related to innovative activity include, for example, time, personal, cultural, and credibility risks (Szatkowski, 2016).

Competency-based trust is expressed in the belief that the entity implementing innovations has the necessary competencies to properly assess the causes, type, and effects of risk and will skillfully manage this risk.

Sankowska (2015, p. 22) noted that "trust is created rather in conditions of relative equality between partners," and the greater the disproportion between them, the greater the likelihood that trust will be replaced by dependence. Such an approach expresses a negative perception of dependence and power, referring to inappropriate interpersonal relationships that use coercive means. Meanwhile, exerting influence manifests itself in various relationships, including non-conflict ones (Laberschek, 2018). Knowledge, and therefore an element of competence, as a potential source of expert power, was noticed by French and Raven (1959, p. 163). They pointed out that when one of the entities exceeds the other in terms of knowledge, and this knowledge is also positively assessed in the context of the adopted standards, it can become the reason for exerting influence. For a resource to become the basis of power and dependence on others, it should be distinguished by its rarity and importance. Therefore, if the competencies are significant and rare for the partner, for example, difficult to copy or replace, and additionally determining the success of innovation implementation, it can be assumed that expert power will be exercised over it. It can be noticed that more important than the similarity of competencies between the partners is the conviction about the similarity of interests, that the trustee is interested in responding to the trust by meeting expectations (Sztompka, 2007). Therefore, it is crucial to believe that all entities involved in creating innovations care about the project's success.

In innovative activity, building trust based on competencies is based on the assumption that thanks to the competencies of its creators, the implemented innovation will meet the expectations of various entities, that is, users, beneficiaries, financing institutions, and the creators themselves. However, competencies are necessary not only directly in the innovation process but also to determine the correct response to the risk associated with the creation of innovation.

9.4 Acknowledgment

The publication was financed from the subsidy granted to the Cracow University of Economics – Project nr 067/ZZS/2022/POT.

References

Bal-Woźniak, T. (2004). O podmiotowych uwarunkowaniach innowacyjności, czyli pierwotnych przyczynach braku aktywności innowacyjnej. *Prace Naukowe Akademii Ekonomicznej we Wrocławiu, 1030*, 19–24.

Bal-Woźniak, T. (2019). *Zarządzanie innowacjami w ujęciu podmiotowym*. Wydawnictwo Naukowe PWN.

Barbalet, J. (2019). Trust: Condition of action or condition of appraisal. *International Sociology*, *34*(1), 83–98. doi:10.1177/0268580918812268

Białoń, L. (2010). *Zarządzanie działalnością innowacyjną*. Wydawnictwo Placet.
Blomqvist, K. (1997). The many faces of trust. *Scandinavian Journal of Management, 13*(3), 271–286. https://doi.org/10.1016/S0956-5221(97)84644-1.
Boyatzis, R. E. (1982). *The competent manager. A model for effective performance*. John Wiley & Sons.
Bukowska, U. (2019). Innowacje społeczne w przedsiębiorstwie jako narzędzie aktywizacji osób niepełnosprawnych biernych zawodowo. *Edukacja Ekonomistów i Menedżerów: Problemy, Innowacje, Projekty, 52*(2), 11–20. http://dx.doi.org/10.5604/01.3001.0013.2340.
Butler, J. K. (1991). Toward understanding and measuring conditions of trust: Evolution of a conditions of trust inventory. *Journal of Management, 17*(3), 643–663. https://doi.org/10.1177/014920639101700307
Cajaiba-Santana, G. (2014). Social innovation: Moving the field forward. A conceptual framework. *Technological Forecasting & Social Change, 82*, 42–51, https://doi.org/10.1016/j.techfore.2013.05.008
Caulier-Grice, J., Davies, A., Patrick, R., & Norman, W. (2012). *Defining social innovation. A deliverable of the project: The theoretical, empirical and policy foundations for building social innovation in Europe (TEPSIE)*. European Commission – 7th Framework Programme. European Commission, DG Research.
Chrzanowski, M., & Zawada, P. (2018). *Otwarte innowacje i ich wykorzystanie w przedsiębiorstwach typu START-UP*. Oficyna Wydawnicza Politechniki Rzeszowskiej.
Clark, M., & Payne, R. (1997). The nature and structure of workers' trust in management. *Journal of Organizational Behavior, 18*(3), 205–224.
Crossan, M. M., & Apaydin, M. (2010). A multi-dimensional framework of organizational innovation: A systematic review of the literature. *Journal of Management Studies, 47*(6), 1154–1191.
Dabić, M., Ortiz-De-Urbina-Criado, M., & Romero-Martinez, A. M. (2011). Human resource management in entrepreneurial firms: A literature review. *International Journal of Manpower, 32*(1), 14–33.
Danik, L., Żukowska, J. (2011). Rola zaufania we współpracy w innowacjach. *Zeszyty Naukowe KGŚ, 32*, 1–20.
De Jong, G., & Klein Woolthuis, R. (2008). The institutional arrangements of innovation: Antecedents and performance effects of trust in high-tech alliances. *Industry and Innovation, 15*(1), 45–67. https://doi.org/10.1080/13662710701858520.
Delamare le Deist, F., & Winterton, J. (2005). What is competence? *Human Resource Development International, 8*(1), 27–46.
Di Battista, S., Pivetti, M., & Berti, C. (2020). Competence and benevolence as dimensions of trust: Lecturers' trustworthiness in the words of Italian students. *Behavioral Sciences, 10*(143). https://doi.org/3390/bs10090143.
Dowell, D., Heffernan, T., & Morrison, M. (2013). Trust formation at the growth stage of a business-to-business relationship. A qualitative investigation. *Qualitative Market Research: An International Journal, 16*(4), 436–451.
French Jr., J. R. P., & Raven, B. H. (1959). The bases of social power. In D. Cartwright (Ed.), *Studies in social power* (pp. 150–167). Institute for Social Research.
Galván, J.A, Casman, E., & Fisher, E. (2022). What skills predict an intern's ability to innovate new products? A quantitative study of innovation capability of Mexican college interns. *International Journal on Interactive Design and Manufacturing, 16*(2), 1301–1320.

Golipour, R., Jandaghi, G., Mirzaei, M. A., & Arbatan, T. R. (2011). The impact of organizational trust on innovativeness at the Tehran oil refinery company. *African Journal of Business Management*, *5*(7), 2660–2667. https://doi.org/10.5897/AJBM10.905.

Grudzewski, W. M., Heduk, I. K., Sankowska, A., & Wańtuchowicz, M. (2009). *Zarządzanie zaufaniem w przedsiębiorstwie*. Oficyna a Wolters Kluwer business.

Hoe, S. L. (2007). Is interpersonal trust a necessary condition for organisational learning? *Journal of Organisational Transformation and Social Change*, *4*(2), 149–156. http://doi.org/10.1386/jots.4.2.149_1

Instytut Badań nad Gospodarką Rynkową. (2021). Drogi do innowacyjnych regionów i Polski. *Pomorski Thinkletter*, *2*(5). Retrieved January 2, 2023, from www.kongresobywatelski.pl/wp-content/uploads/2021/07/pomorski_thinkletter-2-2021.pdf (odczyt z dnia).

Janasz, W. (2005). *Innowacje w działalności przedsiębiorstw w integracji z Unią Europejską*. Difin.

Jasiński, A. H., Głodek, P., & Jurczyk–Bunkowska, M. (2019). *Organizacja i zarządzanie procesami innowacyjnymi*. Polskie Wydawnictwo Ekonomiczne.

Kasprowicz, D., & Murzyn, D. (2014). Innowacje społeczne jako skuteczna odpowiedź na kryzys gospodarczy w Unii Europejskiej. *Prace Komisji Geografii Przemysłu Polskiego Towarzystwa Geograficznego*, *28*, 129–143. https://doi.org/10.24917/20801653.28.8.

Katana, K. (2016). Innowacje w przedsiębiorstwie w kontekście kompetencji miękkich pracowników. *Zeszyty Naukowe Politechniki Śląskiej*, *95*, 159–173.

Kraus, S., Schmid, J., & Gast, J. (2017). Innovation through coopetition: An analysis of small- and medium-sized trust companies operating in the Liechtenstein financial centre, *International Journal of Business Science & Applied Management*, *12*(1), 44–60.

Krot, K., & Lewicka, D. (2015). Wpływ zaufania organizacyjnego na innowacyjność w świetle badania jakościowego. *Studia i Prace Wydziału Nauk Ekonomicznych i Zarządzania*, *39*(3), 65–78.

Krot, K., & Lewicka, D. (2016). *Zaufanie w organizacji innowacyjnej*. C.H. Beck.

Krzyczkowski, M. (2015). *EMAS jako narzędzie wspierające ekoinnowacje, Jesteś kreatorem? Zostań ekoinnowatorem*! Event o Ekoinnowacjach, 24–25 listopada 2015 r., Poznań, 92–97.

Laberschek, M. (2018). *Symboliczne stanowienie władzy w organizacjach*. Wydawnictwo Uniwersytetu Jagiellońskiego.

Lamri, J. (2021). *Kompetencje XXI wieku*. Wolters Kluwer.

Lazányi, K. (2017). Innovation – The role of trust. *Serbian Journal of Management*, *12*(2), 331–344. http://doi.org/10.5937/sjm12-12143.

Lewicki, R. J., & Bunker, B. B. (1995). Trust in relationships: A model of trust development and decline. In B. B. Bunker & J. Z. Rubin (Eds.), *Conflict, cooperation and justice. Essays inspired by the work of Morton Deutsch* (pp. 133–173). Jossey-Bass.

Lewicki, R. J., & Bunker, B. B. (1996). Developing and maintaning trust in work relationships. In R. M. Kramer & T. R. Tyler (Eds.), *Frontiers of theory and research* (pp. 114–139). Sage Publications.

Lipka, A. (2022). *Employee experience. Zarządzanie kapitałem ludzkim w kategoriach rynku doznań*. PWE.

Lundvall, B.-Å. (2007). National innovation systems: Analytical concept and development tool. *Industry and Innovation*, *14*(1), 95–119.

Marciniak, S. (2010). *Innowacyjność i konkurencyjność gospodarki*. Wydawnictwo C.H. Beck.

Mayer, R. C., Davis, J. H., & Schoorman, F. D. (1995). An integrative model of organizational trust. *Academy of Management, 20*(3), 709–734.

OECD & Eurostat. (2008). *Podręcznik Oslo. Zasady gromadzenia i interpretacji danych dotyczących innowacji.* Ministerstwo Nauki i Szkolnictwa Wyższego, Departament Strategii i Rozwoju Nauki.

OECD & Eurostat. (2018). *Oslo manual 2018: Guidelines for collecting, reporting and using data on innovation* (4th ed.). OECD. https://doi.org/10.1787/9789264304604-en

Oei, A. K., & Pratono, A. H. (2020). Trust as a social capital for entrepreneurship to create innovation. *IPTEK Journal of Proceedings Series, 1*, 213–218. http://doi.org/10.12962/j23546026.y2020i1.8490

Oleksyn, T. (2018). *Zarządzanie kompetencjami. Teoria i praktyka.* Wolters Kluwer.

Phills Jr., J. A., Deiglmeier, K., & Miller, D. T. (2008). Rediscovering Social Innovation. *Stanford Social Innovation Review, 6*(4), 34–43. https://doi.org/10.48558/GBJY-GJ47.

Pichlak, M. (2012). *Uwarunkowania innowacyjności organizacji. Studium teoretyczne i wyniki badań empirycznych.* Difin.

Pichlak, M. (2014). Wpływ otoczenia na generowanie i przyjmowanie innowacji w organizacjach. *Przegląd Organizacji, 5*, 7–12.

Pomykalski, A. (2001). *Zarządzanie innowacjami.* Wydawnictwo Naukowe PWN.

Poskrobko, T., & Zielińska, A. (2015). Innowacje w krajach rozwijających się a zrównoważony rozwój, Polityka Ekologiczna a rozwój gospodarczy. *Prace Naukowe Uniwersytetu Ekonomicznego we Wrocławiu, 409*, 277–294.

Poznańska, K. (1998). *Uwarunkowania innowacji w małych i średnich przedsiębiorstwach.* Dom Wydawniczy ABC.

Sankowska, A. (2015). Zaufanie w łańcuchu dostaw. Studia Ekonomiczne. *Zeszyty Naukowe Uniwersytetu Ekonomicznego w Katowicach, 217*, 19–30.

Schumpeter, J. A. (1928). The instability of capitalism. *The Economic Journal, 38*(151), 361–386. https://doi.org/10.2307/2224315.

Sisodiya, S., Johnson, J., & Grégoire, Y. (2013). Inbound open innovation for enhanced performance: Enablers and opportunities. *Industrial Marketing Management, 42*(5), 836–849. http://dx.doi.org/10.1016/j.indmarman.2013.02.018

Skubiak, B. (2016). Innowacje społeczne w teorii i praktyce. *Barometr Regionalny, 14*(1), 29–33.

Stawasz, E., & Niedbalska, G. (2011). Działalność innowacyjna. In K. B. Matusiak (Ed.), *Innowacje i transfer technologii. Słownik pojęć.* Polska Agencja Rozwoju i Przedsiębiorczości.

Szatkowski, K. (2016). *Zarządzanie innowacjami i transferem technologii.* Wydawnictwo Naukowe PWN.

Sztompka, P. (2007). *Zaufanie. Fundament społeczeństwa.* Wydawnictwo Znak.

Taylor, S. P. (2017). What is innovation? A study of the definitions, academic models and applicability of innovation to an example of social housing in England. *Open Journal of Social Sciences, 5*(11), 128–146. https://doi.org/10.4236/jss.2017.511010.

Tiwari, R., & Herstatt, C. (2012). *Open global innovation networks as enablers of frugal innovation: Propositions based on evidence from India* (Working Paper no. 72). Hamburg University of Technology. Technology and Innovation Management. http://dx.doi.org/10.2139/ssrn.2196080

Tsou, H. T., Cheng, C. C., & Hsu, H. Y. (2015). Selecting business partner for service delivery co-innovation and competitive advantage. *Management Decision, 53*(9), 2107–2134. https://doi.org/10.1108/MD-01-2015-0014.

Tyrańska, M. (2021). Podejścia w procesie zarządzania kompetencjami pracowników. In M. Tyrańska (Ed.), *Wybrane zagadnienia zarządzania kompetencjami pracowników w organizacji* (pp. 34–49). C.H. Beck.

Wiśniewska, S. (2015). *Skuteczność niekomercyjnych instytucji otoczenia biznesu we wspieraniu innowacji marketingowych małych i średnich przedsiębiorstw*. Wydawnictwo Uniwersytetu Ekonomicznego.

Wiśniewska, S. (2021). Kompetencje pracowników- wyzwania przyszłości. In M. Tyrańska (Ed.), *Wybrane zagadnienia zarządzania kompetencjami pracowników w organizacji* (pp. 13–33). C.H. Beck.

Zastempowski, M., & Cyfert, S. (2022). The role of strategic innovation activities in creating Spanish agriculture companies' innovativeness. *Agricultural Economics – Czech*, *68*(6), 230–238. https://doi.org/10.17221/66/2022-AGRICECON.

Zhou, K. Z. (2006). Innovation, imitation, and new product performance: The case of China. *Industrial Marketing Management*, *35*(3), 394–402. https://doi.org/10.1016/j.indmarman.2005.10.006.

Zieliński, T. (2012). Zaufanie jako regulator decyzji ekonomicznych (analiza literatury). *Management and Business Administration*, *4*, 73–91.

10 Artificial intelligence as a factor in reducing transaction costs in the virtual space

Jarosław Plichta and Grażyna Plichta

10.1 Rationale for the existence of transaction costs in the digital space

Artificial intelligence, as not only a technological category, has become a matter for consideration by researchers from many disciplines. It seems that increasing the efficiency of human performance through the use of innovative technological solutions is a natural evolutionary process. Interest in and studies on the human brain and its processes have been ongoing since the beginning of mankind. In an era of rapid scientific development and technological advances, studies on this key organ of the human body have accelerated. One of the qualities Homo sapiens possess thanks to the brain is intelligence and the ability to think reflectively. Therefore, enhancing our capabilities through the development of artificial intelligence has become the objective of research and development works carried out by public and private entities.

Research on the human brain is undertaken by scientists from different disciplines, such as linguistics, cybernetics, psychology, sociology, ecology, computer science, etc. It is therefore an area of interdisciplinary research (Chiu, 2021; Steels, 1993). The use of different scientific disciplines is due to the complexity of cognitive and thought processes and the effects of human behavior in the environment in which we live. Therefore, the processes of creating artificial intelligence require the participation of many specialists not only at the stage of its creation, but also at the stages of its application, for example, because of ethical implications.

Although not all the processes and mechanisms of the human brain have yet been explored, the results so far have formed the basis for the creation of devices and technological solutions that mimic its operation. The need for their creation stems from the importance of information and knowledge in the life of modern man. Especially in the twenty-first century, in the digital age, it is becoming obvious to many people that knowledge and the ability to collect and process information are a key factor for progress, solving complex global problems, a subject of cooperation but also an element of competition and domination. The

DOI: 10.4324/9781003311409-11

category of artificial intelligence is not a one-dimensional concept and will certainly have a major impact in the future both on the lives of individual people and on global socio-economic processes.

The areas of AI application are expanding every year, increasingly becoming a general-purpose technology. With lower manufacturing and implementation costs, it additionally enables more accurate predictions and recommendations for solutions needed in decision-making processes. By promising to generate greater productivity and help solve complex decision-making problems, it is stimulating a range of changes in the methods, production, innovation processes, logistics, health care or monitoring of environmental and social risks and management of modern organizations (OECD, 2019).

The emergence of the digital space for the creation and exchange of information was treated in the first phase of its development as a factor positively stimulating socio-economic development, mainly through access to information and dispersed knowledge resources. It was forecast that the Internet would accelerate the development of knowledge accumulation mechanisms and thus accelerate innovation processes and technical progress. Originally, a dedicated tool for students, researchers, the military and as a space for accessing information, the Internet has very quickly become a place of activity for other actors, creating over time a parallel space for economic activities and the development of socio-economic relations. The speed of information flow, the physical accessibility, and the openness of information resources have increased. Many new entities have emerged, offering completely new products and services and innovative solutions to increase the efficiency of the existing, traditional entities.

The potential opportunities to reach previously inaccessible market segments and the assumed economies of scale gave the illusion of low investment compared to the benefits. It turned out that the digital and virtual aspects did not mean that this was a low-cost business and that those operating in it could increase their profitability without limits. The transfer of processes from the analogue world to the digital world has undoubtedly increased efficiency and agility in many areas. However, the functioning of digital markets has highlighted similar efficiency problems as in the real world. In addition, entirely new problems have emerged that are specific to the virtual space. The first Internet bubble at the end of the twentieth century and the overvaluation of many so-called dotcoms were an example of this. The notion of the "New Economy" created at the time disappeared within a few years indicating the real economic nature of the processes in the digital space. The efficiency of actors in the new space was influenced not only by the costs of technology, specialized services requiring new competences, but also by the properties of the specific digital space as a place for exchange and building complex relationships between users. This behavioral aspect has directed the attention of many researchers toward theories that could explain the complex behavior of global network participants and the costs of such activities.

One factor that has certainly had a key impact on the scope of operations of many actors and the scale of complexity of a system, such as the Internet, has been the entry of many billions of people into the virtual economic and social circulation as equal and having large resources participants in global exchange processes. They are now not only consumers, recipients of value, but increasingly co-creators of value in co-creation processes, sharing their resources with other network participants. The processes taking place thanks to the Internet are now a set of conscious individuals making millions of more or less rational decisions every second. Thus, the scale of operation and the size of potential disruptions of the market mechanism are very large. The large-scale manifestation of externally bounded rationality caused by information asymmetry and internally bounded rationality resulting from human cognitive capabilities are the source of transaction costs.

For many years, network participants have been supported by digital devices that enhance their intellectual capabilities. Processors or digital memory stores and decision support software, such as BI (Business Intelligence) systems, have been supporting the efficiency and effectiveness of the human mind and, consequently, human performance for many years. Despite the great capabilities of the human brain, its physical and mental limitations are also recognized. As part of the human organism, the brain certainly needs a lot of energy and rest (Han & Marois, 2013; Klingberg, 2000; Nunneley & Nelson, 1994). Like the human organism, the brain is not a stable organ and is exposed to a number of disturbances and factors that affect its functioning. In addition, the brain is not an autonomous organ, but part of complex psychological, biological, and cultural processes that shape its mechanisms of action. For these reasons, among others, the search for imitations and substitutes of the human brain has begun.

The large number of participants, the increasing volume and speed of information flows, the attitudes and behavior of actors, the specific characteristics of the objects of exchange, and the speed and complexity of processes in the digital world have brought to light the problem of information asymmetry already known from traditional markets (Black, 1998; Kajtazi, 2010). This has revealed a number of other phenomena causing imperfections in digital markets. Despite the fact that the marginal costs of digital products are close to zero, their characteristics and the motives of actors exploiting information asymmetry still remain a source of uncertainty on the part of transaction participants. Despite the automation of many processes, the behavior of actors on the Internet is intentional and the way they use machines or software depends on their programming according to available knowledge, skills but also intentions. Mistakes made by humans can therefore be replicated on a large scale by programmed machines and cause high entropy of the virtual space as a system (Guidotti et al., 2015). In addition to this, in the area of e-commerce we are dealing with successive technological changes, the development of communication tools, such as smartphones, and the transmission of information via the Internet and mobile networks. This requires continuous adaptations and investments, for example, in new software, IT services, or applications to support management processes. These investments are often specific in nature, for example, dedicated software solutions for most large enterprises that are tailored to their individual needs. The IT solutions created quickly age and have a time-limited usefulness, which necessitates further specific investments. For this reason, their alternative use on a large scale is limited. In the case of wrong investment decisions, they can be sunk costs. This results, according to the assumptions of transaction cost theory, in a greater propensity for opportunistic behavior and a desire to discount these outlays in the shortest possible time. This is another potential source of inefficiency in the operation of exchange processes in the virtual space.

In the digital markets, on the one hand, we have a situation of fairly low entry costs. Thanks to universal shop systems or transaction platforms and cloud solutions, it is possible to start up and run a subscription business at a relatively low cost. The relatively low barriers to entry and low initial costs of operating in the e-commerce market have not significantly reduced the risk of abuse (moral hazard) and the phenomenon of adverse selection. The existence of security systems, anti-virus and anti-spyware software and the often prevalent belief in the good intentions of online operators, relieves some users of the need to care for security and exercise caution. Very often, the virtual aspect of behavior and transactions is too weak an incentive to become aware of the real consequences of online activity. The mechanism of exclusion may be due to the general digital exclusion of people who do not have the necessary knowledge or are not able to use modern technologies for technical and financial reasons. Web users may also be separated from a lot of information, especially free information, which is not supported by rather complex search engine positioning techniques and paid advertising targeted at selected, usually the most profitable customers. Another problem is the confinement of users in information bubbles created on the basis of online behavior and interactions with other web users, usually with similar interests, needs, views, etc.

The virtual space and the open nature of many resources appear to have significantly reduced the phenomenon of free riding. Electronic access control systems and far greater ability to track user behavior have largely eliminated free riders who only want to benefit from shared property without participating in its creation. In addition, the introduction of micropayments and subscription models has resulted in a situation that trades off between using transactional platforms and trying to circumvent it is too large. It is more profitable to pay relatively small commissions, at least initially, than to risk getting sanctioned for circumventing their payment, for example, renting premises for tourism purposes outside the official circulation, as the cost of being blocked from the market and going back online may be too high. However, as the last 20 years have shown, the virtual space is not free from the tendency to monopolise, to take ownership of the private resources of network participants, and to create barriers to entry for new entrants through their buyouts and the mass patenting of various IT and technical solutions.

These factors mean that the digital space has required, and continues to require, the introduction of new institutional solutions at a rapid pace, securing the rights of network participants, for example, intellectual property rights. For these reasons, it seems that an institutional approach referring to behavioral aspects on the one hand, but also efficiency and ownership aspects on the other hand, is a good tool to describe and analyze the new phenomena taking place in the digital space, as a complex transactional space (Nagle et al., 2020).

10.2 Transaction costs and exchange relationships on the Internet

The most well-known and comprehensive transaction model was proposed by O. E. Williamson, in which he considered three basic dimensions of transactions (exogenous factors): asset specificity, uncertainty, transaction frequency, and information asymmetry, and endogenous factors that have a fundamental impact on transaction processes, namely opportunism, the internally bounded rationality of exchange actors (Figure 10.1).

The assumption of endogeneity and exogeneity of factors depends on the context of analysis adopted. If we assume that a transaction is the basic unit of analysis, then endogenous factors are directly related to the characteristics of the subjects of the transaction, which are influenced by exogenous factors affecting their behavior, which are integral elements of the model. Transaction dimensions, according to O. E. Williamson's concept, affect the costs of entering into and executing a transaction, the lost benefits resulting from the behavior of the parties to the contract and the costs of creating the institutional system of exchange. These can be divided into *ex ante* and *ex post costs* (Williamson, 1998, pp. 35–37), while departing here from the *explicite* meaning of these terms. *Ex*

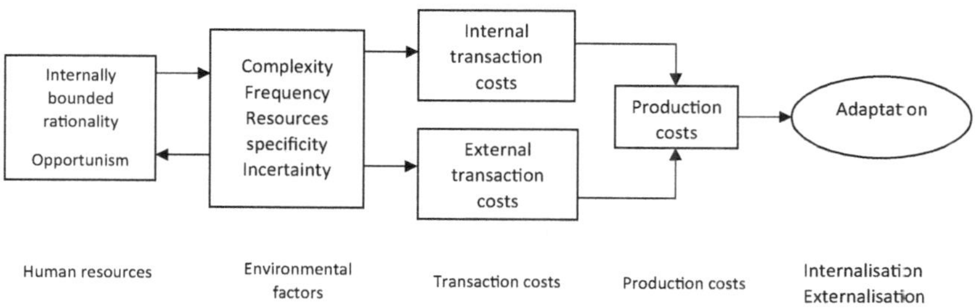

Figure 10.1 Transaction cost economics according to O. E. Williamson – general scheme.
Source: Own elaboration based on Williamson (1975).

ante indicates the possibility of calculating costs and factoring them into the economic calculus before the transaction, *ex post* assumes the absence of such a possibility and the presence of an element of surprise. An example of transaction costs classification is proposed by T. Eggertson who lists the costs of:

- seeking information on prices and the subject matter of the contract (including labor) and on potential buyers, sellers, and their prices,
- negotiations between the contracting parties,
- drafting the contract (conclusion of the transaction),
- monitoring the other side of the contract,
- enforcing the contract and introducing sanctions in the event of its breach,
- protection of property rights from third parties.

(Eggertsson, 2013)

In the virtual space, we are confronted with all the aforementioned costs that can affect the efficiency of actors' operations. Transaction costs, and the agency and ownership transfer costs that are often included, are the result of imperfections in the market mechanism resulting from the possession of incomplete information by its participants. The technological side of the creation, acquisition, collection, processing, or transfer of information is mainly burdened by the physical costs of equipment, energy, labor, etc. Nevertheless, the use of information by the actors of the exchange serves to achieve different kinds of advantages and obtain rents in order to obtain a better negotiating position in the relationship.

As a transaction space, the Internet is a tool for exchange and thus has an impact on shaping the mechanisms that shape social structure and development. The reasons why social exchanges between actors occur are a fundamental research theme not only in economics, but especially in sociology (Blau, 2006; Nowak, 2009). According to some authors, social exchange differs from economic exchange in at least several ways. The first of these, according to P. M. Blau, is trust which is characteristic of individuals and not, as he argued, of impersonal actors involved in economic exchange (P. Blau, 2006). The second is investment in relationships, which is more often emphasized in social exchange than in economic exchange (Eisenberger et al., 1986). Social exchange has a more long-term aspect based on norms of reciprocity, obligations toward others and feelings. Economic transactions tend to be more short-term and based on concrete objects of transaction (Blau, 1964). However, the contemporary approach to economic exchange and economic organizations as part of the social structure has verified these views and organizational behaviors are a product of social relations prevailing within their internal structures, remaining in close interaction with the environment. They are nowadays considered as elements of the ecosystem and institutional environment (Ostrom, 2009). Examples of this approach are corporate development strategies based on the concept of social responsibility, stakeholder theory, or ecological theories. In management and marketing, concepts of customer and supplier relationship management have developed which find extension in stakeholder relationship management (Plichta J. ed., 2022).

Regardless of the approach and scientific discipline, exchange processes are nowadays understood as sets of interdependent sub-processes that form relationships. The interpersonal and interactive nature of these processes is clearly emphasized here. However, it is also pointed out that mobile technologies and the Internet have strengthened the mechanism of atomization and relationship building not between individuals, but between social roles that sometimes form extensive network connections (Wellman, 2001). The social exchange theory treats economic transactions as a special case of more general exchange relations occurring between individuals in different social contexts. Economic relations are not only concerned with the realization of material goals, but also take into account intangible goods, such as symbols, services, property rights, ideas, etc., in these processes (Bourdieu, 2011). Often, material goals, for example, profit, are only a means to achieving intangible goals and satisfying higher-order needs. This is particularly evident in the digital space, where immateriality and symbolism are often reduced to the promise of a physical object. Initial consumer resistance related to distrust of a product offered virtually without first physically inspecting it has been overcome fairly quickly. Nevertheless, this is an area where abuses continue to occur, such as the sale of "fakes" or the incompatibility of the product description with its actual characteristics. Internet and public entities have created a number of institutional solutions to limit the occurrence of such phenomena, for example, price comparison sites for goods, the possibility of returning goods within a given number of days without giving a reason, etc.

Transactions are inextricably linked to the objects, actors, and institutional environment of the transaction. They are an essential element for building relationships. The relationships that arise between the transaction participants and the institutional environment have the characteristics of interactive processes. They depend not only on the characteristics of the specific transaction, but also on the conditions in which it takes place. This refers to the problem, raised among others by Durkheim, of the influence of the social (institutional) structure, as an autonomous entity determining the behavior of individuals in exchange processes, and of culture, as a collective memory remaining beyond the will of individuals (Emerson, 1981; Turner, 2008). From this point of view, transactions not only have a subject and object aspect, but also involve very complex cultural relations that are an integral part of transaction processes. This is particularly true for international exchange in its cross-cultural context and the resulting transaction costs (Gorynia & Mroczek, 2013).

The technological aspect is also of great importance today. The virtual space has also created specific modes of communication and tools for exchange and a specific environment for the activity of participants, often shaping its own norms and rules. The spontaneity of reactions and the freedom of expression offered by the Internet have resulted in larger and larger sets and flows of information under the name of Big Data. This, in turn, is creating more and more information noise. The quantity of information is increasing, which often affects its quality and credibility.

The concept of life, known from dramaturgical theory, as a theatre with actors playing different roles, has emerged very strongly on the Internet in the form of anonymization and avatarization, that is, masking one's identity and performing multiple roles simultaneously at the same time. This postmodern phenomenon has developed largely thanks to the Internet. It creates major credibility problems for actors and disrupts the effective operation of many exchange and relationship-building processes. Blurring and changing one's image online and performing different social roles can also be the source of identity loss or the production of false, acquired identities. This is an example of opportunistic behavior, aimed at conscious or unconscious hiding of information, distorting it or deliberately creating and transmitting false information as, for example, fake news. Opportunistic behavior is the result of information advantage between market players and expression of the desire to gain competitive advantage in exchange processes and the desire to achieve the so-called information rents. The moral hazard is very high, giving a temporary opportunity for some actors to make supernormal profits. However, this is a threat to other actors resulting not only from ethically and formally reprehensible behavior but it also reduces the strength of incentives to act and the need to incur transaction costs to hedge against such actions.

A major problem related to opportunism that has emerged on a large scale on the Internet is the protection and transfer of property rights (Gao, 2006). This refers in particular to digital products, works in graphic form, textual or musical works. The ease with which it was possible to come into possession of various personal copyright creations in the early days of the Internet was very high and this continues to be one of the most important problems concerning the protection of property and ownership rights. As highlighted by many researchers, the problem of property rights over resources is not only a source of inefficiency in the operation of socio-economic systems, but also a major source of conflicts within them (*Property Rights*, 2003; Di Falco et al., 2015; Hafer, 2006).

What favors some of those benefiting from information advantage, who behave opportunistically, is the inspiration to seek innovation and build new business models, such as search engines, news portals, or social media, which, through mechanisms of online credibility through users' personal relationships and their sharing of their own resources, reduce transaction costs (Alston et al., 2018; Baldia, 2013).

The ability to access the vast amount of information gathered on the Internet, the availability of tools to process it and the possibility of communicating with an unprecedented potential number of users have made it possible to increase the level of knowledge, awareness and the number of social relationships. This is a factor that allows access to alternative sources of information and provides a greater opportunity for verification than was previously the case. This also gives rise to a large amount of information about users, their preferences and behaviors and, above all, the relationships they build with other users. It is nowadays a key resource that is not only a commodity, but also a source of profit and competitive advantage (Prescott Michael, 2014).

The cognitive limitations of human beings, pointed out by many scientific disciplines, are the source of the inefficiency and effectiveness of their actions. H. Simon pointed to the internally bounded rationality of actors that causes errors in an ideal world of perfect markets and zero costs of information exchange (Simon, 1955). Although there is an ongoing dispute between the proponents of internally bounded rationality and externally bounded rationality,[1] what is no longer debatable today is the existence of costs that result from actors' decisions that are not completely rational (Chojnacka, 2014; Sagan, 2008). To a certain extent, this problem is solved by the frequency of transactions on the Internet, which, through their repetitive nature, thus make it possible to quickly verify information and the reliability of users. A major opportunity to overcome this problem and reduce the information barrier is the involvement of artificial intelligence.

The new possibilities of the Internet and the situation that Internet users have found themselves in reveal the multifaceted nature of the relationships enabled by the digital space. Users' growing awareness of the consequences of being online is a source of mainly behavioral uncertainty.

The increasing complexity and intangible nature of the objects of exchange make it more difficult to penetrate their properties, which, without increasing expenditure, can result in erroneous decisions throughout the value creation process. The increasing complexity of exchange processes also results in higher and higher costs of adaptation in an environment that is completely new to humans. The emerging problems of assessing the value of products and services and the virtualization of the activities of the actors themselves (location of activities, networking and lack of physical access and contact) can create a sense of uncertainty for many participants in virtual networks and lead them to seek safeguards, which increases the transaction costs of these activities. In practice, the terms risk and uncertainty are used interchangeably (Samuelson & Marks, 1998, p. 323). According to most authors, uncertainty is a broader concept, while risk is derived from it and is measurable in nature (Kaczmarek, 2005). Risk occurs mainly when information is insufficient (i.e., not complete and not consistent), but allows estimating the probabilities of certain phenomena related to an action. Uncertainty, on the other hand, occurs when there is no indication (information) to estimate these probabilities. Both uncertainty and risk are a function of two groups of factors:

- the quantity and quality of information available to the decision-maker,
- the variability of macro- and micro-environmental conditions.

Uncertainties and risks should be considered taking into account the following aspects:

- uncertainty has an informational dimension, its cause being the barrier of access to information or the unreliability of the information obtained (sometimes even the impossibility of selecting appropriate risk estimation techniques because of limited data),
- risk has a financial dimension because it can be measured; this applies when there is information available to assess the losses and gains associated with an investment project, that is, the expected consequences of future decisions (Plichta, 2019a).

From the point of view of transaction costs and relationships between actors, behavioral uncertainty is fundamental and has informational and adaptive aspects. O. E. Williamson referred to behavioral uncertainty as strategic uncertainty (Williamson, 1985). He sees its origins mainly in opportunism. The consequence of opportunistic behavior and attitudes involving more or less conscious action to pursue self-interest and maximize utility is uncertainty about the future behavior of the parties to the exchange. Uncertainty in consumer choices stems from the ever-increasing technical, organizational, and informational complexity, comprising the ever-increasing cognitive complexity accompanying even very simple decisions in the marketplace (Bendor, 2001; Carroll & Teece, 1999). The consumers do not have the time, technical, intellectual capacity to know all the conditions under which they agree to the act of exchange and to estimate the consequences it produces. No consumer is physically capable of reading the contents of leaflets, instructions, warranties, contracts accompanying all the goods or services they use. Few people are comprehensively competent to understand all the technical details and legal conditions of the contracts they enter into.

The virtual space is an environment that fosters information asymmetry, revealing the aforementioned imperfections of exchange processes and often reinforcing them. These processes may be characterized by inefficiency in an economic sense and it may be a sign of the unreliability of the mechanism of value creation and exchange (Constantiou et al., 2001; Kajtazi, 2010). Also, due to the specific nature of investments in new technologies and high expenditures, this can stimulate the creation of barriers to entry for other actors and the monopolization of the virtual space. It is also a source of opportunistic behavior and the threat of hold-up on the part of the keepers of increasingly large sets of information on users.

On the Internet, there are numerous phenomena and examples indicating the rationale for the existence of transaction costs (Plichta, 2011). The most important ones include:

- necessity to bear the costs of encrypting messages and protecting personal data,
- monopolization of access to complete information by search engines,

- fear of unauthorized acquisition of identity and of tangible and intangible resources, for example, intellectual work products or financial resources,
- creating false information and creating alternative, artificial realities,
- deliberate disinformation and manipulation of opinion,
- fear of online behavior and participant information being tracked for use in negotiation and communication processes and trading in personal data,
- threat of unauthorized actors taking control of Internet-connected devices, for example, vehicles, cameras, computers, etc., and strategic control systems, for example, for energy or transport,
- social exclusion of those not using the web and modern communication tools,
- impersonating someone else's identity and exploiting the trust and limited knowledge of Internet users for personal gain, including criminal activities.

In a 2018 proprietary study on transaction costs in the process of building relationships with consumers, only 43% of surveyed young Internet users stated that the virtual space was a good, alternative form to traditional, face-to-face forms of contact. Communication via apps is certainly not conducive to building lasting relationships (only 17.24% of positive responses). Nevertheless, building relationships via apps has a definite advantage over traditional forms primarily due to the possibility of expanding contacts and the flexibility to adjust the time and form of contact. It is also noteworthy that the online form is a better way than the traditional form to verify information about, for example, products, services, or app users (54.83%). Propensity to share was also checked. Close to 75% of the respondents indicate that when using various apps, they tend to share information and resources (e.g., knowledge, experiences, emotions, opinions, involvement, objects, services, etc.) and expect this from other users. However, at the same time, nearly 58% indicate that they are rather oriented toward gaining information and other benefits and do not want to do so in relation to others. Only less than 40% of the respondents want to share selflessly and only 20% would like to pay for it. It can therefore be concluded that in the virtual space there tends to be a belief in the possibility of unlimited use of the resources of others, most often assuming a barter exchange of equivalent resources. However, it should be emphasized that dependence on online resources may cause the risk of the so-called sunk costs. According to 58.6% of the respondents, the lack of social networking applications would result in limited access to relevant information and resources (e.g., products and services) offered by other users. The relationships created and the associated access to various resources, therefore, have the characteristics of specific assets. According to those surveyed, there is a fairly high level of opportunistic behavior in the virtual space. Seventy-eight percent of the respondents say that web app users happen to publish unverified information while looking out for their own interests first and foremost, whereas as many as 69% of the respondents believe that some web app users knowingly provide false information that may mislead others. Internet users are most concerned about the use of their data.

Forty-seven percent of the respondents have concerns about the use of their personal data by the app provider/owner once they have been made available. There is some concern, expressed by as many as 38% of the respondents, about the potential negative behavior of other users, for example, spam, stalking. This shows that there is uncertainty among Internet users. Functioning in the virtual space means, above all, lower physical costs. Communicating and keeping in touch with other users using apps requires less physical effort from 75.9% of the respondents and is financially cheaper for 53.8% of the respondents than traditional, face-to-face forms of contact. For more than 52% of the respondents, it means less mental energy (e.g., thinking, anxiety) to communicate and keep in touch with other users using apps and, for 58% of the respondents, less emotional involvement in building relationships than with traditional, face-to-face forms of contact.

The presented results show the benefits of transacting and building relationships in the virtual space due to savings in physical costs and easily measurable costs, for example, time. In terms of factors that may give rise to transaction costs, there is an ambiguous impact. While, on the one hand, some of them stimulate an increase in transaction costs, for example, opportunistic behavior, others reduce them, for example, savings in mental costs and emotional involvement.

VR and the consumption of digital products are shifting economic and social processes to the level of mental constructs and unreal (non-physical) processes of increasing importance in the global economy, for example, in the financial markets for digital currencies or the execution of transactions without the physical flow of goods and services, based on electronic records. It increasingly enables people, mainly young people, to spend time in alternative realities, often tailored to individual needs and providing the possibility of shaping them according to personal preferences. This applies not only to games, but also to virtual walks or alternative communities, where people can experience situations that are a more attractive substitute for real life.

Virtualization leads to the creation of interpenetrating real and virtual spaces known as Augmented Reality (AR). The overlapping of the two realities blurs the boundaries between the two worlds, which raises the philosophical question of what is reality and experience. This also raises questions about socialization processes and the building of social relationships. The permanence of relationships built in the virtual space and through the Internet is not long and the scale of active relationships does not significantly exceed those formed only through physical contact and direct, personal interactions. However, it should be mentioned that a number of other factors contribute to this, such as: frequency, information content, its quality, reputation, image, mode of communication (text or video), etc. Trust plays an important role in building them and is an enabling factor for entering into transactions and relationships. It is also an important factor influencing transaction costs.

One of the ways to reduce the cognitive complexity accompanying consumer decisions is through trust, that is, the assumption that a person or market exchanger who has an advantage will not use it to harm buyers of goods and services. The factors determining the adoption of this assumption are largely informational and emotional in nature and thus the function of overcoming the cognitive complexity accompanying consumer choices is mainly performed by personal trust (Lewicka-Strzałecka, 2003, p. 198). Trust reduces behavioral uncertainty. However, it should be noted that behavioral uncertainty, trust, and reputation are created and revealed in anticipatory approaches to events. Thus, they are revealed in the process of exchange. Although O. E. Williamson does not define the concept of trust per se, but he points to three categories of trust: calculative trust, personal trust, and institutional trust (Williamson, 1993). Currently, the importance of prioritization of trust and commitment to the relationship as the foundation of mutual commitment between partners and the pursuit of a relationship are emphasized. It is recognized that commitment to trust and relationship building, which reduces the state of uncertainty, encourages the parties to the relationship to act to maintain and invest in the development of the relationship (Plichta & Plichta, 2011; Rudawska, 2008, p. 169; Swiatowiec-Szczepańska, 2012). According to some researchers, such as Fukuyama, communities that create a culture of trust are more effective. However, this hypothesis is not unequivocally confirmed by research (Gray, 1997). Nevertheless, trust has the nature of a social contract between participants in exchange processes as to the expected behavior. This requires, however, a rather complex system of information flow between participants signaling these mutual expectations and norms in the form of institutions creating a framework for such behavior with a system of incentives and sanctions for not complying with them. The absence of institutions and leaving exchange processes to the mechanisms of direct interaction would be, from the point of view of transaction costs, very costly and thus inefficient. An institutional environment based on trust in institutions is therefore crucial to the functioning of exchange processes (Kaasa & Andriani, 2022; Rothstein & Stolle, 2008).

A major contribution of the Internet to socio-economic development is the development of relationships based on the concept of sharing economy. The exchange of information resources between users has, over time, led to the emergence of business models facilitating, on the one hand, the disclosure of their private resources, hitherto inaccessible and unknown to a wider group of potential stakeholders, and, on the other hand, facilitating their exchange. As a result, individual users have become not only recipients of the value previously supplied to them by specialized companies, but also creators and suppliers, acting as prosumers. This has led to the development of markets for new goods and services offered by individuals (market places), which has created a range of new social relationships and structures. It has also created greater opportunities to make better use of existing resources through, for example, second hand markets or the matching of surplus production to the diverse needs of customers located in different parts of the world. This also fits in with the idea of circular economy. Such opportunities correspond to changing social attitudes that experience the consequences of the misuse of natural resources and the effects of environmental pollution and the lives of many people. This seems to be a new type of social relationship on such a scale, which has emerged in the digital age. The development of these relationships indicates, for now, that the benefits outweigh the costs for the participants.

The value co-creation processes can take both traditional institutional forms that build community, for example, educational entities, leisure venues, and modern forms offered by businesses operating via the Internet and using mobile technologies, for example, social networks. They not only organize symbolic exchanges between users, but also enter into and/or act as intermediaries in transactions between them and businesses. By engaging in mutual relationships between users, they simultaneously co-create the value of the services offered by social platforms, for example, recommending products to their friends. Thus, by assessing the quantity and quality of these transactions, the value of the businesses themselves and their profit prospects increase. It is therefore possible to point to a third type of relationship that has been created thanks to the digital space, namely the relationship between the web user as a resource and the value of businesses offering resources in the form of applications or tools that enable online activity. The activity of application users is not only an expression of the attractiveness of the relationship-building tools offered, but is also valued as a potential for generating revenue, for example, from advertising. It is also a source of information that is significantly valuable to advertisers. This creates a symbiotic relationship that can create a dangerous dependency mechanism and an inability to quit. The reinforcement of relationship mechanisms causes users to "lock" themselves into their circles of friends with similar views and preferences. The operation of segmentation algorithms causes information profiling and locks users into the so-called information bubbles, limiting the field of perception. This can result in choices that are inefficient from the consumer's point of view, other than those based on the closest relationships and interests of friends.

10.3 Impact of artificial intelligence on transaction efficiency in the virtual space

From the moment when, in 1950, Alan Turing expressed the opinion that machines could think, works on machine learning began to develop. On the other hand, after successes, such as with the Deep Blue computer in 1990, which won against a human at chess, it became common to talk about artificial intelligence. The term "intelligent" refers primarily to behavior that maximizes protection and survival of individuals in their own environment. While this has usually referred to the physical environment, this aspect is increasingly being broadened to include the virtual space, also requiring intelligence to be involved in activities in this environment. It should be emphasized that intelligence is an individual characteristic of each person, and therefore, in a narrow sense, should refer to individual protection and adaptation (Maturana & Varela, 1987). This approach justifies the existence of an atavistic survival instinct and a preference for the pursuit of broadly understood self-interest in the socialization process. Therefore, intelligence is of existential significance.

The development of artificial intelligence is primarily dictated by the need to increase the efficiency of mental activities and processes currently performed by humans or by autonomous devices created by humans (OECD, 2019, p. 3). Initially, research on artificial intelligence was conducted in two aspects, that is, computational models and artificial models. The former were and are created to represent reality based on the analysis of data and processes, creating a certain image of reality in the form of models, usually digital ones. In the second case, physical models of devices are created whose operation and behavior are intended to reflect the natural phenomena and behavior of, for example, animals or humans (Steels, 1993, p. 5).

The issue of the importance of artificial intelligence has been taken seriously not only by economic actors, but above all by public institutions and international organizations, recognizing the need to create a common global AI policy. According to the OECD's Artificial Intelligence Experts (AIGO), AI is defined as: a machine-based system that can, for a given set of human-defined goals, perform predicted tasks, recommendations or decisions affecting real or virtual human environments. This is made possible by using machine and/or human input representing perceptions of the real and/or virtual environment, processing them as abstractions of such perceptions into models (in an automated manner, e.g., using ML or manually) and using inference from the executed model to formulate recommendations or actions.

Artificial intelligence systems are designed to operate with different levels of autonomy. The taxonomy of AI research distinguishes:

- AI applications, including natural language processing;
- AI systems learning techniques, including neural networks; optimization; and
- research on social issues, including transparency and fairness.

(OECD, 2019, p. 15)

A large role is attributed to AI in the predictive processes as regards behavior, phenomena, and the simulation of various processes requiring the collection and processing of large sets of information. The virtual space is a place of various human and organizational activities, which requires monitoring in terms of compliance with the established legal norms and rules of operation. This applies not only to directly unlawful activities that meet the criteria of criminal offences, but also to discriminatory behavior and those involving the abuse of power against network users. Therefore, specialists see a large role for AI in the system of public control and monitoring of various socio-economic phenomena. AI is therefore becoming an important element of the institutional system, increasing its relevance and efficiency of operation.

The development of artificial intelligence aims, on the one hand, to reflect the characteristics and mechanisms of human action that constitute his unique qualities, but on the other hand, to increase efficiency and effectiveness in areas where human weaknesses become apparent. The premise is to behave and think like a human, that is, by applying the principle of rationality in thinking and acting. AI primarily supports cognitive processes, on the basis of which it extracts features (Feature Engineering), often hidden, and transforms data into information. This makes it necessary to analyze more data, but according to the algorithmic approach, irrelevant information is purged from the data to ensure data reduction. This should result in a more ordered system and a reduction in its entropy. The advantage of using AI is not only the taxonomy and grouping of information, but above all its continuous dynamic adjustment to current data. This is made possible by multi-layered network systems called Artificial Neural Networks (ANNs) that are used, for example, in the recognition of speech, movements, faces, etc., and Deep Learning which increasingly imitates human thought processes. The main advantages of AI are: 24/7 availability, automation, digital assistance, handling of repetitive tasks, reduction of errors/accuracy, increased productivity, more informed decision-making. Currently, AI is most widely used in: the automotive industry, entertainment, healthcare, education, finance and military and cyber security, among others.

The growing popularity and usefulness of AI is confirmed by the latest study among business entities. According to the 2022 McKinsey Company report, the average number of AI functions used by businesses, such as natural language generation and computer vision, has doubled – from 1.9% in 2018 to 3.8% in 2022 (McKinsey, 2022).

The most widespread use of AI in companies is in the automation of marketing and sales activities and the creation of new products. For this reason, among others, marketing automation platforms offered in the area of e-commerce and services offering in-depth segmentation analysis have been growing rapidly in recent years. Although most of the data acquired for this purpose comes from the Internet, the development of AI in the analysis of the behavior of actors in the real space, such as the analysis of behavior during the purchasing process through, for example, bitcoin locator systems or virtual mirrors in fitting rooms, makes it possible to provide comprehensive information. This has become the basis for the development of the omnichannel concept that assumes dynamic and comprehensive customer relationship management which integrates different communication and distribution channels (Plichta, 2016). However, as AI is for the time being an instrument in the hands of humans, its operation can be both

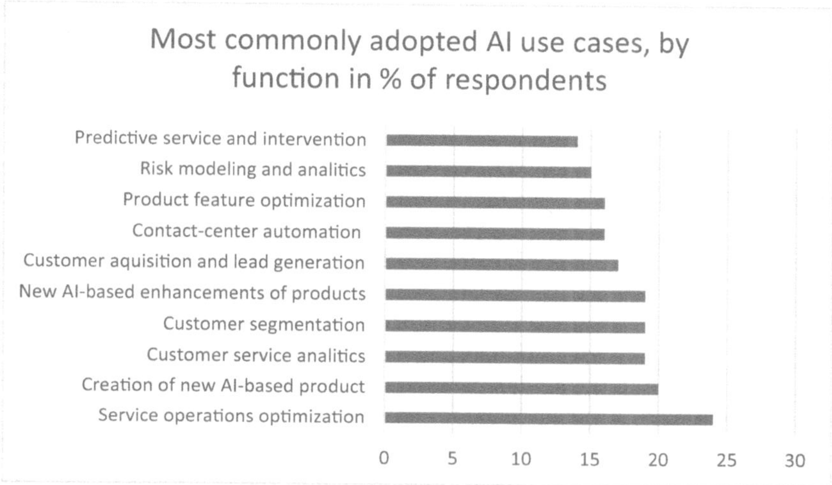

Figure 10.2 *Out of 39 use cases. Question was asked only of respondents who said their organizations have adopted in at least one function.

Source: Own elaboration based on McKinsey (2022).

an opportunity and a threat depending on its purpose and use. Therefore, from the point of view of the efficiency of economic and social processes, not only in the digital space, the question of ownership and accessibility to AI as a resource is crucial. The creation and development of the technology used in the operation of AI usually require large expenditures and at the current stage of development it is rather an investment in specific assets. This means that some of the expenditures and costs may be difficult to recover due to unsuitability in other settings or applications. This effect of potential sunk costs is compensated for by knowledge and know-how of universal and general application, for example, technologies for the production of microprocessors or mass storage. Therefore, the efficiency of these investments is characterized by a certain amount of risk and uncertainty, but at the same time high expected value of potential profits and benefits.

Bearing in mind the process of diffusion of modern technologies, it can be predicted with a high degree of certainty that they are applied in the first phase in strategic sectors for the given country, including the defence sector. Military technologies, for example, have for a certain period of time limited possibilities of dissemination and penetration into the sphere of open economic processes due to state interests, patent protection, and maintenance of strategic advantage. Therefore, AI is at the same time a source of competitive advantage and dominance for many of those investing in its development. This applies to both companies and countries. This situation is a factor that is conducive to opportunistic behavior and creates a situation of information asymmetry (Nagle et al., 2020, p. 5). This reduces the degree of trust between high-tech players, as demonstrated by the international dispute over the scope of application of 5G technology, through which the technology provider could potentially have access to sensitive data and proprietary information.

Although modern technologies have become the domain of private actors in many countries, their dissemination and transfer into the public sphere is most often strictly controlled by the state. Depending on the regime, however, this control may be more or less democratic, which poses the risk of abuse of power in the process of collecting and using sensitive data for citizens. Interference with everyone's private sphere is identified as one of the main risks in the use of AI. It is particularly difficult to protect privacy in the digital space. This does not only apply to traditional identification information but also to unique human characteristics such as retina, facial features, etc.

Human cognitive limitations and the resulting internally bounded rationality can be compensated for by comprehensive data analysis enabling decision-making in different social roles, for example, as a manager, consumer, employee, etc. The problem today is not so much the lack of availability, but the overabundance of information and the time it takes to verify it. Although product and price comparison platforms have existed for many years, their effectiveness is limited and depends on the product features provided and declared by the supplier or manufacturer. These are not always the same and in line with reality. This is often due to the use of different material names, colors, or product varieties. This problem is particularly noticeable in e-commerce, where product descriptions are often adapted to the colloquial perception of consumers by using terms that are understandable and communicative, for example, color names.

To improve cognitive processes, a new generation of devices – bots called algorithmic consumers – are being developed (Gal & Elkin-Koren, 2016, p. 310). In fact, they are automated algorithms in the form of structured decision-making processes that use a set of rules or procedures, such as decision trees, to automatically deliver results based on inputs and decision parameters. They will make purchasing decisions for the consumers by knowing their preferences and selecting the optimal product in the market from their point of view. This does not only apply to the search itself, but also to comparisons and will consequently enable autonomous purchasing decisions, for example, as already used in smart refrigerators which make purchases by themselves on the basis of identifying the absence of the owner's desired products as part of a system called smart home. This not only increases the subjectivity of consumers, but also enables better contact for others in the market and fulfillment of their needs. The progressive monopolization of the virtual space by search engines or transaction platforms makes it impossible to reach the full market offer; hence, this type of personal assistant can also be seen as a manifestation of the liberalization of exchange processes.

This aspect of course raises a number of issues, namely: who will program these bots? Who will own them and the information they collect, and will the consumer have the ability to make these bots learn and adapt the way they operate to the consumer's own needs? These are fundamental questions from the point of view of the efficiency of this mechanism. From the point of view of control and security for society as a whole, this type of resource should remain under social control. An example of the absence of such control is the case of the research agency Cambridge Analytica and the impact of the social media data it obtained on the electoral process in the US (Knowles & Richards, 2021). The ownership of AI technologies by selected market actors will certainly create asymmetry in the market and will be a source of informational rents for them. Thus, one can venture to say that bots should have a broad social function not limited to economic processes only. In this dimension, AI would acquire the status of a guardian of institutional order and institutional trust. Algorithms would be programmed to protect citizens from making mistakes, misdemeanors, or other decisions that are irrational from the point of view of social interest. Flaws in the democratic mechanism could translate into the instrumentalization of AI to maintain power and control over state security structures.

There is another problem which is the issue of decision-making and the autonomy of AI-equipped machines in this regard. An extremely difficult area of decision-making in this regard is the extent of using drones in the military and their autonomy in decision-making and in medical procedures where immediate risk to patients' lives is involved.

A certain solution to break the barrier of access and ubiquity of AI solutions is the open source model that has been developed in this area for several years. Experiences with open platforms and software are both positive, for example, in mobile phone applications, and less successful from this point of view, such as Linux or free OpenOffice. This of course raises the issue of intellectual property and the associated remuneration for the creators and thus the motivation to develop such solutions. From the point of view of transaction costs, the transfer and securing of property rights are one of the key factors in the development and diffusion of innovations.

The main drivers of transaction costs outlined in this article allow us to identify a number of determinants and applications of AI as a tool that affects information asymmetry, opportunism, internally bounded rationality, and thus transaction costs (Table 10.1).

The aforementioned rather simplistic analysis of the impact of AI on the level of transaction costs shows a rather positive impact of AI on the level of transaction costs. However, as can be seen, the exact measurement and determination of this impact require more thorough studies and analysis. It is worth noting that, at the microeconomic level, AI will have a major impact on reducing the physical cost of operations by replacing human labor, automation, increasing performance, effectiveness and, consequently, efficiency. The usability of Business Intelligence and ERPII systems is increasing year on year not only in process

Table 10.1 The impact of AI on transaction cost levels from the perspective of transaction dimensions and characteristics

Dimension/ factor affecting transaction costs	*Positive impact of AI/reduced transaction costs*	*Negative impact of AI/increased transaction costs*	*Balance of costs /benefits*	*Comments*
Asymmetry of information	– – –	+	Positive	One of the main objectives of using AI is to reduce the system entropy
Frequency of transactions	– –	0	Positive	The use of AI essentially aims to reduce the frequency of transactions while better matching them to the needs of the parties
Resource specificity	– –	+ +	Neutral	As innovative products, AI is characterized by a high degree of specificity. On the other hand, the wide access to and cost of this technology may reduce this effect
Behavioral uncertainty	–	++	Rather negative	The assessment results from the collection of a large amount of information and significant interference with privacy and data protection. This can be counterbalanced by individual bots created similarly to antivirus software
Reputation/ trust	– –	++	Neutral	On the one hand, AI can inspire trust and companies may enjoy reputation for rationality. On the other hand, uncertainty about intentions, abuse of information advantage can limit trust
Opportunism	–	+++	Rather negative	Control tools can inhibit opportunistic behavior. Nevertheless, the temptation to use AI in various social relationships will be very high
Moral hazard (hold up)	– –	+++	Rather negative	The implementation of AI involves rather high risk of making decisions for humans, which we already observe as, for example, secondary illiteracy. This can be compensated for by increasing the effectiveness and efficiency of teaching through AI
Adverse selection	– –	++	Neutral	The effects of information bubbles can be compensated for by, for example, virtual assistants providing individualization of information needs
Screening	– – –	+	Positive	The essence of AI application is its ability to acquire and process large amounts of data
Signalling	– – –	+	Positive	Based on segmentation processes and profiling of needs, AI can be used to better position information and communication with users

*impact strength (+/–) – low, (++/––) – medium, (+++/---) – high.

Source: Own elaboration.

improvement, but also in managerial decision-making. While the impact of AI on transaction costs is not unambiguous, the impact on physical production and exchange costs will determine the development of AI.

10.4 Conclusion

While the development of AI does not eliminate the occurrence of transaction costs, under certain conditions it can reduce them significantly. Reducing transaction costs combined with streamlining and increasing the efficiency of physical resource transformation processes will positively stimulate the development of AI. However, the problem of AI has a broader social, economic, and political context which requires a holistic approach and a multi-contextual view that takes into account the relationships between different stakeholder groups.

From a transaction cost point of view, several factors can be highlighted as determinants of this development. These include, among others:

- creation of a friendly and pro-innovation institutional environment with transparent rules for the protection and transfer of property rights, which will allow for the development of innovation and increased accessibility to AI,
- limiting the monopolization of those creating their global business models based on AI technology or the access to information it provides;
- ensuring by public institutions that those using AI are transparent about their activities and that individuals are given special protection;
- equipping individuals with tools to prevent the unauthorized use of AI by various organized actors;
- modification of the mechanisms of democratic systems that use AI for political purposes (Cambridge Analytica) and maintain power through social control and the elimination of political competitors, for example, the Pegasus system;
- introducing AI into educational programs and reducing the problem of digital exclusion;
- stimulating the development of AI in the area of public goods, public services and the activities of social organizations and in solving social problems, for example, well-being of the elderly, disease prevention and treatment processes or environmental protection;
- informing the public about the advantages and disadvantages of AI;
- launching a broad public debate on the human-machine relationship and its ethical and moral implications (the humanoid problem).

Overlooking the aforementioned aspects may reinforce the negatives that cause transaction costs and outweigh the costs over the benefits that the development of AI undoubtedly brings today.

“The publication was co-financed/financed from the subsidy granted to the Krakow University of Economics”

Note

1 Internally bounded rationality assumes that people do not act fully rationally due to "interference" with thought processes at the level of the organism, e.g., physiological or emotional. Externally bounded rationality suggests that people do act rationally but their limitations are due to external factors, mainly limited access to information.

References

Alston, E., Alston, L. J., Mueller, B., & Nonnenmacher, T. (2018). Property rights and transaction costs. In *Institutional and organizational analysis: Concepts and applications* (pp. 58–80). Cambridge University Press. https://doi.org/10.1017/9781316091340.003

Anderson, T. L., & McChesney, F. S. (2003). *Property rights*. Princeton University Press; JSTOR. https://doi.org/10.2307/j.ctv301f7w

Baldia, S. (2013). The transaction cost problem in international intellectual property exchange and innovation markets. *Northwestern Journal of International Law & Business, 34*, (1). https://scholarlycommons.law.northwestern.edu/njilb/vol34/iss1/1

Bendor, J. (2001). Bounded Rationality. In *International encyclopedia of the social & behavioral sciences* (pp. 1303–1307). Elsevier BV. http://dx.doi.org/10.1016/b0-08-043076-7/01100-1

Black, B. S. (1998). *Information asymmetry, the internet, and securities offerings* (SSRN Scholarly Paper No. 84489). https://doi.org/10.2139/ssrn.84489

Blau, P. M. (1964). *Exchange and power in social life*. Wiley.

Blau, P. M. (2006). Wymiana społeczna. In A. Jasińska-Kania, L. NIjałkowski, & J. Szacki (Eds.), *Współczesne teorie socjologiczne*. Scholar.

Bourdieu, P. (2011). The forms of capital. *Cultural Theory: An Anthology*, 81–93.

Broom, C., & Murphy, S. (2015). Social studies from a holistic perspective: A theoretical and practical discussion. *The Online Journal of New Horizons in Education*, *5*(1), 11.

Carroll, G. R., & Teece, D. J. (1999). *Firms, markets and hierarchies: The transaction cost economics perspective*. Oxford University Press.

Chiu, T. K. F. (2021). A holistic approach to the design of artificial intelligence (AI) education for K-12 schools. *TechTrends*, *65*(5), 796–807. https://doi.org/10.1007/s11528-021-00637-1

Chojnacka, K. (2014). Racjonalność decyzji w teorii ekonomii: Kilka refleksji dotyczących wyboru. *Studia Ekonomiczne*, *180*, 35–45.

Constantiou, I. D., Courcoubetis, C. A., & others. (2001). *Information asymmetry models in the Internet connectivity market*. 4th Internet Economics Workshop.

Di Falco, S., Laurent-Lucchetti, J., & Veronesi, M. (2015). *Property rights and conflicts: Theory and evidence from the Highland of Ethiopia Preliminary and incomplete*. https://www.tse-fr.eu/sites/default/files/TSE/documents/conf/energy_climat/Papers/lucchetti.pdf

Eggertsson, T. (2013). A quick guide to new institutional economics. *Journal of Comparative Economics*, *41*(1), 1–5.

Eisenberger, R., Huntington, R., Hutchison, S., & Sowa, D. (1986). Perceived organizational support. *Journal of Applied Psychology*, *71*(3), 500.

Emerson, R. M. (1981). *Social exchange theory. In social psychology: Sociological perspectives* (M. Rosenberg & R. H. Turner, Eds.). Basic Books.

Fiedor, B., & Hockuba, Z. (Eds.). (2009). *Nauki ekonomiczne wobec wyzwań współczesności. Polish Economic Society*. https://ksiazkiekonomiczne.pte.pl/art/show/130/nauki-ekonomiczne-wobec-wyzwan-wspolczesnosci-pod-red-nauk-b-fiedora-i-z-hockuby
Gal, M., & Elkin-Koren, N. (2016). *Algorithmic consumers* (SSRN Scholarly Paper No. 2876201). https://papers.ssrn.com/abstract=2876201
Gao, L. (2006). Intellectual property rights in the internet era: The new frontier, 5 J. Marshall Rev. Intell. Prop. L. 589 (2006). *UIC Review of Intellectual Property Law*, *5*(4), 2.
Gorynia, M., & Mroczek, K. (2013). Koszty transakcyjne jako determinanta formy zagranicznej ekspansji przedsiębiorstwa. *Ekonomista*, *2*.
Gray, K. R. (1997). Review of trust: The social virtues and the creation of prosperity [Review of *review of trust: The social virtues and the creation of prosperity*, by F. Fukuyama]. *International Journal on World Peace*, *14*(1), 84–87. www.jstor.org/stable/20752121
Guidotti, R., Coscia, M., Pedreschi, D., & Pennacchioli, D. (2015). *Behavioural entropy and profitability in retail*. 2015 IEEE International Conference on Data Science and Advanced Analytics (DSAA), pp. 1–10. https://doi.org/10.1109/DSAA.2015.7344821
Gylys, P. (2008). On the scope of the science of economics: A holistic approach: Ekonomicis mokslo dalyko klasimu: Holistinis požiuris. *Transformations in Business & Economics*, *7*(3), 39–52.
Hafer, C. (2006). On the origins of property rights: Conflict and production in the state of nature. *The Review of Economic Studies*, *73*(1), 119–143. https://doi.org/10.1111/j.1467-937X.2006.00371.x
Han, S. W., & Marois, R. (2013). Dissociation between process-based and data-based limitations for conscious perception in the human brain. *NeuroImage*, *64*, 399–406. https://doi.org/10.1016/j.neuroimage.2012.09.016
Kaasa, A., & Andriani, L. (2022). Determinants of institutional trust: The role of cultural context. *Journal of Institutional Economics*, *18*(1), 45–65. Cambridge Core. https://doi.org/10.1017/S1744137421000199
Kaczmarek, T. T. (2005). *Ryzyko i zarządzanie ryzykiem, ujęcie interdyscyplinarne*. Difin.
Kajtazi, M. (2010). *Information asymmetry in the digital economy*. 2010 International Conference on Information Society, pp. 135–142. https://doi.org/10.1109/i-Society16502.2010.6018811.
Klingberg, T. (2000). Limitations in information processing in the human brain: Neuroimaging of dual task performance and working memory tasks. In *Progress in Brain research* (Vol. 126, pp. 95–102). Elsevier. https://doi.org/10.1016/S0079-6123(00)26009-3
Knowles, B., & Richards, J. T. (2021). *The sanction of authority: Promoting public trust in AI*. Proceedings of the 2021 ACM Conference on Fairness, Accountability, and Transparency, pp. 262–271. https://doi.org/10.1145/3442188.3445890
Lewicka-Strzałecka, A. (2003). Zaufanie w relacji konsument-biznes. *Prakseologia*, *143*.
Maturana, H. R., & Varela, F. J. (1987). *The tree of knowledge: The biological roots of human understanding*. New Science Library/Shambhala Publications.
McKinsey. (2022). *The state of AI in 2022-And a half decade in review*. www.mckinsey.com/capabilities/quantumblack/our-insights/the-state-of-ai-in-2022-and-a-half-decade-in-review
Nagle, F., Seamans, R., & Tadelis, S. (2020). Transaction cost economics in the digital economy: A research agenda. *SSRN Electronic Journal*. https://doi.org/10.2139/ssrn.3661856

Nowak, M. (2009). *Instytucjonalizmy w socjologii i ekonomii: Problem i jego konceptualizacja*. Academic Publishing House of the Faculty of Social Sciences, Adam Mickiewicz University.

Nunneley, S. A., & Nelson, D. A. (1994). Limitations on arteriovenous cooling of the blood supply to the human brain. *European Journal of Applied Physiology and Occupational Physiology*, *69*(6), 474–479. https://doi.org/10.1007/BF00239862

OECD. (2019). *Artificial intelligence in society*. OECD. https://doi.org/10.1787/eedfee77-en

Ostrom, E. (2009). A general framework for analyzing sustainability of social-ecological systems. *Science*, *325*(5939), 419–422.

Plichta, J. (2011). Uwarunkowania zachowań oportunistycznych e-konsumenta w transakcjach B2C. *Handel Wewnętrzny*, *3*, 237–242.

Plichta, J. (2016). Rationale for innovation activities in E-commerce in terms of transaction costs as exemplified by home furnishing industry in Poland. In *Knowledge, economy, society: Strategies, concepts and instruments of management/edited by Renata OCZKOWSKA, Andrzej JAKI, Bogusz MIKUŁA: T. I* (pp. 327–336). Foundation of the Cracow University of Economics.

Plichta, J. (2019a). Koszty transakcyjne w procesach współtworzenia wartości przez konsumentów. *Zeszyty Naukowe/University of Economics in Cracow. Special Series, Monographs*, *264*.

Plichta, J. (2019b). Transaction costs in consumer value co-creation processes. *Zeszyty Naukowe/University of Economics in Krakow. Special Series, Monographs*, *264*.

Plichta, J. (Ed.). (2022). *Kluczowe narzędzia i elementy koncepcji co-management w budowaniu relacji kooperacyjnych z interesariuszami*. www.attyka.net.pl/pl/p/-Kluczowe-narzedzia-i-elementy-koncepcji-co-management-w-budowaniu-relacji-kooperacyjnych-z-interesariuszami/125

Plichta, J., & Plichta, G. (2011). Problem identyfikacji czynników wpływających na zaufanie w relacjach wymiennych na rynkach B2C- ujęcie transakcyjne. *Zeszyty Naukowe/University of Economics in Poznań*, *175*, 124–133.

Prescott Michael, E. (2014). Big data and competitive advantage at Nielsen. *Management Decision*, *52*(3), 573–601. https://doi.org/10.1108/MD-09-2013-0437

Rothstein, B., & Stolle, D. (2008). The state and social capital: An institutional theory of generalized trust. *Comparative Politics*, *40*(4), 441–459. www.jstor.org/stable/20434095

Rudawska, E. (2008). *Znaczenie relacji z klientami w procesie kształtowania wartości przedsiębiorstwa*. Academic Publishing House of the University of Szczecin.

Sagan, A. (2008). Racjonalność – Właściwość konsumenta czy modelu badacza? In W. Z. Kędzior & G. Maciejewski (Eds.), *Zachowania konsumentów-Stagnacja czy zmiana?* Publishing House of the University of Economics in Katowice.

Samuelson, W. F., & Marks, S. G. (1998). *Ekonomia menedżerska*. PWE.

Simon, H. A. (1955). A behavioral model of rational choice. *The Quarterly Journal of Economics*, *69*(1), 99–118.

Steels, L. (1993). The artificial life roots of artificial intelligence. *Artificial life*, *1*(1_2), 75–110.

Swiatowiec-Szczepańska, J. (2012). *Ryzyko partnerstwa strategicznego przedsiębiorstw: Ujęcie modelowe*. Publishing House of the University of Economics.

Turner, J. H. (2008). *Struktura teorii socjologicznej*. PWN.
Wellman, B. (2001). Physical place and cyberplace: The rise of personalized networking. *International Journal of Urban and Regional Research*, *25*(2), 227–252. https://doi.org/10.1111/1468-2427.00309
Williamson, O. E. (1975). *Markets and hierarchies*. https://papers.ssrn.com/sol3/papers.cfm?abstract_id=1496220
Williamson, O. E. (1985). *The economic institutions of capitalism*. Simon and Schuster.
Williamson, O. E. (1993). Calculativeness, trust, and economic organization. *The Journal of Law & Economics*, *36*(1), 453–486. www.jstor.org/stable/725485
Williamson, O. E. (1998). *Ekonomiczne instytucje kapitalizmu*. PWN.

11 Trust in robots

The experience of the young generation

Robert Szydło, Małgorzata Tyrańska, Ireneusz Rynduch and Marek Koczyński

11.1 Emerging adulthood

Emerging adulthood, 18–25 years old (Chisholm & Hurrelmann, 1995), is a period of achievement, experimentation, and change (Arnett, 2000). The opportunities in professional life (work), personal life (love), and exploration (Rindfuss, 1991), together with the extended education period and the marriage age (Arnett & Taber, 1994), makes this period of life interesting for scientists. Youn people live without parents and move quickly from one apartment to another due to opportunities and lack of obligations. Self-perception in the emerging adulthood stage is also different from childhood and adulthood. Students do not call themselves children but do not identify themselves as adults. It is a being in between these two stages. According to Arnett, identity shaping in emerging adulthood occurs within three main areas: love, work, and views (Arnett, 2000). Those are not the only areas where young people in emerging adulthood show specific behaviors. These include:

1. Risky behavior such as usage of narcotics, unprotected sex, and dangerous road behaviors (speeding, driving after drinking)
2. Changing the relationship with parents
3. Curiosity about innovation and technology

This curiosity is connected with various innovative approaches.

11.2 The revolutions

Throughout the history of the world, innovation has undoubtedly been a key factor in the development of humanity and commerce, or business. Management sciences undoubtedly highlight the relevance of all industrial revolutions (Olender-Skorek, 2017). Each revolution resulted in the implementation of a unique, previously unprecedented solution that suddenly and dynamically transformed how labor activities are performed or how business organizations

DOI: 10.4324/9781003311409-12

function. The occurrence of three great industrial revolutions is generally acknowledged (Koc & Teker, 2019). The literature allows us to characterize them as well as analyze the impact they had on the world (Popkova & Ragulina, 2019)

1. The First Revolution (eighteenth century) – until this point, people primarily used the power of their muscles and the potential of simple machines to perform labor activities. However, the introduction of the steam engine opened up new products and operational possibilities and fostered the emergence of factories, employing more personnel than the manufactories could afford before (Crafts, 2011).
2. The Second Revolution (late nineteenth century) – the era of electricity, where factories saw the spread of production lines that accelerated the pace of execution – mass production. There was a boom in steel manufacturing and railroad construction. The internal combustion engine became an equally notable invention, replacing steam technology (Mohajan, 2019).
3. The Third Revolution (twentieth century) – some entrepreneurs say it continues today. The genesis is attributed to the spread of personal computers. With the automation of manufacturing processes in the industry, companies with multinational or global operations have become more common (Taalbi, 2019).

Nowadays, there is a growing acceptance of the view that we are living through the Fourth Technological Revolution. It results from widespread acceptance and implementation of solutions implemented in the twentieth century and ongoing development. Computers, machine learning technologies, algorithms, or network systems represent a level of sophistication never seen before (Xu et al., 2018). They can self-learn, repair, update, or suggest solutions for users. Moreover, the widespread trend of replacing human labor with robots is no longer a fantasy but a reality.

11.3 Contemporary usage of robots

Undoubtedly, this is an image reminiscent of popular science fiction movie scenarios. Both in the aforesaid film genre and the real world, it raises the question of trust in the face of such advanced technologies (Karabegović, 2017). However, before the question of whether we, as a civilization, are capable of entrusting our fate to robots can be answered, we must determine what tasks are assigned to them. A very popular area of implementation of robotics and learning systems is the execution of various types of tests and related service control, the so-called Robot Framework (Stresnjak & Hocenski, 2011). Work previously done by humans has been dramatically accelerated while providing increased fault control and tolerance. In practice, all kinds of control analysis, especially in cybernetic systems, are based on libraries of digital data and are largely repeatable. It is, therefore, possible to construct an algorithm that learns a given process and monitors deviations from the standard procedure (Olszewski, 2016). Nevertheless, the use of robots in logistics solutions is popular. This popularization may be related to the primacy of online services, contactless delivery, or other post-COVID trends. However, robots have already been used to load goods onto delivery trucks. There have been significant speed-ups in the pace of work and safety during loading, relieving the burden on manual workers and optimizing the entire logistics process (Park et al., 2021). Seemingly simple solutions, such as equipping already functioning machines with 3D cameras and depth sensors, have resulted in the implementation of technology for tracking specific objects and sorting them according to pre-programmed categories. The work of robots based on such an interface is referred to as pick-and-place (Pellicciari et al., 2013). In addition to relieving the burden on humans, robots can replace them in situations that require extreme precision, even inhuman composure, such as when performing complex medical operations (Zhang & Lu, 2020). Surgical robots are machines that are a kind of extension of the surgeon's hands. A popular one, for example, is the da Vinci system, which minimizes the invasiveness of medical surgery (Beasley, 2012). Thus, the patient is burdened with a lower risk of complications, and the wound healing itself is much faster (Gyles, 2019). Moreover, these types of solutions are conceptually moving toward the development of artificial intelligence and automation and, in the future, to partially replace human labor. The relevance of the development of robotics in the medical field could be seen during the COVID-19 pandemic when hospital staff was globally overstretched. Therefore, it is becoming increasingly popular to engage robots in patient care (Sarker et al., 2021). At present, they mainly perform uncomplicated tasks; delivering medicine, delivering meals, and monitoring basic vital functions. An important function of medical robots, especially for lonely, elderly people, is the role of a companion. Robots of this type are capable of interacting with humans – they respond to voice commands and have touch sensors and microphones for voice communication (Sharkey & Sharkey, 2012). Thus, they can successfully act as a caregiver, a friend but also notify doctors of health changes in the human to whom they are assigned (Vercelli et al., 2018). Another application of robotics related to care, but also the provision of business services, is the popularized cleaning and tidying robots. Smart vacuum cleaners, for example, are popular, using scanning of the environment and built-in sensors and drive to remove dirt from a given flat surface. Moreover, each year brings developments in algorithms, and these improve the precision and quality of the devices (Kleiner, 2018). Today, cleaning robots no longer have problems recognizing and avoiding most obstacles and hazards. What's more, their automation is not just about autonomous movement but also about measuring the level of battery charge and returning to the charging station on their own. Talking about robots, it is impossible to overlook their use in military solutions. This is intriguing since it is the war that has been the driver of innovation throughout human history (Singer, 2008). Today, military robots are no longer a phantasmagoria but a fact. The Avatar III (Conyers et al., 2015), for example, is engaged in maintaining the security of special units through reconnaissance of the area of operations. The DOGO robot, on the other hand, is a tactical solution. It has been equipped with firearms and battlefield monitoring systems. It can also effortlessly overcome terrain obstacles it encounters (Ali, 2021). Most impressive at the moment is a robo-dog called SPOT from Boston Dynamics. Its design allows it to move not only efficiently but also very quickly and with agile movements. It is suitable for reconnaissance, information gathering, and carrying equipment. It can be programmed to carry out autonomous missions (Küçük, 2022). However, security robots do not have to refer to military tasks. Private households can also find uses for the new technologies. Robots act as guards, monitoring the programmed area and reporting to the owners about any changes, unwanted movement, or presence. Homeowners can respond to the transmitted messages on their own or automate contact with the appropriate public services, such as the police or fire department (Sahin & Guvenc, 2007). Robots are often thought of as humanoid machines; however, they don't have to look like that at all. Rising in interest and popularity are autonomous vehicles. This technology, although not widely implemented, is in an advanced stage of testing. The idea is that researchers want to create vehicles that will not require a driver. Autonomous vehicles are expected not only to deliver passengers to the desired destination but to do so safely (Faisal et al., 2019). As numerous tests have shown that intelligent systems for recognizing obstacles, choosing alternative routes, artificial intelligence obeying traffic regulations, being able to react to danger, and autonomous parking systems are already highly developed and effective (Badue et al., 2021). The problem, however, is the need to be almost completely sure of their reliability. At this moment, autonomous vehicles still continue to cause accidents. These minor and rare incidents are very quickly gaining publicity and reaching the masses, who often question the technology (Wagner & Koopman, 2015).

Modern times require modern solutions. Robotics is a field of science that can offer unlimited tools to make human work and life easier. Robots have long since ceased to be only a dream of science-fiction creators and have moved into everyday use. We find applications for them in almost every area of life and business. Starting from the provision of selected services, through medicine, healthcare, and companion functions, to military technology and monitoring our safety. Robots are used to entertain people, to help them in household or work activities. They can remain calm and precise where the human body fails (Heyer, 2010). In conclusion, robotics has enormous potential for applications. At present, however, it is fraught with certain technological limitations, as well as social anxiety. However, moving into the likely future, humanity will become increasingly integrated with robots that will learn our behaviors and need more efficiently. The scope of application of work automation systems, algorithms, or just robots is wide, so it is expected that in the near future, man and machine will act in full synchronization for the common good.

11.4 Methodology

The project should be considered exploratory research, with the main aim of describing the level of trust for robots among students using various independent variables. Four research questions were introduced to address the topic:

1. Does gender differentiate the level of trust in robots?
2. Does age have any correlation with the trust level?
3. Do students with bachelor's degrees have higher trust in robots?
4. Does the origin matters in terms of the trust toward robots?

They were all to describe the level of trust in robots in the field, both in the occupational area and private areas.

In order to achieve the aim of the article, 442 answers were collected by a CSAQ method. The research questionnaire comprises five questions considering the general areas, as mentioned earlier, 22 questions about the selective usage of robots, as well as 6 questions considering the personal data of the respondents. The seven-type Likert scale was used in order to describe each area and usage of robotics.

The research data gathering was conducted between November and December 2022 among students in Krakow City (Poland). Students were asked to fill out the CSAQ online file during classes. Table 11.1 describes the areas of expertise.

Table 11.1 Areas of trust

Occupational		*Privat life*	
Autonomous delivery	Promotion	Recycling and garbage sorting	Home security
Quality control	Graphic design	Cleaning	Rescue operations
Autonomous warehouses	Installation work	Education	Military
Loading and unloading goods	Construction	Autonomous vehicles	Social security and police
Material processing	Food production	Elderly care	Firefighting
Packing goods		Gastronomy	

Source: Own study.

The following independent variables were collected:

1. Gender – described as men and women. Respondents could also choose not to declare the gender but none of them decided to choose this answer
2. Age – respondents were asked to fill the given age by hand in the range from 18 to 26 years old
3. Study level – this variable is represented by two levels bachelor and masters
4. Origin – this variable represents the size of a hometown described as a dichotomic variable village versus city.

Statistical methods were used to meet the aim of the research. Those were:

1. Shapiro–Wilk test of distribution normality
2. EFA
3. Friedman's Anova test
4. Wilcoxon test
5. General descriptive statistics.

All the research and calculations were conducted using SPSS27 software.

The research samples comprised of 189 males (42.8%) and 247 females (55.9%). Six students (1.4%) decided not to associate themselves with any sex. The average age was equal to M=20.64, SD=2.337. Most of the students were during their bachelor's (381 students, 86.2%), 43 students (9.5%) were doing their master's and 19 decided not to give their age. Most of the students came from cities (260 people, 58.8%) whereas 182 students came from villages (41.2%).

11.5 Results

The results are presented with the structure of theoretical-based dimensions, operational usage of robots, and empirical dimensions. Descriptive statistics for areas are shown in Table 11.2.

The mean value of the trust within the occupational area is equal to M=4.9473, SD=.99384 and is significantly higher (Z=−16.203, p<.001) than the mean for

Table 11.2 General descriptive statistics for area

	Mean	*Median*	*Mode*	*Std. Deviation*	*Min*	*Max*	*Percentiles*		
							25	*50*	*75*
Occupational	4,9473	5,0000	5,00	,99384	1,36	7,00	4,3636	5,0000	5,6364
Privat	4,1660	4,2727	4,27	1,08814	1,00	6,82	3,4545	4,2727	4,9091

Source: Own study.

private area is equal to M=4.166, SD=1.08814. The usage of Wilcoxon test was justified because of the lack of normal distribution of both variables (Shapiro–Wilk tests p<.001). The reliability measured by Cronbach's alpha of both occupational and private area are equal to .892. Both dimensions can be considered as reliable.

The U Mann–Whitney test was used to verify the impact of gender on trust within both occupational and private areas. The test revealed that men have a higher trust to robotics than women within the occupational area (Z=–2.855, p=0.004) as well as private area (Z=–2.587, p=0.01). There was no significant correlation between age and occupational area (r_s=0.012, p=0.802) or private area (r_s=–0.011, p=0.821). The difference in trust to robots among the study level was not confirmed statistically in either occupational (H=1.093, p=0.579) or private area (H=.128, p=0.938). The difference within the last independent variable (origin) was also statistically insignificant for both areas (occupational – Z= –,0.656, p=0.512; private – Z= −1.017, p=0.039).

The second phase of statistical analysis is connected with the operational usage of robots. The statistics for robots usage are presented in Table 11.3.

On the scale from 1 to 7, four ways of robot usage were assessed with the mean over 5.2, and those were Autonomous warehouses (M=5.42, SD=1.228), material processing (M=5.33, SD=1.334), packing goods (M=5.27, SD=1.397) and loading and unloading goods (M=5.25, SD=1.276). Also, four usages were assessed on a level below 4, and those were: Firefighting (M=3.91, SD=1.687), home security (M=3.86, SD=1.478), social security and police (M=3.79, SD=1.632), and elderly care (M=3.11, SD=1.482).

The results of the analysis showing the differences in the operational usage of robots described by the independent variables (gender, age, study level, and origin) were presented in Table 11.4. Non-parametric tests of correlation, 2 independent samples, and K independent samples were used.

In fourteen out of twenty-two operational usage of robots, men declared higher trust than women. The biggest difference in the mean rank was in autonomous delivery (55), packing goods (47), and loading and unloading goods (46).

The analysis of correlation of age and various usage of robots revealed a statistically significant difference only in terms of quality control (r_s=.137, p=0.004). It is a weak correlation. The statistically significant test results connected with the study level are presented in Table 11.5.

Only in three out of twenty-two usages, the study level provided a statistically significant difference. In all of the cases, bachelor's students were having higher trust to robots than master's students. The results of the testing of the origin variable are presented in Table 11.6.

Only in two out of twenty-two usages, origin explained the differences with a statistical significance. In terms of cleaning, respondents from the City had a higher trust than respondents from the countryside. The opposite situation was

Table 11.3 General descriptive statistics for robots usage

	Mean	*Median*	*Mode*	*Std. Deviation*	*Percentiles*		
					25	*50*	*75*
Autonomous warehouses	5,42	6,00	6	1,228	5,00	6,00	6,00
Material processing	5,33	6,00	6	1,334	5,00	6,00	6,00
Packing goods	5,27	5,00	5	1,397	5,00	5,00	6,00
Loading and unloading goods	5,25	5,00	6	1,276	5,00	5,00	6,00
Recycling and garbage sorting	5,19	5,00	6	1,395	4,00	5,00	6,00
Autonomous delivery	5,18	5,00	6	1,358	4,75	5,00	6,00
Graphic design	5,14	5,00	5	1,482	4,00	5,00	6,00
Cleaning	5,08	5,00	5	1,424	4,00	5,00	6,00
Promotion	4,90	5,00	6	1,518	4,00	5,00	6,00
Quality control	4,79	5,00	5	1,441	4,00	5,00	6,00
Construction	4,54	5,00	5	1,576	4,00	5,00	6,00
Installation work	4,52	5,00	5	1,446	4,00	5,00	6,00
Education	4,35	5,00	5	1,649	3,00	5,00	6,00
Food production	4,31	4,00	5	1,591	3,00	4,00	6,00
Gastronomy	4,22	4,00	5	1,622	3,00	4,00	5,00
Military	4,21	4,00	5	1,729	3,00	4,00	5,00
Rescue operations	4,07	4,00	4[a]	1,520	3,00	4,00	5,00
Autonomous vehicles	4,02	4,00	5	1,588	3,00	4,00	5,00
Firefighting	3,91	4,00	5	1,687	3,00	4,00	5,00
Home security	3,86	4,00	4	1,478	3,00	4,00	5,00
Social security and police	3,79	4,00	5	1,632	3,00	4,00	5,00
Elderly care	3,11	3,00	3	1,482	2,00	3,00	4,00

Source: Own study.

revealed in terms of graphic designer – people from the countryside demonstrate a higher trust.

The third phase of statistical analysis is connected with the EFA. The results are presented in Table 11.7.

Factor one can be described as the social factor. It comprises seven elements all gathered around usage connected with social security and human aspect. Factor two can be called as the main role in occupation. All the usage from factor two can be fully autonomous. Factor three is also connected with occupational care, but robots are in a supportive role in it. The last factor is connected with marketing roles, but it only comprises two elements. New factors were created based on

Table 11.4 Results of U Mann–Whitney testing for gender

Usage	*Z*	*P*	*Men (rank)*	*Women (rank)*	*Higher trust*
Autonomous warehouses	-,954	,340	224,87	213,62	-
Material processing	-2,797	,005	237,25	204,15	Men
Packing goods	-4,027	<,001	245,55	197,80	Men
Loading and unloading goods	-3,922	<,001	244,54	198,57	Men
Recycling and garbage sorting	-2,758	,006	236,87	204,44	Men
Autonomous delivery	-4,653	<,001	249,67	194,65	Men
Graphic design	-3,217	,001	240,08	201,99	Men
Cleaning	-,485	,628	221,79	215,99	-
Promotion	-,546	,585	222,20	215,67	-
Quality controll	-2,663	,008	236,50	204,72	Men
Construction	-3,746	<,001	243,88	199,08	Men
Installation work	-2,695	,007	236,63	204,62	Men
Education	-1,355	,175	209,35	225,50	-
Food production	-,091	,927	217,89	218,97	-
Gastronomy	-2,897	,004	238,18	203,44	Men
Military	-,330	,742	216,26	220,21	-
Rescue operations	-2,828	,005	237,72	203,79	Men
Autonomous vehicles	-,051	,959	218,15	218,77	-
Firefighting	-3,467	<,001	241,84	200,64	Men
Home security	-3,076	,002	239,29	202,59	Men
Social security and police	-1,183	,237	226,52	212,36	-
Elderly care	-2,645	,008	236,44	204,77	Men

Source: Own study.

the EFA, using the weighted average (where the weights are the factor loadings of each element). The factor descriptive statistics are shown in Table 11.8.

Friedman test revealed that there are significant differences between the factors (X2=447.107, p <.001). The Wilcoxon test revealed differences between each and every factor. Young people have the most trust (mean above 5.0) to robots in terms of occupational jobs where the robots have main role (M = 5.2033, SD = 1.0293) and in terms of marketing (M = 5.0223, SD = 1.326). A bit lower to the occupational aspect where robots have a supportive role (M = 4.38, SD = 1.3163). The lower trust students have for robots in social area (M=3.91, SD=1.228). Results of the personal statistics are presented in Table 11.9.

Men have higher trust in robots in terms of social and both occupational factors. In marketing, there is no significant difference between men and women. The age does not correlate on a statistically significant level with any of the empirical dimensions. In terms of study level, the difference was revealed in marketing factor, where bachelor's students had higher trust than master's students. For the origin (village/city) there was no significant difference.

Table 11.5 Results of U Mann–Whitney tests for study level

Usage	*Z*	*P*	*Bachelor (rank)*	*Wasters (rank)*	*Higher trust*
Rescue operations	–2.477	0.013	217.83	188.76	Bachelor
Firefighting	–1.988	0.047	214.26	190.86	Bachelor
Elderly care	–2.185	0.029	215.64	190.05	Bachelor

Source: Own study.

Table 11.6 Results of U Mann–Whitney test for origin

Usage	*Z*	*P*	*Countryside (rank)*	*City (rank)*	*Higher trust*
Cleaning	–2.201	0.028	205.90	232.42	City
Graphic designer	–1.975	0.048	235.47	211.72	Countryside

Source: Own study.

Table 11.7 EFA results for Varimax Rotation with Kaiser Normalization

	Component			
	1	*2*	*3*	*4*
Social security and police	,842			
Firefighting	,768			
Military	,759			
Home security	,729			
Rescue operations	,699			
Elderly care	,662			
Education	,588			
Autonomous vehicles	,554			
Autonomous warehouses		,822		
Loading and unloading goods		,797		
Recycling and garbage sorting		,785		
Material processing		,695		
Autonomous delivery		,673		
Packing goods		,647		
Quality control		,637		
Cleaning		,471		
Gastronomy			,784	
Food production			,782	
Construction			,619	
Installation work			,612	
Graphic design				,770
Promotion				,760

Source: Own study.

Table 11.8 Descriptive statistics of the factors

	Mean	*Median*	*Mode*	*Std. Deviation*	*Percentiles*		
					25	*50*	*75*
Occupational_main	5,2033	5,2990	7,00	1,02929	4,6192	5,2990	5,9440
Marketing	5,0223	5,0065	5,00	1,32600	4,4967	5,0065	6,0000
Occupational_support	4,3827	4,5009	5,00	1,31634	3,5902	4,5009	5,2803
Social	3,9100	4,0124	1,00	1,22837	3,1294	4,0124	4,7783

Source: Own study.

Table 11.9 Personal statistics and trust

Variable	*Factor*	*Test result*	*P-value*	*Decision*	
Gender	Social	Z=−2.143	.032	Difference	Men higher trust than Women
	Occupational main	Z=−4.202	<.001	Difference	Men higher trust than Women
	Occupational support	Z=−2.763	.006	Difference	Men higher trust than Women
	Marketing	Z=−820	.412	No difference	
Age	Social	$r_s = -0.001$	0.977	No difference	
	Occupational main	$r_s = 0.031$	0.514	No difference	
	Occupational support	$r_s = 0.003$	0.955	No difference	
	Marketing	$r_s = -0.077$	0.107	No difference	
Study level	Social	Z=−625	.532	No difference	
	Occupational main	Z=-.245	.807	No difference	
	Occupational support	Z=-.593	.553	No difference	
	Marketing	Z=-2.315	.021	Difference	Bachelor's higher than Master's
Origin	Social	Z=-.456	.648	No difference	
	Occupational main	Z=-1.483	.138	No difference	
	Occupational support	Z=-1.288	.198	No difference	
	Marketing	Z=-1.953	.051	No difference	

Source: Own study.

11.6 Summary

The conducted exploratory study revealed the level of importance of four factors (gender, age, study level, and origin) for the level of trust toward robots on three

Table 11.10 Statistical significance of the theoretical approach and four factors

	Gender	*Age*	*Study level*	*Origin*
Occupational	Men higher	No	No	No
Private	Men higher	No	No	No

Source: Own study.

different dimensions. Table 11.10 presents the sum-up of the theoretical level.

In general, men present a higher trust toward robots than women do. It might be connected with the fact that males are more likely to prefer robots in general than females (Nomura, 2017) or the fact that the majority of engineering students are males (Hartmann et al., 2007). It gives them better knowledge and understanding of robotic usage. The result is confirmed also in the usage analysis in which in fourteen cases men demonstrated higher trust in robots than women. It is important to state that gender was the only variable that allowed to differentiate the trust toward robots in all three researched aspects. It is due to the fact that emerging adulthood is a fairly stable concept (in the age between 18 and 26) and two variables (age and study level) are all within the emerging adulthood stage. The origin also did not differentiate the level of trust.

11.7 Limitations and future research

The presented research was subjected to a few limitations. Those were:

1. The lack of differentiation of the research sample. The research on such an important topic should be conducted on a larger scale. Presented results should then be treated as the pilot study.
2. The chosen areas of usage of robots do not cover every aspect of life where we are using robots. The research should cover more than only twenty-two areas. It was then the researcher's decision to limit the areas in order to create a research questionnaire that will not discourage the respondents.
3. This exploratory research was focused only on young people in the emerging adulthood stage. It is just a portrait of this particular stage of development. But it is impossible to state that this time of life differs in terms of trust toward robots from teenage time or various stages of adulthood.

The analysis of the limitations helped the authors to plan future research. Those will be among others:

1. Enlarging the research sample in order to achieve a representative research sample for the whole country

2. Analyse various aspects of the robot usage in order to cover more usage areas
3. Conduct the research among other groups such as teenagers, young adults, adults, and people in mature adulthood stage.

11.8 Acknowledgment

The publication was co-financed/financed from the subsidy granted to the Cracow University of Economics – Project nr 067/ZZS/2022/POT.

References

Ali, A. (2021). Artificial intelligence potential trends in military. *Foundation University Journal of Engineering and Applied Sciences* (HEC Recognized Y Category, ISSN 2706–7351), *2*(1), 20–30.

Arnett, J. (2000). A theory of development from the late teens through the twenties. *American Psychologist*, *55*, 469–480.

Arnett, K., & Taber, S. (1994). Adolescence terminable and interminable: When does adolescence end? *Journal of Youth and Adolescence*, *23*, 517–537.

Badue, C., Guidolini, R., Carneiro, R. V., Azevedo, P., Cardoso, V. B., Forechi, A., Jesus, L., Berriel, R., Paixão, T. M., Mutz, F., de Paula Veronese, L., Oliveira-Santos, T., & De Souza, A. F. (2021). Self-driving cars: A survey. *Expert Systems with Applications*, *165*, 113816.

Beasley, R. A. (2012). Medical robots: Current systems and research directions. *Journal of Robotics*, *2012*, 401613. https://doi.org/10.1155/2012/401613

Chisholm, L., & Hurrelmann, K. (1995). Adolescence in modern Europe: Pluralized transition patterns and their implications for personal and social risks. *Journal of Adolescence*, *18*(2), 129–158.

Conyers, S. A., Vitzilaios, N. I., Rutherford, M. J., & Valavanis, K. P. (2015). *A mobile self-leveling landing platform for VTOL UAVs*. 2015 IEEE International Conference on Robotics and Automation (ICRA), pp. 815–822. IEEE.

Crafts, N. (2011). Explaining the first industrial revolution: Two views. *European Review of Economic History*, *15*(1), 153–168.

Faisal, A., Kamruzzaman, M., Yigitcanlar, T., & Currie, G. (2019). Understanding autonomous vehicles. *Journal of Transport and Land Use*, *12*(1), 45–72.

Gyles, C. (2019). Robots in medicine. *The Canadian Veterinary Journal, 60*(8), 819.

Hartmann, S., Wiesner, H., & Wiesner-Steiner, A. (2007). Robotics and gender: The use of robotics for the empowerment of girls in the classroom. In I. Zorn, S. Maass, E. Rommes, C. Schirmer, & H. Schelhowe (Eds.), *Gender designs IT*. VS Verlag für Sozialwissenschaften.

Heyer, C. (2010). *Human-robot interaction and future industrial robotics applications*. 2010 IEEE/RSJ International Conference on Intelligent Robots and Systems, pp. 4749–4754. IEEE.

Karabegović, I. (2017). The role of industrial and service robots in fourth industrial revolution with focus on China. *Journal of Engineering and Architecture*, *5*(2), 110–117.

Kleiner, A. (2018). The low cost evolution of AI in domestic floor cleaning robots. *AI Magazine*, *39*(2), 89–90.

Koc, T. C., & Teker, S. (2019). Industrial revolutions and its effects on quality of life. *PressAcademia Procedia*, *9*(1), 304–311.

Küçük, S. (2022). Introductory chapter: On the verge of a new age–the age of robotic engineering. In *Recent advances in robot manipulators*. IntechOpen.

Mohajan, H. (2019). *The second industrial revolution has brought modern social and economic developments*. https://mpra.ub.uni-muenchen.de/98209/1/MPRA_paper_98209.pdf

Nomura, T. (2017). Robots and gender. Principles of gender-specific medicine. *Gender in the Genomic Era*, 695–703.

Olender-Skorek, M. (2017). Czwarta rewolucja przemysłowa a wybrane aspekty teorii ekonomii. *Nierówności społeczne a wzrost gospodarczy* (51), 38–49.

Olszewski, M. (2016). Mechatronizacja produktu i produkcji–przemysł 4.0. *Pomiary Automatyka Robotyka*, *20*.

Park, J. M., Lee, S. M., & Kim, Y. M. (2021). On the development of robot based automation system for loading cargo in small and medium sub terminals. *International Journal of Internet, Broadcasting and Communication*, *13*(4), 90–96.

Pellicciari, M., Berselli, G., Leali, F., & Vergnano, A. (2013). A method for reducing the energy consumption of pick-and-place industrial robots. *Mechatronics*, *23*(3), 326–334.

Popkova, E. G., Ragulina, Y. V., & Bogoviz, A. V. (2019). Fundamental differences of transition to industry 4.0 from previous industrial revolutions. In *Industry 4.0. Industrial revolution of the 21st century* (pp. 21–29). Springer.

Rindfuss, R. R. (1991). The young adult years: Diversity, structural change and fertility/ *Demography*, *28*, 193–512.

Sahin, H., & Guvenc, L. (2007). Household robotics: Autonomous devices for vacuuming and lawn mowing [applications of control]. *IEEE Control Systems Magazine*, *27*(2), 20–96.

Sarker, S., Jamal, L., Ahmed, S. F., & Irtisam, N. (2021). Robotics and artificial intelligence in healthcare during COVID-19 pandemic: A systematic review. *Robotics and Autonomous Systems*, *146*, 103902.

Sharkey, A., & Sharkey, N. (2012). Granny and the robots: Ethical issues in robot care for the elderly. *Ethics and Information Technology*, *14*(1), 27–40.

Singer, P. (2008). Robots at war. *Wilson Quarterly*, 30–48.

Stresnjak, S., & Hocenski, Z. (2011). *Usage of robot framework in automation of functional test regression*. Proceedings - International Conference on Software Engineering Advanced (ICSEA), pp. 30–34.

Szydło, R., Wiśniewska, S., & Ćwiek, M. (2020). Multidimensional inventory of students quality of life – MIS-QOL. *Sustainability*, *13*(1), 60.

Taalbi, J. (2019). Origins and pathways of innovation in the third industrial revolution. *Industrial and Corporate Change*, *28*(5), 1125–1148.

Vercelli, A., Rainero, I., Ciferri, L., Boido, M., & Pirri, F. (2018). Robots in elderly care. *DigitCult-Scientific Journal on Digital Cultures*, *2*(2), 37–50.

Wagner, M., & Koopman, P. (2015). A philosophy for developing trust in self-driving cars. In *Road vehicle automation* (Vol. 2, pp. 163–171). Springer.

Xu, M., David, J. M., & Kim, S. H. (2018). The fourth industrial revolution: Opportunities and challenges. *International Journal of Financial Research*, *9*(2), 90–95.

Zhang, Y., & Lu, M. (2020). A review of recent advancements in soft and flexible robots for medical applications. *The International Journal of Medical Robotics and Computer Assisted Surgery*, *16*(3), e2096.

Index

Taylor & Francis Group
an informa business
Taylor & Francis eBooks
www.taylorfrancis.com
A single destination for eBooks from Taylor & Francis with increased functionality and an improved user experience to meet the needs of our customers.
90,000+ eBooks of award-winning academic content in Humanities, Social Science, Science, Technology, Engineering, and Medical written by a global network of editors and authors.
TAYLOR & FRANCIS EBOOKS OFFERS:
A streamlined experience for our library customers
A single point of discovery for all of our eBook content
Improved search and discovery of content at both book and chapter level
REQUEST A FREE TRIAL
support@taylorfrancis.com
Routledge
Taylor & Francis Group
CRC Press
Taylor & Francis Group